2/93

The
Migration
of
Managerial
Innovation

John R. Kimberly
Gérard de Pouvourville
and Associates

The Migration of Managerial Innovation

*Diagnosis-Related Groups and
Health Care Administration
in Western Europe*

 Jossey-Bass Publishers
San Francisco

Substantial discounts on bulk quantities of Jossey-Bass books are available to corporations, professional associations, and other organizations. For details and discount information, contact the special sales department at Jossey-Bass Inc., Publishers. (415) 433-1740; Fax (415) 433-0499.

For sales outside the United States, contact Maxwell Macmillan International Publishing Group, 866 Third Avenue, New York, New York 10022.

Manufactured in the United States of America

The paper used in this book is acid-free and meets the State of California requirements for recycled paper (50 percent recycled waste, including 10 percent postconsumer waste), which are the strictest guidelines for recycled paper currently in use in the United States.

10% POST
CONSUMER
WASTE

The ink in this book is either soy- or vegetable-based and during the printing process emits fewer than half the volatile organic compounds (VOCs) emitted by petroleum-based ink.

The poetry of Piet Hein in Chapter Nine is reprinted with permission.

Library of Congress Cataloging-in-Publication Data

The Migration of managerial innovation : diagnosis-related groups and
  health care administration in Western Europe / John R. Kimberly,
  Gérard de Pouvourville and associates. — 1st ed.
      p.   cm. — (A Joint publication in the Jossey-Bass health series and
  the Jossey-Bass management series)
    Includes bibliographical references and index.
    ISBN 1-55542-520-8 (alk. paper)
    1. Diagnosis-related groups—Europe, Western. 2. Organizational
  change—Europe, Western—Case studies. I. Kimberly, John R. (John
  Robert), date. II. Pouvourville, Gérard de. III. Series:
  Jossey-Bass health series. IV. Series: Jossey-Bass management
  series.
    [DNLM: 1. Diagnosis-Related Groups—organization &
  administration—Europe. 2. Diffusion of Innovation. WX 157 M636]
  RA971.32.M5 1993
  338.4'33621'1094—dc20
  DNLM/DLC
  for Library of Congress   92-48670
                                                                  CIP

FIRST EDITION
HB Printing   10 9 8 7 6 5 4 3 2 1   *Code 9318*

A joint publication in

**The Jossey-Bass
Health Series**

and

**The Jossey-Bass
Management Series**

Contents

Preface

How do we account for the fact that a given innovation becomes better accepted and more fully utilized in one setting than in another? This question has spawned vast amounts of research in marketing where the setting is an individual consumer faced with multiple options and making a choice. Marketers have puzzled about the factors that influence individual decision making and behavior in their efforts to clear the way to early and widespread acceptance of new products. The question has also proved of interest to management researchers, for whom the setting is typically the firm. Research in this tradition has tried to determine the relative importance of individual, organizational, and environmental influences on the decisions and behavior of firms considering the possibility of investing in innovations of many types. Although it is obvious that some firms embrace innovation more completely and more quickly than others, determining why that is the case has proved challenging.

When we move from instances of individual and organizational behavior to examine cases in which the setting is the nation-state, the complexity of explanation increases substantially. Yet the question is no less intriguing. Why does a given innovation become more widely accepted and used in one country than in another? To what extent do the explanations lie in cultural differences, and to what extent do they lie elsewhere?

At a point in history when the amount of traffic of all sorts across national borders is accelerating wildly, such questions are particularly significant. What can we reasonably expect when the decision process for an innovation is played out on a national stage? Beyond the obvious assertion that the process will undoubtedly take longer on average than when individual people or firms are the decision units, what more can be said?

This book tries to answer these questions by examining the migration of a particular innovation from the United States to Western Europe. The innovation that is the subject of our analysis is diagnosis-related groups, or DRGs, an innovation that permits detailed analysis of the production activities of hospitals. Developed by academic researchers, the approach was seized on by government officials in the United States as offering a potential vehicle for reform of the system whereby hospitals were paid by the government for services provided to Medicare patients. The approach, which was implemented nationally in the form of the prospective payment system in 1983, became widely discussed and debated in Western Europe. In this book we review the fate of DRGs in nine countries of Western Europe, comparing and contrasting the outcomes and speculating about their implications.

The idea for the book emerged during a sabbatical Kimberly took at the Centre de Recherche en Gestion of the Ecole Polytechnique in Paris, where his host, de Pouvourville, had been working for a number of years on French initiatives with DRGs. De Pouvourville had a good sense of what was happening in other West European countries because of his network of contacts and colleagues in those countries. In May of 1990 we both attended a conference in Montpellier where speakers presented summaries of what was happening with respect to DRGs in a number of countries. It became readily apparent that despite the fact that something was going on in all of the countries represented, the extensiveness, the pace, and the specifics differed considerably from one country to the next. We found these differences intriguing. More important, conference participants seemed to have considerable interest in learning about what was happening in other countries. In the wake of the conference, the possibility of a book was discussed.

Given limited resources and a sense that timing was very important, we decided to try to identify one person in each of nine countries who might be willing to write a chapter on the experience with DRGs in that country. Our choice of countries was largely pragmatic; it was based on what we knew about levels of activity. We chose two countries that were moving ahead rapidly with DRGs, two that we knew had rejected the idea of DRGs, and five that had varying levels of activity and resource commitment. We confined our focus to Western Europe even though we were aware of activity in other countries such as Australia.

Our choice of authors was driven by our belief that they all had to be very knowledgeable about DRGs through involvement in the policy process, consulting, and research. As you will see, each of the chapter authors has had considerable direct experience with DRGs in his or her country, and most are involved in networks that have sprung up in Europe to share information about their experiences. This means, of course, that none of these authors can be considered neutral or dispassionate observers; however, there are few if any people in a given country who know more about the DRG story than they do. As an accuracy check, we asked each author to submit his or her chapter to at least two other knowledgeable individuals for critical review.

Each chapter author was provided with a set of substantive guidelines for preparing the chapter, guidelines that are described and discussed in the first chapter. These guidelines, in effect, represented the variables that we felt were likely to have influenced the fate of DRGs in any particular country and hence provided the theoretical framework for the analyses. Authors were asked to prepare first drafts of their manuscripts over the summer of 1990 and then to attend a meeting in Paris at which the drafts would be discussed and the theoretical framework modified if necessary. Second drafts were requested by February 1991, and chapters were circulated among authors to facilitate communication and to try to encourage comparability in style as well as in content. We wanted to give each author as much autonomy as possible yet at the same time ensure that we would be able to compare individual country experiences and identify points of convergence and divergence in the last chapter.

We are very pleased with the results of this effort. Although the country chapters are not rigorous in the narrow sense of the term, they are carefully researched and present in every case a clear picture of the fate of DRGs through the early summer of 1991. Although written specifically for this volume, each of them could stand on its own as a description of what has happened with DRGs in that particular country. The country chapters also have brief epilogues that update the DRG story in their respective countries for the year or so since the chapters were first written.

Overview of the Contents

The structure of the book, then, is very simple. In Chapter One we review the literature on the diffusion of innovation briefly, discuss DRGs as the innovation of interest in this book, and sketch out the framework we developed for the chapter authors, explaining why we chose to emphasize the particular set of variables we did. Each of the next nine chapters focuses on a particular country. The first three countries to be discussed, England, Belgium, and France, were the first in Europe to become involved with DRGs at a national level. The next two, Sweden and Switzerland, currently are witnessing a variety of experiments regionally and locally, while substantial commitments have been made to DRGs at the national level in Portugal and Norway, discussed subsequently. Finally, decisions have been made in both Denmark and Germany that essentially mean they will move in other directions.

Each country chapter contains a brief description of the health care context—that is, how health care is organized and financed—and subsequently examines the fate of DRGs. The final chapter compares and contrasts these experiences, draws lessons for those who would promote and manage the innovation process, and discusses how what we have learned in the course of this research might redirect innovation research elsewhere.

Audience

The book is intended for three principal audiences: *health policy makers and managers* concerned with understanding the fate of new initiatives and managing the innovation process more effectively; *students* taking courses in health administration, comparative health systems, and/or the management of change; and *researchers* working on problems of innovation, the politics of change, and/or international and comparative health policy and management.

In an era when health reform is high on the political agendas of most Western countries, the book provides an overview of how health care is organized and financed in nine countries outside the United States, and in so doing illustrates a range of alternative solutions. Thus, it will be of interest to those concerned with the general problem of health care reform as well.

Acknowledgments

This project would never have succeeded without a substantial commitment of time, effort, and resources from a variety of individual people and institutions. The authors of the individual country chapters, Anita Alban, Margarida Bentes, James M. Coles, Francis Roger France, Andreas Frei, Bernhard J. Güntert, Torbjørg Hogsnes, Günter Neubauer, Fred Paccaud, Eric M. Paulson, Gérard de Pouvourville, Markus Sagmeister, João Urbano, and James C. Vertrees, all responded both professionally and in a timely fashion to the challenge we set them. The book is largely their doing. Nassera Nacer and Elisabeth Szuskya of the Centre de Recherche en Gestion at the Ecole Polytechnique provided much of the logistical support required by the project, whereas Mission Inter-ministèrielle de Recherche et d'Expérimentation funded travel and translation costs. Michel Berry, then director of the Centre de Recherche en Gestion, provided both encouragement and financial support for the project, as well as a most comfortable office for Kimberly for two years. And the University of Pennsylvania permitted Kimberly to supplement a one-year scholarly leave with a second year's leave of absence, thereby allowing the project to be completed within the original time frame.

To all of the above, we are truly grateful.

December 1992   John R. Kimberly
Philadelphia, Pennsylvania

Gérard de Pouvourville
Paris, France

The Authors

John R. Kimberly is the Henry Bower Professor in the departments of Management and Health Care Systems in the Wharton School at the University of Pennsylvania. Kimberly received his B.A. degree (1964) in sociology from Yale University and his M.S. degree (1967) in organizational behavior from Cornell University. He received his Ph.D. degree (1970) in organizational behavior from Cornell University and has taught at the University of Illinois, Urbana, and Yale University.

Kimberly is interested in problems of organizational innovation and change and is currently investigating how and with what consequences firms internationalize their activities and how health care organizations are responding to total quality initiatives. His most recent books in the area of health care are *The End of an Illusion* (1984, with Jean de Kervasdoué and Victor Rodwin) and *Cases in Health Policy and Management* (1985, with R. Fetter and J. Thompson).

Kimberly has also taught as a visitor at the University of Paris, Dauphine, and at the Ecole Supérieure en Sciences Economiques et Commerciales, Paris. He was a visiting scholar at the Centre de Recherche en Gestion (Management Research Center) of the Ecole Polytechnique, Paris, from 1975 to 1976 and from 1989 to 1991.

Gérard de Pouvourville is research director at the Management Research Center of the Ecole Polytechnique in Paris. He graduated from the Ecole Polytechnique in 1973 and obtained his Ph.D. degree (1978) in management science. He has been studying the management of health care organizations and health

xvii

policy since 1976. His work has dealt with medical manpower planning, financing health care and health policy, the organization of care units in hospitals, the diffusion of innovations in the health care sector, and health economics. He has been a technical adviser to the French Ministry of Health since 1982, mainly on the French DRG program and medical manpower planning. De Pouvourville is a member of the National Scientific Committee of the National Institute for Health and Medical Research and is a faculty member at the National School of Public Health. He is currently the editor of *Sciences Sociales & Santé*, a multi-disciplinary journal devoted to social science applications to health.

Anita Alban is head of the Department of Health Economics at the Danish Hospital Institute in Copenhagen. She received an M.Sc. degree (1975) in economics and a B.Comm. degree (1980) in public management from the University of Copenhagen. She has been a consultant for the World Health Organization since 1985 and for the World Bank since 1988.

Margarida Bentes is a hospital administrator who is currently assistant director of Sistema de Informação para a Gestão de Serviços de Saúde, a research department in the Portuguese Ministry of Health. She is engaged in a series of projects aimed at significant modification of the government health care delivery system, particularly the design and implementation of an output-based funding system for the hospital sector. She was involved in advisory duties for the Secretariat of State for Health in Rio de Janeiro concerning the feasibility of implementing DRGs in Brazil. She is a member of Patient Classification Systems–Europe and of projects in two concerted actions: Euro-DRG in COMAC-HSR and CAMAC in the exploratory phase of the Advanced Informatics in Medicine project.

James M. Coles is associate director of CASPE Research and chairman of CHKS, Ltd., in London. He has been involved in research on the National Health Service (NHS) for twenty years and also has managerial experience in the United Kingdom's

The Authors
The Authors **xix**

health sector. He has written widely on a number of topics including resource management, behavioral aspects of information systems, and the introduction of DRGs within the NHS, and coedited the book *DRGs and Healthcare: The Management of Case Mix* (1989, with M. Bardsley and L. Jenkins). A fellow of the Royal Statistical Society and a member of the Research Committee of the Healthcare Financial Management Association, he lectures regularly in the United Kingdom and internationally on health management issues.

Francis Roger France is a physician and specialist in internal medicine and director of the Medical Informatics Center at the Catholic University of Louvain and of the Central Medical Archives Service of the St. Luke University Clinics in Brussels. He is Professor Extraordinary on the faculty of medicine at the Catholic University of Louvain and a consulting expert to the Ministry of Public Health in Belgium and to the director general of the World Health Organization. France received his M.D. degree (1967) from the Catholic University of Louvain, his M.S. degree (1972) in biometry and epidemiology from the University of Minnesota, and his Ph.D. degree (1982) from the Catholic University of Louvain. He is past president of the European Federation of Medical Informatics and a founding member of the Patient Classification Systems–Europe group.

Andreas Frei is a consultant and project leader at HealthEcon, an independent consulting company that specializes in the health care field. He received his M.A. degree (1983) in economics from the University of Basel. As a former member of the Swiss Institute for Health and Hospital Care, he has extensive professional experience in health services research and hospital financing. He is coauthor of the textbook *Das schweizerische Gesundheitswesen*, which is updated and reprinted every two years, providing the most up-to-date and comprehensive data and information about the Swiss health care system.

Bernhard J. Güntert is senior lecturer at the Research Group for Management in Health Care at the University of St. Gallen. He

graduated from the University of St. Gallen and was then involved in various research projects in the health care field. He
received his M.H.A. degree from Loma Linda University. From
1985 to 1992, he was project leader (and later director) of the
Interdisciplinary Research Centre for Public Health in St. Gallen. Güntert's main field of research is the management and
organization of health service organizations. A major field of
activity is management training on different levels in Switzerland and in Eastern European countries.

Torbjørg Hogsnes is DRG project director at the Norwegian Ministry of Health and Social Affairs in Oslo, where she is leader of
the DRG-based payment experiment. She was educated as a
dentist in 1968 and became a specialist in social dentistry in
1982. Since 1985 she has worked with hospitals in research and
development. In 1990, she joined the Nordic DRG research
group, Resource Management Group. She is also a member of
Patient Classification Systems–Europe.

Günter Neubauer is professor of economics and social policy at
the Universität der Bundeswehr in Munich, Germany. He received his M.A. (1967) and Ph.D. (1971) degrees from the University of Würzburg. Since 1987 he has been a member of Patient
Classification Systems–Europe, and he collaborated on the
CAMAC project from 1988 to 1990. During the same period he
was director of the federally financed test of patient management categories in German hospitals.

Fred Paccaud is a professor at the University of Lausanne and
chair of the Institute of Social and Preventive Medicine at the
School of Medicine, University of Lausanne. He received his
M.D. degree (1977) from the University of Lausanne and his
M.P.H. degree (1982) from the University of Brussels. After some
clinical residencies and a research residency at the Institute of
Social and Preventive Medicine, he was head of the section of
Health Statistics at the Federal Office of Statistics in Bern. He
returned to the Institute in 1987 and became chair in 1988.
Paccaud's main fields of research are: health care research, par-

ticularly in the fields of hospital care, ambulatory care, and preventive interventions (especially cardiovascular diseases, cancer, and AIDS); health information systems aimed at the surveillance and analysis of morbidity and health care; and the epidemiology of reproduction, especially prenatal screening and perinatal and infant mortality in developed countries.

Eric M. Paulson is a researcher at the Department of Social Medicine at Uppsala University, Sweden. He received his M.D. degree (1982) from the University of Lund, Sweden. His present research activities focus on health care policy and improved measures for health care management. Before joining Uppsala University he was a project manager at the Swedish Planning and Rationalization Institute involved in research on DRGs, and he also has experience as a medical director at Excorim, a Swedish medical technology company.

Markus Sagmeister is a medical doctor and a freelance collaborator at the Research Group for Management in Health Services at the University of St. Gallen. He studied medicine at the Universities of Innsbruck and Vienna and received his M.D. degree (1983) from the University of Vienna. After two years of clinical residencies, he studied business administration at the University of St. Gallen, receiving his M.B.A. degree in 1987. From 1987 to 1992, he was project leader at the Interdisciplinary Research Center for Public Health, St. Gallen, and from 1989 to 1992 he was head of its Department of Hospital Management and Health Economics.

João Urbano is a hospital administrator who is currently chief executive officer of Pulido Valente Hospital in Lisbon and director of Sistema de Informação para a Gestão de Serviços de Saúde, a research department in the Portuguese Ministry of Health. He is in charge of a sequence of projects aimed at significant modification of the government health care delivery system. He is a consultant to the World Bank for the Republic of Mozambique and for Venezuela and was involved in advisory duties for the Secretariat of State for Health in Rio de Janeiro concerning the feasibility of implementing DRGs in Brazil. He is a member of Patient Classification Systems–Europe and of projects in two other concerted actions: EuroDRG in COMAC-HSR and CAMAC in the exploratory phase of the Advanced Informatics in Medicine project.

James C. Vertrees is the president of SOLON Consulting Group as well as a senior fellow at the Center for Demographic Studies at Duke University. He is internationally known for his expertise in the design of health care financing and payment systems, program evaluation, and data analysis. He designed the Medicare prospective payment system for hospital payment as well as DRG systems for Pennsylvania and Iowa. He has investigated case mix systems for long-term care and worked on the new ambulatory patient group system for outpatient care. He is currently directing a project to make state-of-the-art health forecasting methods and data sets available to the private sector.

One

Managerial Innovation, Migration, and DRGs

John R. Kimberly
Gérard de Pouvourville

Hardly a day goes by that we are not reminded in one way or another of two very salient facts: we are living in a period of rapidly increasing global connectedness; and change of all sorts appears to be a permanent feature of the human condition. Sometimes the reminders are stark: newspaper headlines and the television news trumpet the fall of the Berlin wall, the disintegration of the Soviet Union, or the discovery of a new technique for genetic engineering. Other times they are more subtle: the "made in China" label on your sweater, the fact that your orange juice comes from Brazil or that the parts for your Ford come from several countries even though it is assembled here in the United States.

In fact, we are bombarded so continuously with these reminders that we become numbed by them, more or less casually accepting their consequences. Yet in a world where technological advance has permitted rapid and frequent communication across national boundaries at the level of the ordinary person, new and different challenges and opportunities arise. Developments of promise in one part of the world become quickly known in other parts, setting off a flurry of activity designed to determine their relevance in the new setting. No domain of human activity stands outside this dynamic. It ap-

1

pears to be equally evident, for example, in biomedical research, education, telecommunications, and retailing.

To take but one case from the realm of management, we
need go no farther than the practices of the Japanese to illustrate the point. Japanese management systems have acquired
near-mythic status outside Japan for their efficiency and effectiveness, and rare is the country that has not sent scouting
parties on missions to ferret out the key success factors enabling Japanese businesses to achieve economic preeminence.
Quality circles and total quality management, to cite two such
factors, have become familiar parts of the managerial lexicon
worldwide.

Scholars interested in the diffusion of innovation would
undoubtedly consider that the increased speed and scope of
communications influence principally the awareness stage of
the process. More communication means that more potential
adopters of an innovation will be aware of its existence sooner,
and overall rates of adoption of the innovation can be expected
to increase as a result. There is considerably more to the story
than this, however. Although it is conceivable that a sort of
snowball effect might propel diffusion more quickly, it is also
conceivable that the association of an innovation with another
country might have the opposite effect. Why should the French,
for example, be expected to embrace an innovation developed
in Germany unless they can somehow make it French? Or the
Americans embrace an innovation developed in Japan without
making it American? Is it reasonable to expect that rationality
will dominate ethnocentrism as innovations migrate?

We are thus confronted by a seeming paradox: awareness
of innovation internationally is greater now than ever before,
but the fact of increased awareness itself may result in re-
calcitrance when an innovation is considered foreign.

(Research on the diffusion of innovative management
techniques across national borders is relatively sparse, but the
interested reader is referred to Kogut and Zander, 1992, or
Westney, 1987, for examples and to Arias and Guillen, 1991, for
an excellent review of the area.)

The Problem of Innovation

Certainly, our fascination with the migratory paradox underlies our interest in the migration of one particular innovation — diagnosis-related groups, or DRGs — from the United States to Western Europe. However, a long-term investigation of the more general problem of innovation has shaped our inquiry as well. This problem has been the subject of literally thousands of scholarly books, articles, and commentaries. As might be expected given the sheer volume of written material, the literature is riddled with definitional ambiguity, competing hypotheses, and contradictory findings. We will not rehearse those here. Instead we will briefly stake out our own position so that you will understand our biases as well as our point of view.

To start with, what is innovation? Is it a process? Or is it a new idea, product, program, or policy? Obviously, innovation can be any of these, but perhaps not all at the same time. For the purposes of theory building and analysis, a choice has to be made. For us, the answer is that innovations are new ideas, products, programs, or policies — that is, things that can be pointed to and whose attributes can be described. For us, invention is the process by which innovations are created, and implementation is the process by which they are put into use.

Most writing on the topic of innovation assumes that innovation is by definition good and thus that more innovation is better (Kimberly, 1981). Given this assumption, the practical problem for the manager or the politician becomes how to increase the system's capacity and appetite for innovation. However, we explicitly reject this assumption. Judgments about the worth of a particular innovation can and do differ substantially from one observer to the next. Some innovations have harmful effects that overwhelm whatever benefits they bring (Abrahamson, 1991). Some are controversial. Evaluations of others change with the passage of time as more experience with them develops. Finally, public pronouncements about value are often little more than political rhetoric designed to build support for investment decisions.

To understand the fate of innovations, one has to under-stand their origins, how they fit into the ebb and flow of in-vention, and how they fit into the structure of opportunity and chance. Innovations do not simply emerge full-blown. As Schumpeter (1934) noted long ago, they are part of a larger pattern of social, political, and economic activity. Their develop-ment may be either encouraged or slowed down, perhaps even stopped, by the interplay of these forces. Yet too often research and writing on innovation, by not addressing this interplay of forces, make it seem unimportant. It is not.

Similarly, the fate of any particular innovation will most likely influence the fate of succeeding innovations in the same domain. Comparisons will inevitably be made and decisions taken based on assessments of past experience. Thus, innova-tions shape the future in ways that are often overlooked by researchers too narrowly focused on the innovation itself.

Innovations are rarely static. They frequently go through many mutations as experience suggests improvements and as use alters initial conceptions of value. Consider the example of the video camera. The consumer who bought a video camera in 1992 got a very different product in many respects than did the consumer who bought one in 1986. Size, capacity, and features changed considerably in a relatively short period of time. The market is a powerful influence on the shape of innovation, and no analysis of the fate of any particular innovation would be complete without taking the fact of use-driven change into account.

Innovations present risks for manufacturers or con-sumers who would invest in them. When they first appear, there often is considerable uncertainty with respect to how well they will perform and what their economic impact on the firm will be. Although the benefits to be gained from early adoption might be considerable, the risks are also high.

The literature on innovation tends to treat the investment decison as a binary one—the firm or the individual consumer either buys (adopts) the innovation or does not. But the reality is frequently more complex. Often investors can hedge their risk by using a series of intermediate strategies, which might be represented by the metaphor of "leasing" instead of "buying." The decision is thus not of the all-or-nothing variety but is actually considerably more complex (and interesting). Analyses of the fate of innovation need to take these intermediate risk-hedging strategies explicitly into account.

Every setting into which innovation is introduced has its own particular set of routines, mix of personalities, hierarchy of priorities, and panoply of political agendas. Their interplay constitutes what we call the context for innovation. Because these contexts both vary from one setting to the next and change over time, and because they constitute the equivalent of the petri dish in which the innovation will either flourish or founder, it is essential that their influence on the fate of innovation be taken into account. Although contextual analysis raises many methodological and epistemological questions, we feel it is the most appropriate form of analysis for the problems we are interested in investigating.

DRGs as Innovation

This book is about the migration of DRGs from the United States to nine countries in Western Europe. Since we find it useful to think of DRGs as a form of innovation, and because the framework that oriented our research was grounded in previous work on this topic, it is incumbent upon us to present our view of DRGs as a form of innovation.

Conceptually, DRGs represent nothing more than a way of thinking about and representing the "products" of a hospital. If you accept the idea that patients with similar presenting problems might be expected to be treated similarly within the hospital, then you might expect that their treatment courses would cost roughly similar amounts of money because they would require similar patterns of resource consumption. This simple but powerful idea emerged from the management literature on production and operations management.

Furthermore, if you accept the idea that the resources consumed by patients with similar presenting problems, other things being equal, can be accurately accounted for, then you might expect that case-mix differences among hospitals could be accurately measured and described.

Finally, if the resources consumed by patients with similar presenting problems can be accurately described, then the work of "product designers" (physicians) can be compared for similar cases in terms of similarities and differences in actual patterns of resource consumption, as can the overall results for one hospital as compared to another.

Although this logic may appear painfully obvious in the 1990s, in the mid 1970s it was anything but obvious. Few if any incentives existed for hospital administrators to analyze the production systems in their institutions in the kind of microscopic detail that an operations management or industrial engineering approach requires, and as a consequence most hospitals in the United States had neither the accounting systems nor the management information systems in place to permit them to do so. Consequently, in the context of hospital management practice in the mid 1970s, these ideas appeared revolutionary even though they had been widely accepted in industry for decades. DRGs represented the application of the logic of production management to the hospital. The approach was developed by a research team at Yale University headed by two faculty members, Robert Fetter, an industrial engineer, and John Thompson, a nurse (Fetter, 1991). Their intent originally was to develop a tool that could improve the quality of internal management in hospitals; the story about how DRGs became incorporated into the prospective payment system and thereby converted to use as a *payment* mechanism provides some fascinating insights into the formation of public policy and has been chronicled in Smith (1992).

DRGs, then, are a sort of patient classification system that groups patients with similar characteristics together. As a management tool, DRGs are designed to permit hospital managers first to understand existing patterns of resource consumption, second to observe anomalies or apparent aberrations, and third to predict patterns of resource consumption in the future based on what is known about the recent past.

To us, there is no question but that DRGs are an innovation in health management. They represent a significant change in the way managers (and others) think about the hospital, its products, and the way in which the production system can be monitored. We make this assertion about the innovation quality of DRGs without, however, attaching any particular judgment to it. Any significant innovation will have its strong detractors as well as its passionate advocates. Our effort here is to avoid any pro-innovation bias and, instead, to try to understand how and why DRGs migrated as they have to Western Europe. Attachment of the label "innovation" to them does not, therefore, imply a value judgment; how potential users of DRGs impute value, however, will inevitably affect their fate.

Although DRGs represent an innovation, the ideas upon which they were built were not, in themselves, new. DRGs are connected directly to two domains of activity, the one in health economics and the search for production functions (or their equivalent) in hospitals, and the other in industrial engineering and the drive to develop microanalyses of resource consumption by firms. Furthermore, they emerge in the context of previous efforts to determine hospital case-mix differences and their consequences for institutional management. As is the case with most innovations, the innovation here is the way in which ideas and techniques from differing domains were combined and made operational for the purposes of hospital management.

How will DRGs shape the future? Although we cannot make specific predictions, it is clear that the development and migration of DRGs have had an enormous impact on how people think about the management of health care institutions. In our judgment, the impact is irreversible. We simply cannot envision a return to the old system, in which physicians independent of institutional managers are at once the product designers, the de facto resource allocators, and the sole evaluators of results. DRGs, in conjunction with other forces, have put a train on the tracks. How far the train will go is unclear, as is its precise direction, but it most certainly will not return home.

DRGs have certainly evolved since they were first developed at Yale. Not only have they been modified and revised based on experience and feedback, but they have also been used in ways, as noted above, not originally intended. So both their structure and their use have been modified over time. In fact, one might argue that the survival potential of any innovation is greater to the extent that it can be adapted for use in local circumstances. As you will see in Chapters Two through Ten, different countries have adapted DRGs for use in quite different ways, and the fact that they are a bit of a moving target appears to have worked to their advantage.

You will also see in the following chapters how the risk that is inevitably associated with investment in nearly any innovation has been hedged in various countries. Although relatively heavy investments have been made in two countries on a national scale, and decisions to move in different directions have been made in two others, in the majority of countries a variety of testing and experimentation is being carried out. In some cases, this experimentation is basically political, designed to provide an opportunity to gain the support of essential constituencies; in others it is more technical in nature, designed to permit examination of the performance characteristics of the tool; and in still others it is some combination of the two. What is striking is the degree of hedging that we observed in the majority of cases.

Finally, in considering DRGs as an innovation, you will see the importance of context as an influence on their fate. For us, context has several dimensions, including the extent to which decision making in any particular country's health system is relatively centralized or decentralized, the extent to which there is tangible and widespread discontent with the current health care system, and the extent to which increasing costs are driving the search for solutions. Each of these dimensions is an important piece to the puzzle. Their particular configuration varies from one country to the next, but the nature of the configuration shapes outcomes. To be able to compare outcomes, then, we must first understand how the pieces fit together in each country.

Key Attributes of DRGs

Everett Rogers, a longtime student of innovation and assimilator of scholarly research on the topic, used the extensive body of empirical and theoretical literature to construct an elegantly simple framework for analysis. He argues that adoption of an innovation is a function of the characteristics of the innovation itself, the characteristics of the potential adopter or adopting system, and the interaction between the two (Rogers, 1983).

This framework served as a point of departure for our analysis of the diffusion of DRGs. Earlier in this chapter we described certain attributes of DRGs themselves. We will return to this theme in the last chapter, but for the present, the most significant attributes to bear in mind as you consider their fate in different countries are that both their form and their use are malleable and that their construction requires both significant amounts of information about hospital activity *and* considerable technical sophistication in statistics and computing. Furthermore, their construction in the United States involved, from the very beginning, substantial and continuing input from physicians.

The scholarly literature on innovation strongly suggests that to the extent that a given innovation is capable of being modified to suit local circumstances, its chances of widespread diffusion are enhanced, other things being equal. The specifics will vary from one innovation to the next, but the basic idea is that differences in the context will create different needs and that an innovation will diffuse if it can be adapted to meet these changed circumstances. In a sense, the message is diametrically opposed to that sent by Henry Ford when he declared that one could buy his car in any color as long as it was black.

Where innovation is concerned, there is always a tension between how much the system must change to incorporate the innovation and how much the innovation itself may be modified to mesh well with the system as it is. Rogers (1983) uses the word "reinvention" to refer to the oft-observed tendency of users of innovation to mold an innovation to meet system expectations or requirements. We would argue in the case of DRGs, then, that their fate in any given country will partly depend on perceptions of their malleability in both form and use.

The construction of DRGs themselves requires relatively large amounts of reliable information on hospital discharges from significant numbers of hospitals. If such information is not available, the innovation cannot be implemented, no matter how desirable it may appear to be. In the mid 1980s, there was considerable variation among the countries included in this book with respect to availability of reliable, computer-accessible information on hospital discharges.

In a similar vein, construction and use of DRGs has certain technical requirements in the areas of both statistics and computing. In the absence of these skills and facilities, the innovation cannot be implemented, again no matter how desirable it may appear. As might be expected, there was also considerable variation among the nine European countries with respect to the statistical and computing capabilities available in the mid 1980s.

Construction of DRGs also requires literally hundreds of clinical judgments to be made as the classification process proceeds. To ensure the validity of the tool itself, these judgments need to be made by qualified physicians. Of course, to ensure acceptance of the tool, physicians in general have to be convinced of its clinical appropriateness and relevance.

Characteristics of the Setting

As important as the attributes of the innovation itself are the structure and dynamics present in the setting into which they are introduced. At the outset of our research we identified a set of factors that we felt were important characteristics of the settings and that might be expected to vary from one country to another. We then asked each chapter author to try, insofar as possible, to address each of these factors in his or her chapter. Factors included were the health policy context, the technical context, the path of entry of the innovation into the country, the roles played by key consitituents, the existence and influence of champions for the innovation, and the emergence and role of networks of supporters both within the country and without. Each of these is discussed briefly below.

Health Policy Context

At the national level, there are considerable differences among the nine countries included in our research in the way in which health policy is created and administered. These differences have consequences for the way in which priorities are defined, decisions are made, and resources are allocated within the health sector. Additionally, the total amount of resources available to that sector are a reflection of social and political choices that vary from one country to the next. We anticipated that such differences might well be related to the search for innovation and the receptivity to DRGs.

The search for innovation might also be a function of what some have called performance gap or a sense that the system is inefficient and/or ineffective and thus in need of improvement (Zaltman, Duncan, and Holbek, 1973). Hence, we tried to include a global or necessarily crude estimate of the relative satisfaction or dissatisfaction expressed within countries regarding the performance of their health care systems.

An innovation that promises to lead to better management of health care institutions might be expected to be particularly attractive to countries facing financial crises in their health care systems. We use the word "crises" advisedly, recognizing that crises are often manufactured for particular political ends, as Alford (1975) has demonstrated convincingly. Nonetheless, in an atmosphere of financial crisis an innovation that portends relief might be especially welcome.

Technical Context

As noted above, the DRGs require certain levels of information on hospital activity as well as some sophistication in statistics and computing in order to be constructed and used. It was not obvious to us at the outset that these technical requirements would be met in every country. Furthermore, we hypothesized that the greater the investment required to build the minimum technical capabilities, the greater the chance that efforts to derail the introduction of DRGs would be successful, and/or the greater the chance that perceptions of cost would dominate perceptions of potential benefit, thus diminishing enthusiasm for the investment. For this reason, we attempted to examine systematically (albeit imperfectly) the nature of the existing information infrastructure and the extent of available technical capabilities in each country prior to the time at which DRGs were first introduced.

Path of Entry

An innovation does not migrate across national borders in vacuo. It moves through carriers, much as disease does in epidemiological models. Although we had no particular a priori theories to guide us here, we did have a strong intuition that the way in which DRGs entered a particular country might well influence their fate. We reasoned that there were at least four possible channels: academic researchers, government officials, consultants, and businesspeople. We reasoned further that if the sole point of entry was academic research, then, absent some strong and most probably idiosyncratic connections between individual researchers and policy makers, the chances of diffusion at the national level were relatively circumscribed.

Methodologically, determination of precisely how and when DRGs entered any given country was problematic, to say the least. Yet we believed that it was important, both as a theoretical and as a practical matter, to attempt to make such a determination. As to theory, we felt that we were in promising new territory; as to practice, there were potentially interesting lessons to be learned for those who would promote the spread of innovations across national borders. Thus, mindful of the difficulties, we plunged ahead.

Key Constituencies

One finding that has been replicated time and time again in studies of innovation and the change process is that the behav-

ior of those people directly and indirectly affected by the innovation will largely determine its fate (Kanter, 1983). To the extent
that such people are active and enthusiastic supporters, the
innovation will be implemented and used; to the extent that
there are pockets of active and enthusiastic resistance, the innovation's fate is less certain.

This finding needs to be qualified in many ways. Perhaps
most important, *any* innovation that disrupts the existing fabric
of relationships among parties is bound to be controversial.
Some parties will see their own agendas being furthered by the
new initiative, while others will see theirs being placed at risk.
Thus, one can always expect pockets of both active and passive
resistance when the prospect of innovation looms on the
horizon.

The inevitability of controversy in the face of innovation
led us to believe that the most reasonable research approach
would be to define the sets of actors who were most likely to be
affected by the introduction of DRGs and to encourage chapter
authors to pay particular attention to the roles they played.
Authors were encouraged to add others where appropriate and
to try to distinguish behavior that was role-defined from that
which was individually defined and institutionally defined. Although this latter exercise is a very tall order (indeed, impossible
to execute perfectly), we felt the distinction was important to
attempt.

The categories of actors included in the framework were
physicians, hospital administrators, government policy makers
and bureaucrats, consultants, academics, and entrepreneurs.
We realized, of course, that not everyone in any given category
will speak with one voice, but we felt that points of controversy within groups would represent interesting additional
information.

Role of Champions

Another finding that emerges consistently from research on
innovation is the importance of champions or true believers
(Van de Ven, Angle, and Poole, 1989). Champions are those
individuals who, for one reason or another, are dogged support-

ers of an innovation and who are prepared to invest extraordinary amounts of personal time, energy, and reputation to ensure its implementation. They may, in some cases, be the inventer. But more often than not they are men and women who see advantage, personal and/or systemic, from introduction and use of the innovation and who are willing to take substantial personal risks to see it used. To be effective, champions have to be credible in the system, have to have access to senior executive support within the system, and have to be willing to persist in the face of what often appear to be overwhelming negative odds.

We have attempted where possible to determine whether DRG champions existed in particular countries and what roles they played where they existed. Our view is not that the fate of innovation rests with the behavior of particular individuals but that there are roles that need to be played in the process of diffusion by particular individuals if that process is to result in widespread use.

Networks of Support

Introducing innovation into a setting can be a lonely undertaking. To the extent that the advocates of innovation are relatively unconnected, the challenge of diffusion increases in magnitude. To the extent that supporters are linked both to other supporters within the system and to others in similar roles in other systems, the chances for building momentum increase.

In the case of an innovation that migrates across national borders and where what we called earlier the migratory paradox may be at work, the development of networks of support may boost the probability of success. This is true regardless of whether that support be in the form of sharing of technical information, of communication regarding successes and failures, or of recruitment of like-minded colleagues.

The final variable in our framework, then, is the development of such networks both within a particular country and among different countries. Chapter authors were encouraged to document any such developments within their countries and to

Figure 1.1. Influences on the Fate of DRGs.

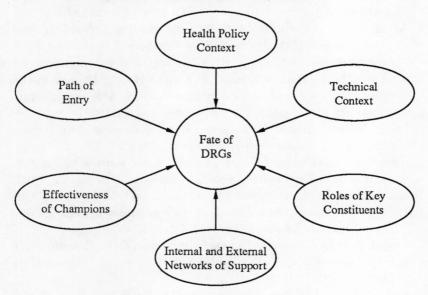

document participation by any of their colleagues in international undertakings as well.

This completes the framework we used for our examination of the migration of DRGs to Western Europe. This framework is presented fully in Figure 1.1. Although we were presumably tracking a single innovation, it did, in fact, prove to be somewhat malleable in both form and use, as you will see in the following chapters. Although the fate of DRGs varies considerably from one country to the next, there are some intriguing patterns observable when one compares the experiences of all nine. It is to these patterns that we turn our attention in the final chapter.

References

Abrahamson, E. "Managerial Fads and Fashions: The Diffusion and Rejection of Innovations." *Academy of Management Review*, 1991, *16*(3), 586–612.

Alford, R. *Health Care Politics: Ideological and Interest Group Barriers to Reform.* Chicago: University of Chicago Press, 1975.

Arias, M., and Guillen, M. "The Transfer for Organizational Management Techniques Across Borders: Combining Neo-Institutional and Comparative Perspectives." Paper presented at the INSEAD Conference on Organization Theory at the Crossroads: European Contributions to the Science of Organizations, Fontainebleau, France, November 1991.

Fetter, R. (ed.). *DRGs: Their Design and Development.* Ann Arbor, Mich.: Health Administration Press, 1991.

Kanter, R. *The Change Masters: Innovation and Entrepreneurship in the American Corporation.* New York: Simon & Schuster, 1983.

Kimberly, J. R. "Managerial Innovation." In P. C. Nystrom and W. H. Starbuck (eds.), *Handbook of Organizational Design.* New York: Oxford University Press, 1981.

Kogut, B., and Zander, U. "Knowledge of the Firm, Combinative Capabilities, and the Replication of Technology." *Organization Science*, 1992, *3*(3), 383–397.

Rogers, E. *The Diffusion of Innovation.* New York: Free Press, 1983.

Schumpeter, J. A. *The Theory of Economic Development.* Cambridge, Mass.: Harvard University Press, 1934.

Smith, D. *Paying for Medicare: The Politics of Reform.* New York: Aldine-DeGruyter, 1992

Van de Ven, A., Angle, H., and Poole, M. S. *Research on the Management of Innovation.* New York: HarperCollins, 1989.

Westney, E. *Imitation and Innovation: The Transfer of Western Organizational Patterns to Meiji, Japan.* Cambridge, Mass.: Harvard University Press, 1987.

Zaltman, G., Duncan, R., and Holbek, J. *Innovations and Organizations.* New York: Wiley, 1973.

Two

England: Ten Years of Diffusion and Development

James M. Coles

By the very nature of the process, those who would write about the diffusion of an idea — in this example case mix systems and diagnosis-related groups (DRGs) — are also taking part in it. However, some will have also been active in the program of analysis, evaluation, and dissemination surrounding the development of the idea. The reader should recognize that this chapter was written by someone who has been involved with case mix work in the United Kingdom for over ten years, and while rigorous steps have been taken to keep subjectivity to a minimum, certain lines of interpretation will inevitably be the author's own views. Substantive facts have largely been obtained from written documents and confirmed in discussion with some of those involved.

The chapter has four main sections. The first provides a short background to health care in England and gives a number of basic facts concerning health care expenditure and activity. The second section examines in rather more detail the considerable amount of change that has occurred in the National Health Service (NHS) in England over the last decade. These first two

Note: The author wishes to thank Hugh Sanderson, Tim Scott, and Linda Jenkins for reviewing this chapter.

sections provide the context within which to consider the development of case mix management, and in particular DRGs, in England. The bulk of the chapter is concerned with this development. The fourth and final part of the chapter is somewhat speculative in that it attempts to examine some major themes in case mix in England throughout the 1980s and identify whether and how these are likely to progress over the next five to ten years.

Outline of Health Care

The period from the beginning of the 1980s, which has seen the start of the diffusion of case mix issues in the United Kingdom, has also been one of considerable turmoil in health service. A number of major organizational changes occurred throughout the decade that clearly had an impact on the way this innovation developed. Although by the start of the 1990s private hospitals were playing a more significant part in certain areas of health care (for example, in elective surgery and in care of the elderly), by far the greater part of health services in this country continue to be provided by the NHS, and thus it is on the NHS that this chapter focuses. Table 2.1 presents, by way of background information, some basic facts about the NHS during this period.

The National Health Service Act of 1946 required the minister of health to promote the establishment in England and Wales of a comprehensive health service designed to secure improvement in the physical and mental health of the population. The service itself, which was a development of trends that had been growing over the previous few decades, came into being in 1948. However, it was new in that it was to be available to the whole population and free of charge at the point of service. It would be funded from general taxation, and the country's hospitals, vested in the minister, would be run by local boards that were agents of the minister rather than having the autonomy that the previous authorities had. Family practitioner services were also brought within the scope of the act, with all members of the population eligible to register with a general practitioner and receive care, by and large freely.

The relationship between the Department of Health and

Table 2.1. Key Health Care Figures for England.

Country area	130,439 sq. km.
Total population (mid 1987 est.)	47.407 million
Population over 75	3.189 million
Percent of population over 75	6.73%
Average income per household, 1986	£5,711
Average income, nonpensionable adult, 1986	£9,786
Average per-capita expenditure on health, 1987	£432
Average NHS per-capita expenditure on health, 1987	£377
Percent of GNP devoted to health care, 1980	6.46%
Percent of GNP spent by NHS, 1980	5.97%
Percent of GNP devoted to health care, 1987 (est.)	7.06%
Percent of GNP spent by NHS, 1987 (est.)	6.17%
No. of nonpsychiatric hospitals, 1988	1,282
No. of nonpsychiatric beds, 1988	212,019
No. of beds in acute specialties, 1988[a]	128,000 (approx.)
No. of beds in acute specialties per 1,000 inhabitants, 1988	2.7
No. of cases treated,[a] 1987–1988	5.13 million (approx.)
No. of cases treated per 1,000 inhabitants, 1987–1988	108.2
Average length of stay, 1985[a]	7.6 days
No. of physicians, 1987	
Hospital medical staff	38,018
Community services medical staff	2,839
Primary health—GP principals	25,082
No. of physicians per 10,000 inhabitants, 1987	
Hospital medical staff	8.02
Community services medical staff	0.60
Primary health—GP principals	5.29

[a] Acute specialties include all specialties except geriatrics, younger disabled maternity, mental handicap, and mental illness.

Source: Data from *Health & Personal Social Services Statistics*, 1991; *Compendium of Health Statistics* (7th ed.), 1989; *Annual Abstract of Statistics*, 1990; *Britain 1991*, 1991.

the NHS (now run by Regional and District Health Authorities, Family Health Services Authorities, and the newly created NHS Trusts) has often confused observers of the English system. In general the duties of the minister (now secretary of state) for health are exercised on his or her behalf by these authorities. However, because the minister remains accountable to Parliament both for the broad development of health services and for their provision, authorities can be directed on the way they carry out their functions, and, if necessary, these functions can be managed directly. The Department of Health, as well as running some central functions (for economy or convenience), looks after the development of national policies and priorities, the overall administration and allocation of resources, and central personnel requirements, including training and liaison with health authorities. Formerly, the health authorities were member bodies to whom the professional managers reported. They have recently been reconstituted more on the lines of boards of commercial companies, with both executive and nonexecutive members. The chair's appointment is approved by the secretary of state.

The principles of the NHS have remained unchanged since its inception. Its organization, however, has been examined and modified almost continually. This is probably due to concerns about the relatively high proportion of public expenditure the NHS consumes and to doubts whether the various structures have proved to be the most efficient way of using these resources. For example, the fragmented organization of hospitals, family doctors, and, in some cases, social services (provided by local government) has been thought open to improvement, while another favorite topic has been the appropriate scale of the operational authorities. Was it the 388 separate Hospital Management Committees that existed in the early days, or the 90 Area Health Authorities that existed between 1974 and 1982, or is the correct level somewhere between the two?

It was against this background that the firmly monetarist government of Prime Minister Margaret Thatcher came to power in 1979. The Thatcher government was committed to reducing public expenditure but not to following all of the suggestions (particularly those involving additional expenditure) put forward by the Royal Commission on the National Health Service that was just reporting (HMSO, 1979) and that had been set up by a previous Labour government.

Key Changes in the NHS

Many lecturers in health services management in the United Kingdom have at one time or another shown a transparency with a quote from a Roman author who lived in the first century A.D. The reason for this rather strange diversion lies in the similarity between what Petronius had noted about the Roman army and what was going on in the NHS in the late 1970s and throughout the 1980s. To Petronius it appeared that every time the Roman army got itself organized in a particular fashion, someone would come along with a new perspective and seek to reorganize the whole institution yet again. Petronius comments on the restlessness within the human spirit and our need to continue to search for a supposedly better way of organizing ourselves.

This search for improvement is most persistent in those areas about which we, as a society, care most deeply. Unfortunately, these are often also the areas that attract the greatest political attention when they threaten to become an embarrassment to the government of the day. Across the western world these two features are nowhere more noticeable than in the area of health care. Most people, whether or not they pay for treatment directly, wish to ensure that they can obtain adequate health care for themselves and their families when they need it. Even where the responsibility for the provision and financing of health care resides with third parties (such as insurance companies or private hospitals), the government of the country is generally held responsible by the population if it fails to ensure that the superstructure is appropriate to meet its needs.

Petronius would probably not be surprised to learn that since the reorganization of 1974 the NHS has been turned upside down by further major reviews instigated by the government in 1982, 1984, and 1989. Each of these has involved major restructuring and, although listed here as occurring in a single year, has taken two to three years to implement. Indeed, you could say that during the Thatcher years there was hardly a day when the NHS was not being substantially altered. Yet, if we go back to the Conservative party's manifesto of 1979, very little was said about health directly. The emphasis of the national agenda at that time was the economy, defense and international alliances, and the encouragement of self-help through personal incentives. The intention, as far as the welfare services were concerned, was to ensure that their provision was concentrated on people in real need.

The impetus for change in 1982 came largely from within the NHS and, although appearing radical at the time, has certainly turned out with hindsight to be minor compared with what was to follow. It was generally recognized that the bureaucratic structure of regional, area, and district organizations, which was set up in 1974 and sat above the direct care-giving hospitals and clinics, was too cumbersome. Overlapping responsibilities and reporting mechanisms and a panoply of committees were to be simplified. In the end, it was the area tier that was dismantled, with most of its responsibilities being given to new, statutory district authorities. The overriding emphasis at that time was on devolution, with the operational units taking on a larger managerial function but still following the byword of the 1974 reorganization: consensus.

The reorganization of 1984 resulted from a management inquiry set up in February of the previous year to look at the effective use and management of people and other resources. The inquiry team were all businesspeople, a fact that reflected the then-current perception that the public sector might benefit from a more businesslike approach. The report itself (Griffiths, 1983) also stepped outside of the usual bureaucratic approach in that it was written in the form of a personal letter to the secretary of state. The letter identified the need to devolve responsibility as far down the line as possible but recognized that, at that time, such devolution was occurring much too slowly. The team proposed a small management board at the Department of Health to run the NHS according to strategy set by a supervisory board under the secretary of state. The major thrust of the report, though, focused on a clearly argued need to dispense with the consensus style of management and to identify a single general manager at each level from the management board down to the single hospital. Each general manager would be accountable for all activity undertaken at his or her level, and the existing functional managers would report to this general manager. It was also recognized that clinicians, who allocated many of the hospital's resources, should be encouraged and enabled to take a more active and responsible part in management, particularly at the unit or hospital level. This involvement was to be facilitated within the hospital organization with the development of what was called "management budgeting," whereby clinicians would have power over, but also be accountable for, financial resources.

The prime ministerial review of 1988, which resulted in the white paper *Working for Patients* (HMSO, 1989), arose following a campaign in the press attacking the lack of available resources to meet what clinicians and other critics considered were reasonable demands for health care. The government, which argued that it had put more money into health than ever before, was unable to defuse the situation until the review was announced. As well as stressing further the need to give local staff as much responsibility as possible, the review aimed to give patients greater choice and to produce greater satisfaction and reward for NHS staff who successfully responded to local needs. While it is not clear that the proposals that are currently being enacted will achieve these aims, they are producing probably the most fundamental reorientation of the health service since its inception. In the case of many services, money is following the patient, with hospitals now becoming income-earning as opposed to allocation-funded bodies. There is greater delegation of responsibility to the local level, the most extreme example currently being the new self-governing NHS Trusts.

The balance between devolution and accountability for public funds is of course a difficult one. The changes brought about in 1982 and 1984 were supposed to enhance local decision-making powers, although many observers (Bussey, 1985;

Dixon, 1983) saw the accompanying upward reporting requirements as substantially decreasing this effect. Critics of the new
white paper proposals also suggest that, together with the loss of
local members from the managing health authorities, the current changes represent a significant diminishing of local
accountability for the type, quantity, and quality of the service
provided. The government would argue, however, that a controlled move to a market orientation enables the population to
influence these matters more easily.

    The reorganizations of the 1980s have all addressed three
major themes:

• Devolution of responsibility while retaining accountability
• Appropriate management style, including the increased
  role of clinicians
• The requirement for enhanced information systems, including financial information

    Additionally, there have been various examinations of the
method of financing the NHS (Enthoven, 1985). While funding
largely through taxation still appears sacrosanct, discussions
about the best way to produce incentives to improve the use of
resources have continued unabated. In common with all Western countries, the United Kingdom sought throughout the 1980s
to limit what seemed to be an inexorable rise in the cost of
health care. Although the NHS was already highly successful in
limiting the growth in overall costs through the Treasury's cash
limit system, it would be naive to suggest that England was not
examining developments that were taking place at the same
time in other countries, especially the prospective payment
system being introduced in the United States. It is reasonable to
assume that the development of case mix classification systems
in England has been considerably shaped, over this decade, by
the emphasis given to each of the three major areas identified
above. While, as we shall see later in the chapter, much of the
developmental and evaluative work in these areas was undertaken by research groups, agendas in the area of health services
research themselves influence and are influenced by the issues

of the day. It is difficult to imagine, for example, that developments would have followed the same path if greater involvement of doctors in management had not been sought by the policy makers at the Department of Health, or if it had not been recognized that information systems (and the power of computers) had to be enhanced in the NHS throughout the 1980s. It is therefore worthwhile to look at each of the three main themes identified above in slightly more detail.

Devolution of Responsibility

District health authorities were established in the 1982 reorganization, ostensibly to increase local accountability for health care. Previously, districts had been the managerial level and had reported upward to area authorities, which had the statutory responsibility for the planning and provision of services. The 1982 changes also sought to develop the role of the individual hospital, or service area, which was to have stronger management and the responsibility to manage its own budget. Clinicians were to play an increased role in management through new unit management teams. Accompanying these changes was a need for greater accountability upward, all the way to the secretary of state's accountability to Parliament. To bring about this change, a review mechanism was introduced so that each level monitored the plans and performance of the next level down the hierarchy. A higher level of information management was needed to support this process, and detailed comparative performance indicators were produced. These were by no means perfect as there were no quality-of-care indicators and an insufficient allowance was made for differences in case mix and for the functional nature of the cost information.

The latest white paper has carried devolution a great deal further by encouraging hospitals and other units (those at a similar level to the units of 1982) to set themselves up as self-governing trusts. While still within the NHS and providing free services to patients, they were allowed to untangle themselves from the bureaucracy by being accountable directly to the secretary of state for the development and achievement of their

business plans. This move has also encouraged increased competition for resources between units, and although NHS trusts
will continue to be upwardly accountable, it is not wholly clear
what information will be required from them and how openly
available this will be.

Management Style

The move to general management was brought about by the
Griffiths report of 1983, and as a result a single manager became
responsible for all activities at a particular managerial level
(such as a region or a district). Most top managers at the various
levels were given short-term renewable employment contracts
with agreed objectives for them to achieve. The managers were
thought to have greater freedom to achieve these objectives
since the perceived constraints of consensus (slowing down or
dilution of decision making) were removed. Additionally, a system of performance-related pay for senior managers was slowly
introduced throughout the health service, again to motivate the
achievement of quantifiable objectives.

     While these initiatives had a noticeable effect, it was also
clear that doctors, who had largely remained detached from
mainstream management, could thwart the new, more ag-
gressive style of management for good or for ill. Mechanisms
therefore needed to be found to involve the medical staff more
fully in management. A local initiative (Smith and Chantler,
1987) was taking place at about the same time in the Lewisham
and North Southwark Health Authority to achieve similar par-
ticipatory ends. Guy's Hospital in London, which had an academic link with Johns Hopkins Hospital in Baltimore, Maryland, decided to model its management on this U.S. hospital
and in 1985 introduced a structure incorporating clinical directors who would basically run small, output-oriented "businesses." They would agree on expenditure and activity plans and
would have a senior nurse plus a business manager to assist
them. During the second half of the 1980s, many hospitals
experimented with similar models focused on clinical directors.
Some are still skeptical about this style of management, but the

principles have recently received general support from the British Medical Association. The larger role of doctors in the management of our health care institutions is now widely accepted, but, not surprisingly, such doctors are demanding relevant and timely information to support them in their efforts.

Development of Information Systems

The 1980s saw an increasing importance attached to the need for reliable management information within the health service. Throughout this period, computing power increased dramatically and prices tumbled so fast as to make computers accessible to many departmental budgets. While this development had some disadvantages—such as the replicated development of similar systems in many hospitals or a lack of consistency in data elements and their definitions—there is little doubt that the power of these machines brought a sophistication to data handling and manipulation that was not practicable at the start of the decade.

For an example of this one only has to look at the history of clinical budgeting and patient-costing experiments in the early 1980s (Perrin, 1988). These experiments showed that it was technically feasible to collect information adequate to the detailed costing of patients but that in many service departments such information was only available in manually produced records. As the decade progressed, management demanded that these systems became more computer-based, and the stimulus of the Resource Management Initiative from 1986 onwards ensured that the pace of this development quickened throughout the NHS. As we shall see, the initiative played a major role in the development of case mix thinking in England.

All three of the themes discussed above are continuing to evolve within the new purchaser/provider and contracting-for-care NHS of the 1990s. Although we have had a nationally agreed and mandated set of data on hospital discharges for a considerable time now, its value as a management tool at the local level has not always been appreciated. During the last half of the 1980s, managerial development required that the quality of such data be improved and their potential use be more widely understood. The political agenda, the managerial agenda, and the increased information capabilities have all come together to play their part in shaping current developments in case mix management, and DRGs in particular.

History of DRGs

The need to identify the requirements of a varying mix of hospital patients has long been recognized within the NHS. By the 1960s hospitals had been required to report their activity by certain defined categories (for example, specialties) to which each practicing clinician had been assigned when appointed. Financial reporting also sought to take into account what was thought to be legitimate variation in cost performance by grouping similar hospitals before embarking on any comparisons of efficiency. However, these bands were rather broad, with each hospital being described as acute, mainly acute, long-stay, and so on and subgrouped by size.

This level of definition looks, from thirty years on, to be very crude, but it should be remembered that neither the information systems within the NHS nor the computing technology at that time could support anything much more refined. In the late 1960s and early 1970s researchers began to show that useful analyses of data could be produced at the specialty level. Feldstein (1967) produced an economic analysis of differences in hospital costs that identified how much might reasonably be explained by a difference in specialty mix. Barber and Johnson (1973) concentrated on the efficiency with which beds were used and produced a method for displaying a number of associated statistics on one chart. Varying levels of performance could be expected for different specialties. For example, data on short-stay specialist surgery would look very different from that on chronic medical conditions. These kinds of presentation quickly found favor with many hospital managers, who used the available information to monitor their performance.

Once specialty data became reasonably well understood, it was not long before it was recognized that it did not go far

enough. Further standardization was needed before the efficiency of, for example, gynecological or ophthalmic care could
be compared at a number of hospitals. Unfortunately, there was
little progress in this area. In a few individual studies different
case types were examined using the shortened categories of the
International Classification of Diseases (the so-called A list), but
this was often unsatisfactory since it was difficult to determine
the statistical or clinical validity of these studies. The typical
hospital continued to have little or no grasp of the cost of any
clinical care group, either at the patient or the specialty level.
Costing was performed by function or department.

In the 1970s a number of isolated experiments examined
the feasibility of disease and patient costing (Babson, 1973;
Harper 1979; Mason, Perry, and Skegg, 1974), but the lessons
from these were not followed up, either because of lack of
technology or because of disinclination on the part of managers
and/or politicians. Financial reporting remained dominated by
the functional approach, and even today hospital accounting
systems are still largely geared to that approach, with the costs of
the hospital product (case type) being derived secondarily.

During this time, attempts were made to involve clinicians in resourcing issues, primarily as a means of trying to
ensure that the best decisions were made concerning the use of
finite resources. Further regression models for specialty-costing
were developed, while Magee and Osmolski (1978) worked with
individual hospitals to seek a better apportionment of specialty
costs than might be obtained through regression models. Wickings and others (1975) sought even greater costing accuracy,
arguing that, at least for direct costs, apportionments were an
unsatisfactory way to construct clinical budgets. This latter research was carried out at the level of the individual clinician and
hence would allow intra-specialty comparisons. However, it did
not at that stage seek to look at the case mix issue in greater
depth.

As time moved on, the development of these systems
gained momentum, some of which must be attributed to the
rapid development of microcomputing beginning in the early
1980s. It is hard to believe now that the forefront of this tech-

nology in 1980 was the Apple IIe with 64 or 128K of memory, while the IBM personal computer with its many clones did not have an impact in the United Kingdom until 1982.

Picking up on these technological advances, in the early 1980s the Department of Health embarked on a wide-ranging review of the NHS's information needs. Commonly known as the Körner review after its influential chairwoman, it tried to define information requirements at the operational level, suggesting that higher levels of management should meet their needs for information by summarizing that already collected (Department of Health and Social Security, 1982). Although this principle was later somewhat derailed, the group's work was very important in the development of NHS information. As we move into an era of contracting for hospital services, it is very difficult to contemplate how such a move might have been undertaken without a preliminary exercise similar to the Körner review. In particular, the group recommended the introduction of a specialty costing return from every health authority. This recommendation was subsequently implemented in 1987 and formed the basis on which the first round of contracts were priced in 1991.

Early Research

While mainstream health service planners were looking at the specialty level as the answer to the need for case mix adjustments in planning, researchers and academics were aware of the pioneering work that was going on at Yale University under Robert Fetter and John Thompson and of the New Jersey experiment in prospective payment (Iglehart, 1982). Between 1979 and 1981, the School of Organization and Management at Yale was very helpful in providing working papers and reports to those interested in case mix in the United Kingdom, while the seminal supplement to the February 1980 edition of *Medical Care* (Fetter and others, 1980) probably reached an even wider audience. Of course, at this time much of the work was based on the original 383 DRGs and on ICD8 clinical coding.

The initial entry of DRGs into the United Kingdom was

therefore made through the research fraternity in 1981. Two research groups were largely instrumental in this introduction. The London School of Hygiene and Tropical Medicine, which is part of the University of London, has a long tradition of training specialist doctors from both the United Kingdom and abroad in the areas of public health, community medicine, and epidemiology. A senior member of staff at that time also had key responsibilities in maintaining the classification of operative procedures that was used throughout the NHS, while many research projects of the school relied on a national data base of hospital activity known as the Hospital Inpatient Enquiry (HIPE).

The other research group, Clinical Accountability, Service Planning and Evaluation (CASPE), had its beginnings in a project in the mid 1970s that sought to improve resource management by providing clinicians with more information about the resources they committed while also giving them added incentives. The Department of Health (and Social Security, at that time) agreed to establish a research program to expand this work, and CASPE was set up in 1979 to work with a number of health authorities in experiments to give hospital consultants budgetary responsibility. It rapidly became clear that the inclusion of a case mix factor would be valuable in this work, although there would clearly be logistical problems in bringing this about. Following correspondence between me and Fetter and Thompson, CASPE set up a meeting with them in July 1981.

Toward the end of 1981, a group at the London School department of community medicine submitted a proposal to the Department of Health to apply the DRG approach to the national HIPE sample (a 10 percent sample of inpatient records). After the proposal was finally accepted, work was carried out throughout 1982 and into 1983, and a report was produced early the following year (Sanderson and Andrews, 1984). Similar results to those noted in the United States were seen, except that many DRGs showed a rather broader length-of-stay distribution (due in part to our different health care structure), while a number of groups showed an unacceptably high level of variation. The report showed that DRGs were a great advance on the currently available approaches to service planning, but it also identified a number of technical problems associated with their use on United Kingdom data. Some of these were linked to the different computer hardware being used in the United Kingdom—IBM mainframes were uncommon in the NHS at that stage, while microcomputers had yet to take off on both sides of the Atlantic. More important, though, the grouping mechanism used in the United States to assign patients to DRGs was totally foreign in that it used a different classification system (ICD9-CM) from those used to code the English records (ICD9 and OPCS). The London School research group, which was led by Hugh Sanderson, had to decide how to deal with this discrepancy. Using a broad definition of DRGs, the group produced a computer program that assigned DRGs directly from the U.K. codes. This was an invaluable tool in the first years of research work until a microcomputer grouper became available. This latter grouper, like most subsequent ones, used U.S. software that could map U.K. to U.S. codes. The pros and cons of each approach—especially loss of specialty versus direct comparability—have not been fully examined.

CASPE's work was with individual hospitals in local district health authorities and centered on providing clinicians with information and other support to enable them to run their own budgets. Case mix was clearly an important component of these budgets, and during 1982 and 1983 the CASPE team undertook some small, informal studies using sample data from hospitals. Eventually, the Department of Health agreed to let CASPE formally evaluate whether the underlying case mix treated by consultants would change if they were given control of their own budgets. The study commenced in late 1983 and was based on three experimental districts, each matched with a comparable control district. The results showed no evidence to suggest that the case mix changed as a result of incentives newly introduced in the experimental sites, but there was some evidence that the use of resources declined at these sites when standardized for the types of cases treated.

The CASPE research team undertook a good many other analyses that helped to lay the foundations for the use of DRGs in the United Kingdom. While the formal study was under way, interest in the performance and potential of DRGs (and case mix tools in general) grew rapidly, and the study consequently broadened so that as much information as possible could be obtained about case mix effects. Among the activities undertaken was a review of the quality of medical coding and an assessment of the effect of poor coding on DRG assignment; the identification of good and bad length-of-stay distributions within DRGs (similar evaluations were undertaken by the London School team); comparisons of frequency of case types and lengths of stay between districts (including the differences between teaching and nonteaching districts); and experimentation with different methods of trimming outliers and the subsequent effect on case-mix descriptions.

As well as describing the case mix of hospitals or clinical specialties, the CASPE research group tried to look at the assessment of costs by case type. This proved somewhat difficult since in the NHS in the early 1980s costs were only known at the functional departmental level (for example, nursing), while the relationships between cost and volume were generally not understood at all. Work on the development and evaluation of cost-allocation models was therefore often undertaken using a top-down approach. These simple models were tested for validity and in sensitivity analysis appeared suprisingly robust. While in the early 1990s we are moving toward more sophisticated costing techniques, it should be remembered that many doctors and managers will need to be trained in costing concepts and understand and agree that such concepts are appropriate before the derived costs are accepted.

The research team also compared U.K. cost estimates with the relative cost weights from the United States and did some specific studies in examining ward nursing costs by DRG and on the cost of specific procedures within DRGs.

Following the July 1981 meeting, CASPE and the London School maintained contact with Yale, and on a number of occasions in the next few years we welcomed Fetter and Thompson over to the United Kingdom. Additionally, I visited Yale in 1983, and subsequent visits were made by members of the CASPE group, by Hugh Sanderson, and by officials from the Department of Health and the Welsh Office. By the mid 1980s Yale was on most health officials' agenda if they were planning a visit to the United States.

Early Dispersion

During 1982 and 1983, interest in DRGs in the United Kingdom was largely focused on a few people within the two research groups and one or two isolated individuals around the country who had learned of the Yale work by reference to U.S. journals. It is probably fair to say that it was not long before the two research groups recognized the potential applications of case mix systems within the NHS and were enthusiastic about the possible use of DRGs. There are three reasons why this system of case mix descriptors became the first choice for further work:

- It had been tested most widely.
- It used only readily available information.
- It combined clinical and resourcing considerations.

When Graham Winyard, who worked with Hugh Sanderson at the London School, moved to being district medical officer at the Lewisham and North Southwark Health Authority, he met up with Tim Scott, one of the interested but isolated individuals referred to above, and case-mix developments took another step. Scott, who was at that time a financial planner, wrote to me and suggested that a wider network be set up to discuss approaches to the use of DRGs. Subsequently, CASPE and Sanderson established a user group to discuss technical issues associated with DRGs in England, and an interest group for those people who wanted to keep up with developments but were not currently working with any data. The interest group fell apart very rapidly as members either joined the user group or were placed on an information list that subsequently became the foundation of the *DRG Newsletter* circulation list.

The first meeting of the user group took place in June 1983, and we were fortunate in having John Thompson and

Larry MacMahon from the Yale group present. Nine other members from the two U.K. research groups and three health authorities attended. Later meetings included members from other health authorities and the Department of Health's Operational Research Service. The user group met bimonthly, with some meetings open to a wider audience. A number of seminars were organized (CASPE Research, 1984, 1985, 1986), either to provide general information or to address a single topic such as costing. During this period we welcomed visitors from a number of countries, including the United States and Australia. Among the U.S. visitors were Susan Horn and Wanda Young, who proposed alternative or complementary systems to DRGs.

Over the course of the next year interest in case mix developments grew rapidly and produced demands for information from clinicians, treasurers, managers, planners, and others. To meet this need, the *DRG Newsletter* was launched in June 1984. Its editors were Linda Jenkins, who was CASPE's case mix research manager, and Hugh Sanderson. Since 1984 it has been published three times a year.

By midway through 1985, this wider communication network had produced more activity, albeit of a somewhat uncoordinated nature and with few resources being made explicitly available for it (other than in a few research grants). The original U.K. case mix assignment program was made available to anyone in the NHS who wanted to apply it to produce a case mix data base to address a particular issue. The first result of this wider diffusion was to make the user group more difficult to organize, as a result of which its meetings became less frequent. More important, however, it promoted a wider set of applications for DRGs than would have been possible in the smaller group. For example, Tim Scott had moved to the Northwestern Regional Health Authority and was looking at case mix within a specialist children's hospital, Alex Glaskin was trying to describe the work load that was likely to accompany the building of a new hospital, Toni Newman was undertaking a detailed patient costing exercise, and Gwyn Bevan was examining the greater costs and severity of a London Teaching Hospital. CASPE, like a number of management consultancy firms, was assisting districts with DRG studies to look at, among other things, patient flows across district boundaries.

Thus, during the mid 1980s the development of DRGs in the UK was largely based in research work or exploratory use by individuals in the planning departments of a few health authorities. No directives came through from the executive side of the Department of Health on the need for such case mix measures, and only limited resources were made available to develop their potential. An important result of this was that during this period the pioneer users were dependent on the original U.K. assignment program that had been developed by the London School in 1983. Use of this software continued up to 1988, and the expanding number of users meant that some program support became necessary. This was provided free, again by the CASPE and London School research groups, but it became clear that in the longer term this approach was not sustainable. The program, which had been developed as a research tool, needed a more rigorous validation than had previously proved possible, while among the users there was a growing feeling that the best approach to grouping was the mapping of codes and the retention of U.S. definitions, a rather different approach from that used in the existing program.

Altogether, these users had by 1987 assigned DRGs to at least twenty-five data bases at the national, regional, and district level, with at least twenty of these containing more than 20,000 records each. With the exception of a small number of these data bases, most were produced to address issues of a fairly general nature, that is, to assist with planning or to compare work loads over time.

European Network

In other parts of Europe there was much interest in the very major funding changes then being undertaken in the United States, and it became clear that good medical records with appropriate patient classification were a necessary and important force in these changes. At a number of international meetings between 1983 and 1985, researchers and others who had been working independently in their own countries on case mix issues first got together to share their findings. The first of these took place at the University of Leuven, Belgium, in April 1983 under the auspices of Francis Roger France and looked at the application of patient classification systems to management and budgeting issues. It included representatives from Belgium, the United Kingdom, Switzerland, and Scandinavia.

In 1985 the Council of Europe commissioned a study that looked at the degree of medical records computerization in hospitals. One by-product of this was a recognition of the diversity of classification systems that existed across Europe. Not only were different versions of the International Classification of Diseases used in different countries to code diagnoses, but most of these countries also used their own systems for classifying procedures. The study showed that eleven countries in Europe were investigating the potential of DRGs.

At this point, a European network involving eighteen countries began to develop. Known as Patient Classification Systems–Europe (PCS-E), its prime aim was to stimulate links across national boundaries and encourage the application of classification systems. The group, which was largely self-financing, organized meetings, took part in conferences, and encouraged collaboration. While individual members were influential within their own countries, the group did not have any particular locus within the wider framework of the European Community and depended on the skills of individuals to develop its influence. PCS-E has offered a more satisfactory forum to discuss case mix issues than other more general settings such as medical informatics or health computing conferences. Inevitably, with so many countries participating, a certain amount of duplication of programs has occurred. However, in some respects this has been helpful since reconsidering difficult subjects can often take discussion a stage further.

Shift to Centralized Leadership

The latter part of 1986 was to prove a watershed for the development of case mix in England. Prior to this time DRGs were by and large the property of researchers and a small number of enthusiasts working in a few health authorities. With the Thatcher years in full swing, many clinicians and other health workers were worried about how moves to get the health service to face economic reality might be implemented. In particular, they were concerned that the horror stories (mostly exaggerated, it should be said) about the effects of the change to prospective reimbursement in the United States should not be repeated in any changes planned for the United Kingdom. Because of this link between DRG classification and payment systems, many planners within the health service were wary of DRGs. Quite possibly this was one reason for the Department of Health's low-key approach to the use of patient-based case mix information for any particular application. The development of management budgeting, for example, did not depend on patient-based information, while the Körner systems that were implemented in April 1987 focused primarily on information aggregated from the patient level. Although individual patient abstracts were retained within the hospital's patient administration systems, few people thought that case mix standardization of individual records had much relevance outside of a costing system.

During the early years, contact had been maintained between U.K. researchers and the Yale group. Apart from informal meetings, at least two U.K. researchers (Linda Jenkins and Tim Scott) attended the Yale Executive Program during the summer. This intensive program used case studies to look at the role of case mix analysis in addressing structural and strategic problems in hospitals.

Additionally, the very informative reports and technical appendixes of the Prospective Payment Assessment Commission (1991) gave insight into how the DRG system changed over time (in order to reflect changing clinical practice) and what refinements were being made to the methodology of incorporating the classification within the U.S. funding system. A very noticeable feature of the U.S. approach was the sizable investment in structures to maintain and monitor the use of DRGs from a central perspective. These were put in place at the outset, in marked contrast to the largely hands-off approach to case mix development in the United Kingdom. Our interest in these areas led CASPE to meet with the commission's chairman, Stuart Altman, on a number of occasions in order to find out more about how the commission functioned.

Late 1986 was marked by two major events. First, the Department of Health launched the Resource Management Initiative (Department of Health, 1986). The groundwork had been carried out by Ian Mills, the new director of finance on the NHS management board, and was aimed primarily at regaining the confidence of clinicians in resourcing discussions, which had largely been lost in the over-accountancy-oriented approach of management budgeting. The initiative itself was similarly aimed at improving resourcing decisions through clinical involvement but sought to do so first by addressing the need for a suitable organizational structure and second by providing a data base that clinicians felt was adequate to answer resourcing questions. From the very outset Ian Mills was certain that the data needed to be based on the individual patient record and that there should be some recognition of the diagnosis or medical procedure (in other words, the case type of the patient). While the Department of Health was determined not to be prescriptive about which case mix measure to use, it became clear that DRGs were among the most favored in that they provided a common vocabulary for clinicians and managers, they had relevance to resource use, and they had been tested more widely than other measures.

The second major event was an international conference held in London in December 1986 under the auspices of the Yale School of Organization and Management (Health Systems Management Group, 1986). The timing of the conference, so soon after the launch of the Resource Management Initiative, ensured attendance by influential members of all health care disciplines as well as a relatively high profile in the journals. These two events therefore considerably raised the profile of case mix within the management of health care and ensured further development over the coming years.

Although 1986 provided the watershed between predominantly research-led activity and activity organized and funded directly by the health service (Table 2.2), it was to be some time before any significant change could be detected. In many respects this was not surprising. The implementation of the Körner information systems in all U.K. hospitals would preoccupy the minds of information specialists for a large part of 1987. At the same time, the six pilot sites that would make the first inroads into resource management were busy producing project plans, recruiting staff, and determining strategies for approaching a task in which case mix developments played only a small part. As well as developing an approach to case mix, the pilot projects were to specify hardware, implement a nurse management system, and ensure that clinicians remained sympathetic to their overall proposals. With this large agenda to complete, it was not surprising that CASPE and other researchers continued to play an important part in maintaining the visibility of DRGs by writing articles and organizing meetings and conferences.

During 1987, the Resource Management Initiative team at the Department of Health started to assume part of this role in that it commissioned the Yale Executive Program to be run in the United Kingdom with around fifty senior health service managers present. The purpose of this move was to illustrate the potential of case mix management at the operational level. Additionally, the team took on a much greater role in directly commissioning and funding particular case mix work. Around this time the resource management team obtained from the NHS the services of two supporters of DRGs, John Catterall, previously a regional director of finance, and Tim Scott. This had the important effect of consolidating the position of case mix in future developments.

The Department of Health now took steps to enhance the involvement of some of the regions in case mix developments and to commission a large-scale evaluation of the DRG approach using U.K. data. Not surprisingly, Fetter and the Yale group were given this latter task. They had by that time already undertaken similar work in other European countries; in fact, the United Kingdom was perceived as having dragged its heels

Table 2.2. The Incorporation of Research into Centrally Led Developments.

Year	Research Group–Led Developments	Departmental Commissions	Policy Developments
Pre-1981	Specialty costing Patient costing Clinical budgeting		1974 reorganization (consensus management)
1981	London School feasibility research[a] Evaluation studies Case mix in clinical budgeting[a]		Körner information
1982–1983	User group founded Newsletter founded Conferences and meetings Isolated applications International connections		1982 reorganization (devolution to units) Regional reviews and performance indicators Griffiths report (general management; management budgeting)
1986	Application studies Alternative classifications Publications	Resource management Yale contract U.K. grouper Cost models Expert group	Resource management (doctors in management) HISS
1989 to date	Grouper comparisons Refined DRGs[b]	Coding and training support Roll-out to more sites Central and regional support Case mix office	Working for patients (purchaser/provider split; contracting; GP fundholders; NHS trusts)
1990s?	Specialist areas (e.g. pediatrics)[b] Case mix in other sectors Nursing and case mix[a] Costing Links to quality	English case mix groups Case mix management and training in data usage	

[a] Research funded by Research Management Division, DoH
[b] Commissioned by Resource Management Directorate

in committing itself to large-scale work. The work itself was largely unexciting and comprised only the early stages of the standard Yale contract (Fetter, 1988). The Yale team was to assign DRGs to patient data from four regions, assess the technical difficulties that were experienced, and examine the quality of the resultant groups. Except for the scale of the work, such evaluations had already been carried out by the English research groups. However, it is recognized that the Yale stamp was probably politically necessary.

As mentioned earlier, there had already been discussion of the appropriateness of producing mapping tables to translate ICD9 diagnoses and OPCS operation codes to the ICD9-CM codes used within the Yale grouper, and prototype tables had been produced. This work was consolidated by the Fetter team. Despite continuing problems with records that did not contain a coded diagnosis, Fetter's team was able to assign nearly all records to a DRG and found similar resource use patterns as in the United States. In absolute terms, England had a lower rate of treatment and longer lengths of stay, but overall the important conclusion was reached that the basic DRG model was appropriate for English data.

A more detailed piece of work was carried out in 1988 by Hugh Sanderson, who examined high-volume DRGs to assess the sensitivity of the assignment process to the relatively poor coding standards that were (and to a lesser extent still are) common in the United Kingdom. Systematic biases, lack of specificity, and other problems led Sanderson to conclude that coding quality needed to be improved substantially if resource management was to succeed in its aims. This finding should not be underestimated in its importance since many early attempts to gain clinical enthusiasm for case mix analysis in England had been thwarted or at least delayed by the poor coding of records. Results based in 80 percent of cases are unacceptable to clinicians, while inaccurate data quickly undermine credibility. Further work on the clinical acceptability of the groups identified over sixty where improvement was thought necessary. Twenty of these would be susceptible to coding improvements, while the others would need some structural amendment of the DRG definitions, such as subdivision or regrouping.

As the resource management sites began to be established in 1987 and 1988, it became clear that there was little technical support available from commercial computer companies, partly because the issues were very complex and partly because the return on software was likely to be limited. Yale, as part of its contract with the Department of Health, made the 1985 version of its grouper available, together with mapping tables for diagnosis and procedure conversion. The procedure tables were updated when OPCS introduced new versions and later incorporated in a new grouper written by Healthcare Knowledge Systems (now CASPE HKS).

While grouping capabilities developed apace in the United Kingdom, knowledge about DRG-related costs grew much more slowly. After Körner instigated specialty costing in April 1987, people looked to two methods to bring costs to a DRG level: individualized patient costing (drawing on resource management information) or a top-down cost-modeling approach. Since the information systems to support patient costing were not available to most, it is not surprising that much of the work to date has been based on cost-modeling approaches. In 1988 Fetter's Yale cost model was evaluated in the Northern Region using data collected from the Freeman Hospital in Newcastle, one of the resource management sites (Robson, 1988). Modifications that were necessary focused on relating the detailed U.K. functional cost centers to rather fewer categories as well as on the appropriate treatment of general service overheads. This early work was presented to and discussed by a costing group set up by the Department of Health to look specifically at costing issues. This group was a precursor to an expert group that met frequently from October 1988 onwards to advise the NHS director of financial management on case mix matters and that eventually subsumed the costing group.

Alterations continued to be made to the Yale model, eventually resulting in a specification that was made available to software producer Thorn EMI, which had previously produced a specialty cost model. It was intended that the DRG model could be an add-on to the existing software. As of this writing, the new software had been available to the service for over a year (since January 1990), but there is little evidence to show that it has been used very widely.

With a view to developing a more appropriate approach to costing (the Yale model and others developed at this time drew on U.S. resource use weights), the Department of Health asked management consultants Ernst and Whinney to examine the feasibility of producing English-based measures of relative resource use (National Health Service Management Executive, 1989a). A survey of 40 English hospitals in early 1989 demonstrated that the necessary information was not available to produce such cost weights. However, the consultants were able to apply detailed Maryland weights to cost data from these hospitals, thus increasing the level of knowledge about DRG-specific cost estimates in the United Kingdom. Further work to refine the cost model was commissioned in 1989.

The period from 1986 to 1988 was therefore marked by a significantly greater interest in case mix developments at the executive level of the NHS. The previously research-led user group found its role being taken over by the Department of Health and in 1988 metamorphosed into an expert group. The expert group's role has been to advise the NHS on case mix matters from a national perspective.

CASPE has continued to play an important part in these initiatives and has taken the lead in disseminating information about case mix developments in the United Kingdom. Since 1986 the *DRG Newsletter* has been published without interruption and its circulation has grown to over 1,500 recipients in twenty-seven countries. CASPE's research unit has become a focus for enquiries and visitors from overseas who wish to discuss case mix matters. In particular, this period saw a growing interest among NHS managers, who became a more significant part of the newsletter's circulation list. Additionally, articles on DRGs and other case mix systems began to appear more frequently in the U.K. journals, and toward the end of 1987 CASPE was commissioned by the *Health Services Journal* to write a series of eight articles on DRGs and possible application areas (CASPE, 1987). Earlier that year, CASPE had published the first substantive book on DRGs and their application in a non-American setting to be published outside the United States (Bardsley, Coles, and Jenkins, 1987).

European collaboration continued to be strong, with increased communication between researchers in different countries, both at PCS-E meetings and at major informatics conferences. The European Community began to develop an interest in health as a major issue on the European agenda and in particular recognized the importance of developments in informatics in optimizing the use of health care resources. This concern was focused in the request for bids against the Advanced Informatics in Medicine program, which resulted in U.K. participation in a number of international research projects in the 1989–1990 period. Two of these specifically focused on the value of inpatient classification systems (especially DRGs), while a number of others looked at classifications for outpatients and primary care.

Improvements in Data

The next stage in the evolution of the use of case mix (and DRGs in particular) in England can be identified with the start of the roll-out of the Resource Management Initiative from the six pilot sites to the 260 major acute hospital sites in the NHS. The first phase of this roll-out was made up of fifty hospitals that had been identified as having an infrastructure capable of supporting the developments and of making reasonably fast progress. The Department of Health provided these sites with a range of support material, such as grouper software, DRG definition manuals, and so on (National Health Service Management Executive, 1989b).

The primary aim of enhancing the quality of the underlying data was addressed in a number of ways from 1989 onward. In the early stages of roll-out the Department of Health held seminars emphasizing the importance of consistent coding, encouraged the use of automatic encoders, and distributed a specially commissioned computer training package for coders that identified the importance of accurate coding as a prerequisite for case mix management. In 1990 CASPE HKS was commissioned to run a training program for regional clinical coding tutors, whose role would be to disseminate good practice and organize similar training programs at the district and hospital level. Ongoing support is currently being provided to these programs, while general medical records consultancy is being undertaken in a number of regions. The Department of Health has also distributed specially adapted ICD9 manuals incorporating approved coding conventions in order to remove any ambiguities that have grown up over time in particular areas.

Beyond clinical coding, the Department of Health began to sponsor a series of technical workshops to develop case mix expertise across the NHS. These were aimed primarily at information scientists, although a key element was the involvement of managers in the use and interpretation of information. By the end of 1990, nearly 100 participants from most of the English regions had been through these programs.

In supporting the introduction of case mix concepts within the NHS, the Department of Health recognized that the NHS needed to have ready access to people who would be able to tackle any problems that arose. To this end, selected individuals were given responsibility as case mix contacts in each of the fourteen English regions. These people were to field queries from individual sites and were also to create a network of communication both across the country and between the Department of Health and the hospitals. Additionally, a guide to DRG grouping was published (Jenkins, McKee, and Sanderson, 1990), and two hot lines were set up toward the end of 1989 — one to address technical issues associated with the grouping software, the other to assist with clinical or other queries relating to the coding and grouping definitions used.

During 1990 and 1991, DRGs came under increasing scrutiny as national involvement with them increased. The Resource Management Initiative team encouraged more detailed investigations of alternative case mix systems and provided some funding to this end. An evaluation of Yale's refined DRG structure (which, being more complex, yields some 1,100 case mix groups) showed that improvements over the basic DRGs were somewhat marginal. Specific groups were improved by the greater attention paid to co-morbidities, but it was generally felt that most of the benefits had already been obtained by the DRG revisions that were made to derive the 1988 grouper. The use of Medisgroups, an alternative patient classification system, had also suggested only marginal improvements for significantly greater investment in data collection. Patient management categories have a number of supporters within the United Kingdom and will undoubtedly be examined further, as will disease staging. Patient management categories are perhaps more closely allied to resourcing issues, but even so the categories are primarily clinically oriented and their relationship to resource use in many areas is as yet unclear. A wider international study of case mix measures is being undertaken in Ontario, Canada, and England has contributed some sample data to this hoping to gain some useful comparative information. However, the original paradox remains in looking for improvements on DRGs: measures that require more clinical information are more costly and difficult to achieve, while improvements in clinical coding need to be demonstrated before some other classifications can show their full potential.

Since 1990, the Department of Health has shown considerable interest in a classification known as "read codes," originally developed for use within primary care practices. The attraction of these codes lies in the multiaxial approach, with codes for signs, symptoms, and treatments as well as diagnoses and procedures, and also in the use of simple synonyms linked to clinical terminology and codes. These codes can be used within many of the case mix systems, but again their benefits over existing classifications and encoding software have yet to be demonstrated.

In early 1990, the Department of Health took a somewhat radical step in its search for improvements to DRGs and, in particular, its effort to increase clinical acceptability. A case mix development program was established primarily to look at the weak areas of the original classification, but it effectively encour-

aged the construction of a new set of case mix descriptors.
Thirteen projects were commissioned that encompassed both
the known weak areas and also some others (for example, oph-
thalmology) that had not previously been identified as problematic. The time scale for reporting on these projects was fairly
limited (around six months), and to date (August 1992) there has
been little indication that these new groups have any greater
degree of resource homogeneity. The new groups have been
combined into an overall classification called English case mix
groups, which is currently under further study (National Health
Service Management Executive, 1991). Officially, this is seen as
the start of a continuing process of refinement to arrive at
groups more appropriate to English practice and more acceptable to clinicians. At present the Department of Health is not
favoring these groups above other systems, although a grouper
will be offered to districts and hospitals as an optional alternative case mix classification, while the DRG grouper will also
continue to be available. However, in order to maintain comparability across national boundaries (another departmental
objective is to be supportive of the European Community initiatives), mapping capabilities to a standard DRG classification
will need to be maintained. In the longer term, the price of
maintaining two systems running in parallel will be considerable; if only one system can be afforded, the survivor is likely to
be that found most useful in the new contracting processes
(although of course political expedience might also win out).

The current position in England with respect to DRGs
and case mix management in general is one of continued experimentation and a major undertaking in education, both of clinicians and of managers. As a result, in late 1992, case mix
development had not attained that degree of stability that could
be seen in the United States or, to a lesser extent, Canada. The
country with a mature approach to case mix will have a sound,
reliable, and consistent approach to data collection, good software tools to manipulate data, and information-oriented managers educated to obtain the maximum benefit, in terms of total
patient care, from the output of these systems.

In England, we are making considerable strides in our

ability to obtain good patient activity data. We have a nationally agreed data set operating in all NHS hospitals (with interest also being shown by some of the private hospitals), and many of the Department of Health's initiatives with respect to improving the quality of clinical coding should bear fruit in the next few years. The collection and collation of information on activity (and hence resource use) in service departments such as nursing and pharmacy is less complete. While the Resource Management Initiative seeks to extend coverage across many departments and across all acute hospitals, progress so far has been fragmented. This has meant that there has been little opportunity to investigate DRG costs on a widespread basis other than through a top-down cost-modeling approach. However, decisions about how to collect information and attribute costs need to be addressed within the overall context of the objectives for case mix management. For example, are case mix effects being identified to assist in the contracting process, to improve the internal management of hospitals, or to allow hospitals to be compared on efficiency and effectiveness?

In the long run, the software needed to carry out these aims should be readily available. At present, however, the organization of information and computing services in many hospitals means that access to case mix assignment software and previously processed information is somewhat restricted. End users such as clinical departments do not always have immediate access to this type of management information or to software to enable them to manipulate it.

While all these areas might be expected to show development over the next few years, the NHS's shift toward more information-oriented management may prove less tractable. Concepts like weighting factors, case mix indexes, and variance analysis are alien to the majority of top managers. Before case mix systems can be thought to have come of age in England, managers must be persuaded of the place of such concepts in the overall management of health services. They must understand that the assessment of these factors cannot be left to accountants of information specialists and also be confident in their own capabilities to interpret the messages from the information. Quite how fast these ideas and skills will develop is difficult to predict. On the one hand, there is resistance to changes that might reduce health care management to a system dominated by numbers; on the other, there is a recognition that the financial imperatives accompanying the newly introduced contracting process are likely to demand attention to case mix issues in the not-too-distant future.

Given these factors, the pattern that case mix activity in England has followed up to this time is not surprising. Paucity of data relating to resource use has meant that much of the work has focused on length-of-stay studies. The scale of these studies varies depending largely on access to data, with individual districts being, by and large, only interested in their own hospitals. Regions, on the other hand, have tended to apply the DRG assignment across a range of districts and consequently have access to larger data bases. Work within districts has primarily focused on the demands of the Resource Management Initiative and quite often has been limited to a first inspection of local data rather than being linked to a specific application. These explorations have been a way of evaluating DRGs but have also highlighted deficiencies in data quality that districts have subsequently sought to correct before embarking on any ambitious analyses. They have also been used to help managers and clinicians talk about case mix concepts in general.

At the regional level, where scale can overcome some of the data inaccuracies, the initial evaluations have led to the use of DRGs to address a number of fundamental issues that have long been on regional agendas. In so doing they are adding a greater level of specificity to existing issues rather than identifying or creating new issues. For example, cross-boundary flows of patients, regional specialties, and the additional cost of teaching hospitals all have financial consequences for health care purchasers and providers, and analysis of these issues is given an extra dimension by incorporating a case mix component. Some regions have taken an interest in each of these areas, while others have sought to use case mix tools as an aid to their monitoring role. In this latter respect it is still early days, since the quality of data across districts is widely variable and appropriate comparison against budgets and contracts will not be possible until these issues are fully addressed.

At the Department of Health, the current thrust is twofold: to encourage the general improvement of data quality and the assessment of new case mix groups and to support international collaboration within the European Community. A major project was undertaken in 1990 within the Advanced Informatics in Medicine (AIM) program (the HOSCOM project) to investigate the feasibility of obtaining a standard minimum data set across a fairly large number of European countries (the United Kingdom included). This data set would have consistent data elements and coding protocols and would therefore enable comparative analyses of practices in the different countries. The department has also looked at a number of conditions in more detail and has compared activity measures by department (for example, pathology or nursing). A feasibility study (Roger France and others, 1991) provided positive results and encouraged England and Belgium to investigate the possibility of setting up a wider collaborative study within a few years.

The Future of Case Mix

What is on the case mix agenda in England in the next few years? Indeed, will case mix even be an issue, or will further changes in the health care system, perhaps occasioned by a change of government, simply displace it?

It is always dangerous to suggest that something is an inevitability, but I do believe that there is no chance of the clock being completely turned back, irrespective of what happens to the organization and provision of health care in the United Kingdom. It will be impossible for managers to run hospitals, control their resources, and contract for services without some understanding of the consequences of treating different case types. Although as late as 1992 the first round of contracting largely ignored case mix, the increasing availability of data by case type over the next few years will ensure that it is used. The likelihood that case mix information will remain unused is negligible, particularly when it can be shown to add weight to an argument for more resources.

While some pundits envisage the various case mix initiatives being made obsolete (or at least watered down) should the government change within the next few years, my own opinion is that some of the ideas now being implemented, including the purchaser/provider split, will remain whatever party is in power. If this is correct, the very fact that contracts must take work loads into account means that discussions will eventually include information on case types and quality levels. Additionally, both of the major parties have long been committed to the idea of local resource management, which was the spark that ignited the case mix fuse. There is therefore every chance that case mix measures will continue to be available to health care managers and that the more able managers will use them to secure and deploy appropriate resources.

Whether the case mix measure in use in England will be DRGs is less clear. Competing measures include disease staging and patient management categories, as well as the newer English case mix groups (ECMGs). While still to be adequately tested for resource homogeneity, they could claim greater clinical acceptability and therefore might compete with DRGs for use in England. For international comparisons, however, it seems likely that DRGs will remain the common vocabulary. However, since both DRGs and ECMGs are derived from the same diagnostic and procedure codes, there is no reason why both classifications cannot exist side by side (except for a continuing need to maintain mapping tables to support a U.S. DRG grouper or to write a U.K. version).

Whichever case mix system is used, it must be reviewed regularly to ensure that the classification remains up-to-date in relation to changing clinical practice. In order to achieve this a suitable infrastructure needs to be established. England has made good progress in this area with the expert group set up by (but independent from) the Department of Health, together with the National Case Mix Office, which is run by Hugh Sanderson. However, these initiatives do not as yet have sufficient resources to fully cover the role that the U.S. Prospective Payment

Assessment Commission plays in commissioning economically based research. Nor does it have the monitoring capabilities of the U.S. peer review organizations to ensure that quality of care remains high. As contracting develops and the split between the purchasers and the providers of health care develops in the United Kingdom, there will be an increasing need to establish an organization to take on these roles. Whether this is done centrally or develops through the demands of individual purchasers remains to be seen.

If the scenario painted earlier in this section is correct, the use of a case mix system such as DRGs or ECMGs in resource management and in contracting will require continuing effort in the development of costing methodologies. However, such developments must not take place in a sterile environment. They should incorporate the best of the various cost-modeling approaches with the benefits of local information and the flexibility that managers based in local health authorities typically demand from software.

A final area that I am sure will see development in England over the next few years is case mix classifications in other areas of care. The Department of Health has commissioned research to see whether these primarily medically dominated classifications adequately reflect the major nursing resource. This, of course, is important in itself but will become more so as the need to have satisfactory case descriptors in other areas of care becomes more important. The barriers between types of care—day surgery, outpatient surgery, and inpatient care; primary and secondary care; long-term and acute care—are becoming blurred. With the increased focus on contractual arrangements, it will be important that it be possible to plan care for particular case types irrespective of where that care is provided. A fragmented approach merely concentrating on inpatient care could lead to overall distortions in both the financial consequences of contracts and the planning of services if such care can be provided in a number of settings. An evaluation of the so-called ambulatory visit groups is currently under way in the East Anglia Regional Health Authority (1989).

Epilogue

During the latter part of 1991 and early 1992, the NHS has been in a period of consolidation, wrestling with the realities of the NHS reforms (which were implemented beginning in April 1991) rather than the theory. At the same time, and not surprisingly, the NHS came under political pressure to ensure that there were no horror stories — hospitals running out of money, operations being canceled for financial reasons, children dying — before the then-imminent general election.

It was known quite early on, in the period of the so-called phoney election (September 1991–February 1992) that the two main political parties would develop the NHS in very different ways if elected. While the NHS reforms continued to be implemented as set down by the Department of Health, the enthusiasm for innovation was somewhat stifled in case it all had to be reversed after the election. In particular, the newly created NHS Trusts were threatened with losing their increased autonomy and often chose to keep a low profile in advance of election day.

To the surprise of many, including the opinion pollsters, the incumbent Conservative party was returned to office in April 1992 with a clear majority, thus ensuring that the fledgling reforms would continue and giving the prospect of some stability to the NHS. For the next five years, the course has been set for all hospitals and other health care groups — health centers, clinics, ambulance services — to move toward NHS Trust status. The election also sounded the all-clear for the development of the contracting process itself.

It is probable that the election result has promoted the development of case mix measures and case mix–based information systems in England during the 1990s. However, it is clear that health service managers would have increasingly required information systems to identify patient types no matter how the election turned out, simply in order to gain a better understanding of the cost, efficiency, and quality of the service they provide. During the last year, emphasis on the quality of coding as a precursor to the provision of adequate case mix and contracting systems has continued. The National Centre for Coding and

Classification is seeking to expand, in a structured way, the number of codes used to describe clinical work and interactions between different parts of the health system. This would enable different grouping systems to be employed using the same data and should also facilitate linkage between primary and secondary care information, as well as that collected by different clinical professions on the same patient. As part of this work a new project, supported by the Conference of Royal Medical Colleges, has been started to define a common system of clinical terms.

The new case mix system originally known as English case mix groups is now called health resource groups (HRGs). Compared to DRGs, HRGs are more directly related to specialties and vary in their construction between specialties. The National Case Mix Office recognizes that HRGs may well need refining or enhancing, particularly in areas such as radiotherapy and oncology, and a second version was slated for release in 1993. Grouper software is available for HRGs, and hospitals are being encouraged to use one or both of the HRG and DRG systems to examine their data, with neither being unduly promoted.

The emphasis in the first year of the contracting process was on block contracts. That is, purchasers bought a block of care (for example, all inpatient maternity care) for a given price without defining further the makeup of that block. The exception to this has been in extra-contractual referral cases, which, as their name implies, are cases treated outside the normal contracting process (usually because of emergency treatment or an unusual physician referral). Hospitals have published their price lists for these cases, which are normally described by diagnosis or procedure (though often not by a recognized case mix system), but these show a high and unexplained level of variability. Some of the variation can be attributed to different definitions of the care package, but much of the residual is likely to derive from different costing protocols.

While contracting for the 1992-1993 year showed slight signs of moving to an increased definition of case types, some of the larger teaching hospitals seemed unwilling to include some of the higher-cost cases within block contracts.

Managers interested in progressing in case mix analysis still have a number of choices open to them. They have grouping software to produce DRGs or HRGs available to them through the Department of Health, or they might choose to investigate other systems such as the refined DRGs, the New York all-purpose grouper (which incorporates pediatric groupings), or more data-intense systems such as APACHE III, patient management categories, or disease staging. With respect to resource use analysis, DRGs are probably still more widely used than HRGs, due in part to the wider availability of the grouping mechanism and in part to uncertainty about the homogeneity of HRGs. DRGs may not be perfect, but their deficiencies are at least well known. The Audit Commission has taken this latter view in commissioning CASPE to produce hospital profiles standardized for case mix across a large number of English hospitals. It was recognized that HRGs might be more appropriate for any future work, but in 1992 there was more certainty about DRGs.

As far as hospital management itself is concerned, it is clear that there are a growing number of hospitals actively involved in looking at some or all of their data on a case mix basis. While there is no consensus about the best system either for assessing efficiency within hospitals or for addressing issues of quality related to resource use, much of this involvement is being stimulated from within the units rather than from outside. Overall, progress since this chapter was written may not have been dramatic, but it would seem that the subject is maturing nicely.

References

Annual Abstract of Statistics, 1990. London: HMSO, 1990.

Babson, J. H. *Disease Costing.* Manchester, England: Manchester University Press, 1973.

Barber, B., and Johnson, D. "The Presentation of Acute Hospital Inpatient Statistics." *The Hospital,* 1973, *69,* 11–14.

Bardsley, M., Coles, J., and Jenkins, L. (eds.). *DRGs and Health Care: The Management of Case Mix.* London: King Edward's Hospital Fund, 1987.

Britain 1991. London: HMSO, 1991.

Bussey, A. "NHS Reorganisation—Getting Down to Units." *British Medical Journal*, 1985, *285*, 663–664.

CASPE Research. "DRGs in the NHS?" Proceedings of a seminar, London, 1984.

CASPE Research. "Diagnosis-Related Groups and Resource Management." Proceedings of a seminar, London, 1985.

CASPE Research. "An Evolving Strategy for DRGs." Proceedings of a seminar, London, 1986.

CASPE Research. "Advances in Health Services Management Using DRGs." (Eight collected articles) *Health Services Journal*, Sept.–Dec. 1987, 1074–1075, 1108–1109, 1141, 1166–1167, 1261, 1322–1323, 1382, 1408–1409.

Compendium of Health Statistics (7th ed.). London: Office of Health Economics, 1989.

Department of Health. *Health Services Management: Resource Management (Management Budgeting) in Health Authorities*. HN(86)34. London: Department of Health, 1986.

Department of Health and Social Security. *Steering Group on Health Services Information: First Report*. London: HMSO, 1982.

Dixon, M. "The Organisation and Structure of Units." In H. I. Wickings (ed.), *Effective Unit Management*. London: King Edward's Hospital Fund, 1983.

East Anglia Regional Health Authority. *Introduction to Ambulatory Visit Groups*. (Proceedings of a seminar.) Cambridge, England: East Anglia Regional Health Authority, 1989.

Enthoven, A. C. *Reflections on the Management of the National Health Service*. London: Nuffield Provincial Hospitals Trust, 1985.

Feldstein, M. S. *Economic Analysis for Health Service Efficiency*. Amsterdam: North Holland Publishing Co., 1967.

Fetter, R. B. *The Development of a DRG-Based Cost Accounting, Budgeting, and Management Information System for Hospitals in England—Technical Report Phases 1 and 2*. New Haven, Conn.: Health Services Management Group, School of Organization and Management, Yale University, 1988.

Fetter, R. B., and others. "Case Mix Definition by Diagnosis-Related Groups." *Medical Care*, 1980, *18* (Supplement), 1–53.

Griffiths, E. R. "NHS Management Inquiry." Letter to Norman Fowler, Oct. 6, 1983.

Harper, D. R. "Disease Cost in a Surgical Ward." *British Medical Journal*, 1979, *278*, 647–649.

Health and Personal Social Services Statistics, 1991. London: HMSO, 1991.

Health Systems Management Group. "The Management and Financing of Hospital Services." Proceedings of a conference, Yale University, New Haven, Conn., 1986.

HMSO. *Royal Commission on the National Health Service.* London: HMSO, 1979.

HMSO. *Working for Patients.* London: HMSO, 1989.

Iglehart, J. K. "New Jersey's Experiment with DRG-Based Hospital Reimbursement." *New England Journal of Medicine*, 1982, *307*, 1655–1660.

Jenkins, L., McKee, M., and Sanderson, H. *DRGs—A Guide to Grouping and Interpretation.* London: CASPE Research, 1990.

Magee, C., and Osmolski, R. "A Comprehensive System of Management Information for Financial Planning, Decision Making, and Control in the Health Service." Technical paper for the Royal Commission on the National Health Service, London, 1978.

Mason, A., Perry, J., and Skegg, J. "Disease Costing—A Review." Unpublished paper, 1974.

National Health Service Management Executive. *A Report on DRG Activity and Cost Work Undertaken in the NHS: Constructing English Estimates of Relative Resource Use.* London: Ernst and Whinney, 1989a.

National Health Service Management Executive. *Resource Management Initiative—Information Package—Acute Hospitals.* London: Resource Management Directorate, 1989b.

National Health Service Management Executive. *Proposals for English Casemix Groups.* London: Resource Management Directorate, 1991.

Perrin, J. *Resource Management in the NHS.* Wokingham, England: Van Nostrand Reinhold, 1988.

Prospective Payment Assessment Commission. *Report and Recommendations to the Congress, Mar. 1, 1991.* Washington, D.C.: ProPAC, 1991.

Robson, M. P. *Production of DRG Costings Using Cost Model— Progress and Issues Raised.* Northern Regional Health Authority, 1988.

Roger France, F. H., and others. "Hospital Comparisons Using a Euro Health Data Base for Resource Management and Strategic Planning." *Health Policy,* 1991, *17,* 165–177.

Sanderson, H. F., and Andrews, V. "Monitoring Hospital Services: An Application of DRGs to Hospital Discharge Data in England and Wales." Occasional paper, London School of Hygiene and Tropical Medicine, London, 1984.

Smith, N., and Chantler, C. "Partnership for Progress." *Public Finance and Accountancy,* Nov. 6, 1987, pp. 12–15.

Wickings, H. I., and others. *Evaluating Management Information Presented to Clinically Accountable Teams.* London: Brent Health District, 1975.

Three

Belgium: Steady and Incremental Activity

Francis Roger France

The Kingdom of Belgium, which became an independent state in 1831 and a federal state in 1989, occupies an area of about 30,000 square kilometers. A high population density gives it almost 10 million inhabitants. Fifty-six percent of the population speaks Flemish, whereas the Walloons (32.9 percent) speak French. The capital city of Brussels has a mostly French-speaking population of nearly one million. Belgium comprises three regions—Flanders, Wallonia, and Brussels—and three communities—Flemish, French, and Germanic.

This complex structure has influenced the organization of the health care system and the division of responsibilities for it. Thus, while social security remains national in scope, planning and budgeting for hospitals and major capital equipment for them is in the hands of the regional governments. There are currently six ministries that have some responsibilities in the field of public health as part of their portfolios. The largest share of financial resources for health care is controlled by the national Minister of Social Affairs and Public Health.

Note: The author wishes to express his gratitude to Mrs. M. C. Closon and to J. L. Willems, who kindly agreed to review this chapter and offer their comments.

Since 1945, Belgium has had a particularly extensive social security system. Nearly all of the population, including the self-employed, has gradually been covered by a national system of sickness and disability insurance. The roots of the modern social security system go back more than a century. It was during the era of Napoleon III, not long after the country's independence, that the *mutuelles* (mutual-benefit societies) came into being in Belgium. At that time, workers could associate for the purpose of pooling and sharing their health care costs, but were forbidden to do so for the purpose of forming a labor union. The first Belgian mutual-benefit society opened in a Louvain printing works around 1850.

As Belgium's present-day health insurance institutions have evolved over the intervening years, many have developed close links with the traditional political parties. There are Christian Democratic, Socialist, Liberal, and politically neutral mutual-benefit societies, not to mention numerous other smaller organizations. In other words, although health insurance is mandatory in Belgium, each person is free to affiliate with the insurance body of his or her choice. Private, profit-making health insurance firms have only a marginal role in Belgium (for supplemental coverage).

In 1964 Edmond Leburton, the president of the Socialist mutual-benefit societies who had been named minister of social insurance, was worried by those societies' deficit. He felt that the fact that the costs to the Socialist mutual-benefit societies were higher than those for the Christian mutual-benefit societies was unfair, given the principle of worker solidarity. Although the higher costs reflected objectively higher risk because the Socialist societies covered workers in the mining and metalworking industries, whereas the Christian societies insured primarily white-collar and agricultural workers, Leburton felt that the State should intervene in a way that would equalize costs.

In that same year, a law was passed in Belgium regulating the fees for medical services. To the great surprise of other countries, this law encountered solid opposition from physicians, who did not hesitate to go on strike. A compromise settlement was reached in the so-called St. John agreements whereby physicians agreed to accept a fixed payment for services rendered.

Belgium, like Germany, has a long tradition of bargaining among the social partners. Both the physicians and the mutual-benefit societies are represented in an institution called the National Health and Disability Insurance Institute (INAMI). All medical services and surgical procedures have been classified according to a precise nomenclature, and each service or procedure has been assigned a letter code. The price to be associated with each letter code is the subject of annual bargaining. The resulting negotiated fee schedule for medical procedures is the same for all mutual-benefit societies and all hospitals.

Health care costs are financed in part by this fee-for-service reimbursement, based on a preestablished nomenclature and a fee schedule agreed annually between physicians and mutual-benefit societies, and in part by the hospitalization per-diem rate, which varies from hospital to hospital. The latter rate is adjusted each year by the Ministry of Public Health as a function of the various specialties and activities in each hospital and as a function of conformance to standards as reported by the hospital inspectors. Unlike their counterparts in countries that, like the United Kingdom, have national health systems without fee-for-service reimbursement, Belgian physicians have accepted controls by inspectors concerning both medical services as defined by INAMI and conformance to standards set by the ministry.

Another characteristic of the health care system in Belgium is the lack of any true competition between public and private hospitals. The system of reimbursement is such that the public or private character of the initial investor in a hospital makes little difference. Thus, the two state-owned university hospitals, the public social aid centers, and the hospitals founded by religious organizations or insurance institutions are all financed essentially by fee-for-service and per-diem rate reimbursements.

Compared to the national health systems, a fee-for-service system has the enormous advantage that each procedure performed on a patient is documented, whether the service is provided in a hospital or on an outpatient basis. Data of this kind has long been sadly lacking in, for example, Denmark and the United Kingdom, where it has been possible to obtain only resource consumption data by hospital department or by region.

On the other hand, in the open-ended system in Belgium, which operates without a budget determined in advance, the rapid increase in the number of services provided and procedures performed has been causing exponential growth in the overall cost. The proliferation of hospitals and hospital beds during the 1960s and the lack of financial encouragement for home care and nursing homes have only aggravated the explosion of health care costs.

It was this development that in 1983 led the then-minister of social affairs and public health, J. L. Dehaene, to reconsider the way health care was being financed, beginning with revisions at the hospital level. From the moment he joined the government, he made known his intention to introduce a prospective budget for reimbursed services, particularly laboratory procedures, in the form of fixed annual ceilings — in other words, an overall budget. Ceilings could subsequently be applied to other areas of activity such as medical imaging, and even to the entirety of hospital care services. Dehaene made the further decision to reduce the number of beds by assigning quotas to hospitals. He set the minimum hospital size at 150 beds, which gave rise to numerous negotiations with a view to merging existing health care institutions or even closing some of them (Table 3.1).

The current (1992) minister of social affairs and public affairs, Philippe Busquin, has continued a policy of rationalizing the country's health care facilities. He has also taken an interest in adjusting per-diem reimbursement rates to reflect the case mix of hospitalized patients rather than other criteria based on historical bargaining or the volume of procedures performed in the past.

Introduction of DRGs

Diagnosis-related groups (DRGs) first surfaced in Belgium at the end of the 1970s when Robert Fetter of Yale University spent a

Table 3.1. Key Health Care Figures for Belgium.

Country area	30,518 sq. km.
Population	9.928 million
% of population over 75	6.5%
Average per-capita income, 1987	$7,403
% of GNP spent on health care, 1987	6.2%
Number of acute-care hospitals	330
Number of acute-care hospital beds	
1984	69,416
1989	61,454 (– 8.7%)
Ratio of acute care-hospital beds to population	
1984	7 per 1,000
1989	6.2 per 1,000
Number of acute-care hospital admissions, 1988	1.529 million
Average length of stay in acute-care hospitals, 1988	11.25 days
Ratio of physicians to population	34 per 10,000

year's sabbatical at the Catholic University of Louvain with Jan Blanpain, a specialist in hospital management at the university's School of Public Health. At that time, Fetter's ideas had not been well received either in Belgium or in the United States, where his model appeared to be too simple to be used as a basis for hospital management. Fetter's macromodel also ran counter to the existing operational research systems based on micro-models, such as those of Charles D. Flagle at Johns Hopkins University in Baltimore, Maryland. Besides, as Fetter and his colleagues have regularly emphasized, DRGs were intended in the first place not for hospital financing but for improving hospital management.

Two factors explain the gradual increase in interest in DRGs in Belgium within the framework of a revision of the system for financing health care. The first and most important factor was the choice of this information system in 1983 by the United States government for its prospective payment program for Medicare claims. The generalized use of DRGs in the major-ity of U.S. states then allowed the method to pass the critical threshold of acceptability as a standard of comparison between hospitals. On scientific grounds, the method deserved to be tested in Belgium as well, without necessarily arousing fears of a financing system identical to that used in the United States. However, it was clear that other classification systems also deserved to be investigated. So long as DRGs remained purely a topic for research, there were only favorable opinions concerning studies on the validity of such a system. Belgium's policy in this regard was not as forceful as that adopted by the French Ministry of Social Affairs, which indicated the course to be followed in a much more imperative manner and, as a consequence, met with much more resistance.

The second factor was the gradually increasing availability of case mix data in Belgium. This was a direct consequence of the need to restrain the rapid growth in health care expenditures. The first step had been to set an overall budget for clinical laboratory work, but reimbursement based on previous expenses could only reward those laboratories that had been spending the most. An external criterion such as patient pathology was thus becoming desirable. (Up to this time, the Belgian system of health care reimbursement was essentially based on a nomenclature of *procedures* and took no account of *diagnosis*.)

In 1968, an abstract of the patient medical record called the clinical abstract had been introduced at the French-speaking Catholic University of Louvain so that the university could conduct clinical epidemiological research and obtain hospital activity profiles. This was a local initiative by J. J. Haxhe, who was in charge of planning for the new Saint Luke hospital (900 beds) that was to be built in Brussels (it was inaugurated in 1976). The patient medical record was perceived to be fundamental to modern hospital management, and I was engaged by the new hospital's medical directors to make an interdepartmental proposal for a computerized record. As points of departure, I took three elements: the single medical record; an abstract of this record used by the Mayo Clinic of Rochester, Minn.; and a model abstract used by the Commission on Professional and Hospital Activities of Ann Arbor, Mich., which was similar to the Mayo Clinic's but which distinguished the principal diagnosis for use by hospital management. I proposed a clinical abstract by medical specialty with a uniform structure. It was to be coded using the Ann Arbor commission's Hospital International Classification of Disease Adapted (HICDA) code (translated into French) for two reasons: first, because the precision of the diagnoses in the HICDA code was better than in the then-current ICD8 code; and second, because the HICDA code would allow comparisons on an international scale, which were not possible with INAMI's code (Roger, Joos, Servais, and Legrain, 1986; Roger, Joos, and Haxhe, 1988).

The proposed model was accepted by the directorate of the university clinics at the Catholic University of Louvain. It was then extended to all the university hospitals between 1971 and 1973 by the Ministry of Science Policy*; and following that, to the nonuniversity hospitals and about fifty general practitioners between 1974 and 1980. The Medical Informatics Center at the Catholic University of Louvain; in collaboration with the universities of Leuven, Ghent, and Brussels, was responsible for coordinating the work of implementing this model.

At the same time, the Commission of the European Communities, through the Directorat Général XIII (DGXIII), had charged a group of biomedical experts with the task of developing standards for medical records. A minimum basic data set was proposed to the commission and became its recommendation (Lambert and Roger, 1982). This data set was designed not only for clinical and epidemiological research but also for management and evaluation of patient care services at all levels. It served as the basis for the definition of the minimum clinical abstract that was standardized for all hospitals in Belgium in 1983. Given the intention of the minister of social affairs to link case mix to hospital financing and to use this instrument for internal management and planning, adoption of the minimum

*In 1969, the Belgian Cardiology Society (SBC) had become greatly alarmed at the spread, encouraged by the physicians union (Dr. A. Wijnen), of a program for automatic interpretation of electrocardiograms offered by a private company, Cardionics. One result was a recommendation by the SBC to the National Council on Science Policy (report of Dr. F. H. Roger) which eventually led to a "national programme to promote research in medical informatics," funded out of unused reserves held in case of natural catastrophes.

clinical abstract became mandatory in all university hospitals in 1985. Gradually, between 1986 and 1989, 110 nonuniversity hospitals were encouraged to introduce the abstract on a voluntary basis using personnel specially trained for this purpose. (These were formerly unemployed workers retrained and paid by the state.) In 1986, 60 percent of Belgian hospitals were collecting data for the minimum clinical abstract (Roger and others, 1987).

Beginning in 1979, the ICD9-CM code was made mandatory in the *Moniteur Belge* for all hospitals wishing to encode diagnoses. The decision to promulgate the ICD9-CM code in the *Moniteur Belge* resulted from a recommendation by the University Commission of the National Council of Hospitals, a body composed of university hospital medical directors, following research conducted under the sponsorship of the Ministry of Science Policy. This code had been used by all Belgian hospitals that had participated in the Science Policy Research Program since 1971. The work in that program had been coordinated by me as in 1970 I had undertaken a comparison of the ICD9 and ICD9-CM codes at the Mayo Clinic. It had emerged from this comparison that the ICD9-CM code better met the demands of hospital specialists and, above all, that it contained a classification of procedures that enabled comparisons with U.S. hospitals. The members of the group supervising the Science Policy Research Program had then pronounced in favor of the ICD9-CM code rather than face the necessity of constructing conversion tables (ICD9 and INAMI to ICD9-CM) to permit international comparisons. At that point in time, the choice of code was a question of clinical research, activity profiles, and quality of care — not yet a question of DRGs.

The Medical Informatics Center at the Catholic University of Louvain translated the complete ICD9-CM code (both diagnoses and procedures) into French and introduced supplementary codes (3,550) in response to demand from clinicians. The resulting code, called Hospital Adaptation of the International Classification of Diseases and Operations, has been widely distributed in Belgium and France (Roger, Joos, Servais, and Legrain, 1986).

At the beginning, DRGs elicited interest from only a few researchers. Thus, the first versions of the grouper were used at the Catholic University of Louvain on an experimental basis starting in 1981. It was not until 1987 that this university team was given the task of coordinating a research project linking the minimum clinical abstract to financial data, initially data on clinical laboratory costs. Given the narrowness of the field of application and the interrelations with other sectors of medical activity, the university research team, in collaboration with the Free University of Belgium (ULB, Erasme Hospital) and Catholic University of Leuven (KUL, Gasthuisberg) teams, chose DRGs in order to be able to proceed to interhospital comparisons of all kinds of medical services as well as lengths of stay.

As a result of the pilot project comparing the three university hospitals, the usefulness of the minimum clinical abstract was recognized, not only for internal hospital management but also for overall financing of health care services and, most especially, for evaluating the quality of care and for tracking epidemiological trends (Closon and Roger France, 1989). The DRG method was applicable in all of Belgium's different milieus — whether French- or Flemish-speaking, predominantly Catholic or nondenominational — and it gave distinctly higher percentages of explained variance for clinical laboratory costs than any other method proposed by INAMI.

Subsequently, in 1988 and 1989, the study was extended on a voluntary basis to 40 hospitals selected from among more than 100 that had asked to be included. It should be recalled that at this point it was a question only of research and development work on an infrastructure that might subsequently be applied in the hospitals. No doubt this is what explains the great enthusiasm of hospitals to participate. After a round of conferences on the subject led by me and J. L. Willems, hospital managers were eager to understand the advantages as well as the limitations of DRGs — the better to attack or defend them, according to how they saw their interests. In any event, they did feel themselves to be party to a process of working out a new system of financing.

Tables 3.2 and 3.3 give an example of the study results obtained in those 40 hospitals. Table 3.2 separates surgical and nonsurgical (medical) cases, while Table 3.3 contrasts university and nonuniversity hospitals (Closon, 1991). These tables give the percentage of the variance of expenses that is explained by several different methods of grouping pathologies: DRGs, refined DRGs (RGN), and New York DRGs (NY). The data are for the second quarter of 1988. Some key study findings include the following:

- In Table 3.2, the percentage of explained variance in most categories of expense is two or three times higher for surgical cases than for medical cases. These results are consistent with the information provided by analysis of the coefficient variation for these two types of cases.
- The refined DRGs give better results than the DRGs or the New York DRGs, especially in the university hospitals.
- Table 3.3 shows a higher percentage of explained variance in hospital expenses at the university hospitals, especially using refined DRGs.
- In both tables, explained variance is higher for the total bill than for the length of stay.

The minimum clinical abstract was made mandatory for all Belgian hospitals in June 1990.

Roles of the Principal Actors

As is often the case with any major change, it was at the level of a few very motivated individuals, unsatisfied with things as they were, that new models of data gathering and management were first proposed and tested in Belgium. In this particular case, there was a conjunction between the proposals of a researcher at the Catholic University of Louvain (me) and the willingness of a hospital director (J. J. Haxhe) to implement those proposals locally. With the support of the science policy and public health authorities, the new information system incorporating the minimum clinical abstract was gradually accepted by the majority of hospitals and eventually made mandatory.

At the national level, the minister of science policy in the

Table 3.2. Analysis of Variance of Expenses for Surgical and Nonsurgical Cases.[a]

	Surgical Cases			Nonsurgical Cases		
	DRG	RGN	NY	DRG	RGN	NY
Number of stays	76,055	76,089	75,905	119,884	119,833	120,029
Expenses	Percentage of Variation					
Days of hospitalization	51.6%	52.4%	50.8%	26.8%	32.7%	24.1%
Bills	60.0	59.7	62.0	21.5	33.6	23.6
Fees	68.2	70.6	69.9	24.4	35.3	24.2
Laboratory	39.7	47.0	46.8	20.1	31.8	21.3
Radiology	34.8	39.1	34.8	38.1	39.4	34.4
Surgery	74.1	74.8	74.6	17.0	21.9	16.2
Internal medicine	21.5	24.8	21.3	26.6	27.4	23.5
Intensive care	46.7	50.0	49.2	15.5	27.3	15.7
Pharmaceuticals	32.3	38.8	36.9	14.3	25.8	19.2
Blood products	22.4	31.0	30.3	7.5	22.8	11.2

Note: DRG = diagnosis-related groups; RGN = refined diagnosis-related groups; NY = New York DRGs.
[a] Figures for 40 Belgian hospitals; 2nd half of 1988.

Table 3.3. Analysis of Variance of Expenses in General and University Hospitals (40 Belgian Hospitals, 2nd Half of 1988).

Expenses	General Hospitals			University Hospitals		
	DRG	RGN	NY	DRG	RGN	NY
Number of stays	130,262	130,170	130,244	65,677	65,752	65,690
Days of hospitalization	36.7%	40.6%	35.3%	38.6%	43.3%	34.5%
Bills	56.2	55.4	53.8	53.1	57.0	52.8
Fees	52.7	56.1	50.5	58.3	61.5	56.1
Laboratory	29.9	38.0	31.4	36.8	45.6	40.1
Radiology	34.4	37.9	32.4	41.7	43.8	37.8
Surgery	69.6	71.2	68.0	79.4	79.2	78.1
Internal medicine	24.1	24.9	22.7	32.3	36.3	27.9
Intensive care	27.9	34.7	27.3	38.0	44.6	25.5
Pharmaceuticals	22.2	29.9	25.3	33.7	39.8	36.7
Blood products	16.3	25.4	22.7	24.3	32.8	30.2

1970s, Théo Lefèvre, played a key part in enabling the collection of basic data to be gradually extended. He also subsequently authorized the use of case mix methods on financial data, in the form of a summary of services performed (the so-called minimum financial abstract). After 1981, the Science Policy Ministry judged that the clinical abstract's promise had been sufficiently demonstrated and that financing of its further development should come from industry or the public authorities. In the event, it was the Ministry of Public Health that financed continued research and gradually generalized the minimum clinical abstract.

With a view to finding a new system of hospital financing, the Public Health Ministry first financed a research project in three hospitals of different philosophical views (St. Luke University Clinics, Erasme Hospital, and Gasthuisberg Hospital). No single method was favored a priori. The DRGs were chosen as a tool of comparison but not imposed on the hospitals. The reason they were chosen was, above all, their ready accessibility at an affordable price. This case mix method is well documented, operational, and in the public domain. It has been used by numerous hospitals in numerous countries, which makes it possible to make international comparisons. Patient management categories and disease staging based on the ICD9-CM code could have been used in Belgium if they had been more accessible, less expensive, and nonproprietary. The software for these two methods cannot be obtained as readily as the DRG grouper software. Moreover, the requirement that the data be sent to the United States for the analysis of results was not acceptable in Belgium, where the users wanted to keep control of operations. These case mix variants have been used on a selective basis for a few diagnoses, of which diabetes is one (Beguin and others, 1991). If access to them could be had on terms comparable to those for DRGs, these variants could still find wider use in Belgium.

The creation of an oversight committee within the Ministry of Public Health was very favorable to the progress of these efforts. This committee was composed of a staff member from the office of the Minister of Social Affairs (J. Hermesse), a repre sentative of the Public Health Administration (H. Splingaer), various university researchers (I, A. De Wever, J. Willems), and a representative from INAMI (J. Praet). The oversight committee met on a regular basis to assess the progress of the research project and to ensure that it was followed through in a coordinated fashion.

The minimum financial abstract was created to record data for each hospital stay in relation to each minimum clinical abstract. The financial abstract was a summary of the various categories on the bills—laboratory, radiology, operations, and so on. It thus became possible to relate these elements to the pathologies recorded for the same patient. At the same time, the nursing profession, in order to be able to demonstrate the value of nursing services, had requested the creation of a minimum nursing abstract, to be based on selected data used in studies that had been conducted in the United States and Canada. The minimum nursing care abstract thus records a whole series of nursing care activities related to the degree of dependency of the patient—assistance in feeding, ambulatory assistance, and so on. It is collected by unit of care provided rather than by hospital stay and takes account of the number of nursing personnel involved in providing the services recorded.

Overall, the development approach that was adopted in Belgium rested on demonstration of convincing results, rather than on imposition of ready-made solutions from on high. The Ministry of Public Health was very sensitive to the need to provide hospitals with both regular feedback on the ongoing research and a training program to promote knowledge of the new techniques. The research coordinators (I and J. L. Willems) made numerous presentations to the hospitals. From 1988 on, information sessions were held every six months at the ministry in order to familiarize physicians and hospital managers with the new methods. Only personnel who had taken courses in the new coding methods at one of the Belgian universities and who had received a certificate of qualification after completing certain practice exercises would be paid by the ministry.

In this whole process, no contract was signed with any U.S. or other foreign team of experts. The models were readily accessible from the literature. The DRG grouper was available at a very reasonable price (from Health Systems International), and using the ICD9-CM code in French translation allowed the grouper to be applied in Belgium immediately, both for diagnoses and for operations. In addition, the summary of charges for services permitted attribution of relative cost weights based, as in the United States, on the system of reimbursement.

I and J. Hermesse, as members of the oversight committee, had had contacts with Robert Fetter since 1984, but it was not necessary to establish research contracts for the mapping of the codes or for the grouping of pathologies. ("Mapping" here refers to the tables of correspondence between the local codes for diagnoses and operations and those in the ICD9-CM code or DRG codes, depending on which version of the grouper is chosen.)

Current Infrastructure and Development

The infrastructure for gathering billing data has a long tradition in Belgium, but for the minimum clinical abstract it is practically brand-new. Before it was generalized, the infrastructure for the clinical abstract was initially based on voluntary trials conducted in forty university and nonuniversity hospitals. During the research project, two teams, headed by me (for the French-speaking region) and J. L. Willems (for the Flemish-speaking region), were responsible for coordinating data gathering from the various hospitals. The teams worked in close collaboration using similar software programs. They benefited from the economic models developed by M. C. Closon (1991) and from the system courses on data coding and quality assurance of the clinical abstracts developed by C. Beguin (Beguin and others, 1989) and M. Meurisse (Meurisse and others, 1991) on behalf of all the hospitals in the country.

To receive financing for the minimum clinical abstract (at the rate of 5,000 Belgian francs per bed), each hospital must employ a staff member who has received a certificate for taking the course in coding at one of the Belgian universities. Now that the system has been generalized to all hospitals in the country, it is the Ministry of Public Health that is in charge of centralized data gathering. A surveillance commission (chairman, J. Tielemans) has been set up to assure confidentiality of the data and oversight of its applications. For the moment, the link between the minimum financial and clinical abstracts has not been maintained in data gathering at the national level.

For the purposes of hospital financing, and because payment based solely on historical consumption runs the risk of being perversely prejudicial to those who restrained their prescriptions in the interest of economy, the government decided to take account of the case mix. This decision has been reaffirmed in official declarations of the two most recent Belgian governments. The case mix has been taken into account indirectly, based on surgical operations and the type of specialty, given that the financial and clinical abstracts have not been available in all hospitals. The INAMI experts have, however, concluded that the use of DRGs would enable the case mix structure to be captured in finer detail. They have therefore recommended the use of DRGs when the minimum clinical abstract does become available in all hospitals. Research has been pursued in Belgium using the newer versions of DRGs — in particular adjacent DRGs, version 6.0 of the DRG grouper, and New York DRGs — as well as other case mix systems, when available, such as disease staging for certain disorders such as diabetes (Tables 3.2 and 3.3).

A study aiming to evaluate the actual costs by type of disorder, rather than simply the billed charges, is currently under way in a small number of hospitals, sponsored by the Ministry of Public Health.

European interhospital comparisons were made as part of the Advanced Informatics in Medicine research project during its 1989-1990 exploratory phase. Known as the Hospital Comparisons in Europe project, these comparisons included seven countries: Germany, Belgium, Denmark, Spain, Holland, Italy, and the United Kingdom (Roger France and others, 1991). A European health data base was first created at Utrecht in Holland in order to make real comparisons (macrocomparisons) and to determine the practical difficulties and differences among the seven countries. Up to the present, this effort has had to be limited to length of stay and case mix since the documentation on resources and costs in other countries remains too disparate and fragmentary. More detailed studies (microcomparisons) have also been conducted on particular diseases and procedures, such as diabetes, hip fractures, and cardiac valve replacements, with a view to visualizing the differences in practices and use of resources and furnishing indications regarding management and quality of care. Both macro- and microcomparisons have been conducted in order to test the cost and resource models that have been worked out and to define evaluation criteria for quality of care.

Current Controversies

The present separation of the data on patient pathologies and resources in Belgium does not facilitate the use of clinical and financial abstracts for health care financing. Moreover, hospitals have to decide individually on the code for operations in the clinical abstract. Formerly, surgical operations had to be coded according to the ICD9-CM, but since the generalized use of the clinical abstract began, they may be coded according to either the INAMI nomenclature or the ICD9-CM. Use of the INAMI codes by certain hospitals necessitates a conversion table between those and the ICD9-CM codes if DRGs are to be applied directly. This work is currently in progress.

Verifying the quality of the information, and in particular the relation between operations or specialized techniques on the one hand and patient pathologies on the other, requires instruments developed for the purpose. The DRG surfaces once again in this connection. Moreover, researchers continue to be interested in the newer versions of DRGs in the United States because these are better at taking into account particular pathologies that consume large amounts of resources, such as AIDS, certain types of leukemia, and multiple-trauma cases.

The difficulty of using the minimum clinical abstract directly under current conditions has induced many hospitals participating in research on abstracts to proceed voluntarily to

DRG-based comparisons of 1989 and 1990 data, which they have continued to collect according to service, using the ICD9-CM codes for diagnoses and operations. This exercise was conducted in 1991 on a strictly voluntary basis in collaboration with the Catholic University of Louvain and KUL. It was financed by each participating hospital.

In another connection, there has been a renewal of interest by hospitals in using DRGs for internal management purposes. DRGs are, in fact, the only instrument available for comparing differences in practice between hospitals. A number of hospitals, including the St. Luke University Clinics, have set up a strategic plan called St. Luke 2000. Under this plan, the strategy choices for the next ten years (promoting or reducing transplant operations, enlarging ambulatory care facilities, reducing certain medical procedures, and so on) will be based on comparative data for the St. Luke clinics and all other university hospitals taken together. Each service within the hospital has received a readout of its activity by DRG and, within each DRG, by pathology, for the disorders most frequently encountered, along with information about emergencies, geographic origin and destination of patients, stays of long and short duration, and so on. Specific surveys of attending physicians and patients, as well as a log of all consultations (diagnoses made and techniques performed) in the previous fifteen days, round out this information and decision-making system. The reports have been provided to all physicians and hospital administrators in order for them to give their opinions to an administrative council, which was originally scheduled to decide on a course of action at the end of 1991. Although the decision has not yet been made, the exercise has helped to familiarize physicians with DRGs. DRGs are also in use at a number of other hospitals, such as KUL at Ghent, where version 6.0 of the DRG grouper has been purchased. At these other hospitals, however, there is as yet no strategic plan based on DRGs.

Elsewhere, the data that has been gathered is to be analyzed either by the staff of the Ministry of Public Health or by the minimum clinical abstract research coordinators (I and J. L. Willems), who are responsible for providing feedback to the hospitals. An information bulletin financed by the Ministry of

Public Health was started in 1991, as were new research and development programs on data quality controls in the hospitals, internal feedback, and criteria of comparisons. Also undertaken in 1991 were educational programs using simulation to see the effects of decisions to modify behaviors; tables for conversion from INAMI codes to ICD9-CM codes; performance indicators; and studies of correlation between the minimum clinical and nursing care abstracts. These studies have been extended to seven faculties of medicine in Belgium, in Antwerp, Brussels (two), Ghent, Liège, and Louvain (two), as well as to the Institute of Hygiene and Epidemiology of the Ministry of Public Health.

At the national level, the obstacles to DRGs are now the physicians and, at the same time, the mutual-benefit societies. The physicians are fearful of the budgetary ceiling and the possibility, all too easy in Belgium, of using DRGs to regulate the budget. On the other side, the mutual-benefit societies are worried at seeing payments for health care services related to case mixes that they cannot control on a patient-by-patient basis. A debate has thus ensued over the question of respect for the secrecy of an individual patient's medical records, as well as over the control of the data base by the state rather than by the insuring institutions. The fact that the minimum clinical abstract was made mandatory by royal decree has only intensified these fears and further heated up the debate.

The future of DRGs in Belgium will most likely depend on how acute the financial problems are in the hospital sector. Solutions acceptable to all parties should improve the climate in the direction of more openness. Continuation of research and coordination of teaching at the European level could be an additional factor in unblocking the situation in Belgium, if uniform data-gathering standards are progressively adopted and if management based on case mix methods becomes a routine instrument in several countries, despite the diversity of economic measures that could be taken (Roger France and Santucci, 1991; Thayer, Boulay, and Roger France, 1991).

Stalling on a Solution

As we have seen, both the idea of classifying patients by disease and the idea of DRGs were at first relatively unopposed by the hospitals and the mutual-benefit societies. In 1990, however, the situation seemed to change suddenly. What happened?

The explanation appears to be the passage from the voluntary and experimental character of the research phase to the mandatory character of implementation as a part of a new system of financing hospital care. From 1970 to 1990, there had been participation by each of the social partners with a view to testing new ideas and new information systems. The clinical abstract that came to be used in Belgian hospitals during the 1970s opened the way to experimentation with systems of classifying pathologies. It seemed natural that DRGs should be tested, especially in Belgium, where data was available on resources used by patients. With help from the universities and financing from the government, the hospitals willingly conducted this kind of research work. The situation was not yet engraved in stone; every alternative was still possible; each party could still have hopes of one day controlling the new information system.

The royal decree of 1990, which made the minimum clinical abstract mandatory in all hospitals and changed the information flow by centralizing the abstracts at the Ministry of Public Health (and without any further mention of the minimum financial abstract) gave the state part of the means it would need for a new policy of financing acute-care hospitals and assessing the quality of care they provide. However, passing from experimentation to generalized use is not that easily done. The mutual-benefit societies are raising doubts about the ability of one ministry to manage such a data base effectively, given the difficulties of obtaining the credits needed for rapid deployment of data processing resources as well as the ponderousness of public administrations generally.

The mutual-benefit societies' current blocking of classification systems based on case mix seems intended to take advantage of possible administrative weaknesses in order to regain control of the medical data. This in turn, by linking the clinical and financial abstracts on a patient-by-patient basis, would give the societies control over physicians' practices. The medical profession is unanimously opposed to the prospect of this kind of bureaucratic control of medical practice. It continues to prefer control by a public administration on a hospital-by-hospital basis, using anonymous data.

The hospital managers, for their part, would like to be able to participate in managing the data. The university research teams continue to be active in seeking solutions, helping to perfect the tools, to propose alternatives, and to choose the classification system.

From this perspective, each of the partners appears to have an interest in delaying a definitive solution, so long as what remains of the fee-for-service reimbursement system can be maintained with partial measures — budget ceilings for laboratory tests, reductions in the number of hospital beds, and so on — but without an explosion in hospital costs. The Belgian experience may seem surprising, especially in the United States, where it has apparently been easier to introduce DRGs than to close hospitals and reduce hospital beds, as was done in Belgium.

Epilogue

In December 1991, elections were held in Belgium. Although a new government was installed, it remained a coalition between the Christian Democrats and the Socialists. The new government is determined to reduce the growth in health expenses, particularly for medicines. These expenses increased by almost 20 percent in the three years preceding the election. Furthermore, fixed ceilings are planned for expenses in radiology. In general, it is becoming more and more necessary to take case mix into account in order to allocate resources.

Data for the minimum clinical abstract are now successfully processed by the Ministry of Public Health for more than 85 percent of hospital inpatients in the country. ICD9-CM codes are used for surgical procedures by more than 85 percent of hospitals and for diagnoses by 100 percent. Twenty percent of hospitals use the INAMI nomenclature for surgical procedures. Computer programs for hospital and internal departmental management have been developed in many institutions.

The Ministry of Public Health is supporting a number of

research and development projects. One major goal is to distribute uniform ICD9-CM codes (translated into French and Dutch) to hospitals. Another is to produce error-checking programs and feedback software in order to enable local and national comparison of results. The seven faculties of medicine in the country are working simultaneously on these developments.

The Ministry of Public Health has also initiated research into the influence of pathologies on consumption of drugs, based on DRGs, refined DRGs, and other criteria (medical specialty, admission into the intensive-care unit, and so on). This work is made possible by the availability of a financial record summary data base, which is generated on a voluntary basis by about forty hospitals. Another research project intends to estimate real costs by groups of pathologies.

A bulletin on hospital record summaries (including the minimum clinical abstract, financial abstract, and nursing abstract) is compiled every three months for all hospitals. It contains articles on various topics (resource management, quality of care, data confidentiality and reliability), as well as examples of practical applications and uniform coding rules.

In other words, the situation continues to evolve very progressively in Belgium. Although the team that collects data at the Ministry of Public Health is small, it is very efficient and works in a collaborative spirit with the hospitals. However, data from the minimum clinical abstract will not be used for hospital financing until the national data bank reaches an adequate level of quality for all the hospitals in Belgium. The general feeling is that this goal should be reached in 1993 or 1994.

References

Beguin, C., and others. "Quality of Hospital Data: How to Measure and Improve It?" In F. H. Roger France, G. De Moor, J. Hofdijk, and L. Jenkins (eds.), *Diagnosis Related Groups in Europe*. Ghent, Belgium: Medische Informatica/Informatique Médical, 1989, 16–24.
Beguin, C., and others. "Euro Health Data Base for Hospital Macro- and Micro-Comparisons in Europe: Diabetes Mellitus

as an Example." In K. P. Adlassnig, G. Grabner, S. Bengtsson, and R. Hansen (eds.), *Medical Informatics Europe 1991: Lecture Notes in Medical Informatics*, Vol. 45. Berlin: Springer-Verlag, 1991, 641–645.

Closon, M. C. "Le financement des hôpitaux en fonction de la structure des pathologies" (Financing of hospitals as a function of case mix). Doctoral dissertation in public health, Catholic University of Louvain, Brussels, 1991.

Closon, M. C., and Roger France, F. H. "Case-Mix and Severity of Cases for Hospital Financing and Quality Assessment." In F. H. Roger France, G. De Moor, J. Hofdijk, and L. Jenkins (eds.), *Diagnosis Related Groups in Europe*. Ghent, Belgium: Medische Informatica/Informatique Médical, 1989, 49–55.

Lambert, P. M., and Roger, F. H. *Hospital Statistics in Europe*. Amsterdam: North Holland–Elsevier, 1982.

Meurisse, M., and others. "Case-Mix for Prospective Hospital Financing in Belgium: Data Collection and Basic Descriptive Data." In K. P. Adlassnig, G. Grabner, S. Bengtsson, and R. Hansen (eds.), *Medical Informatics Europe 1991: Lecture Notes in Medical Informatics*, Vol. 40. Berlin: Springer-Verlag, 1991, 162–167.

Roger, F. H. "Le résumé du dossier médical: Indicateur informatisé de performance et de qualité des soins" (The medical record summary: a computerized indicator of performance and quality of care). Doctoral dissertation, Faculty of Medicine, Catholic University of Louvain, Brussels, 1982.

Roger, F. H. "Medical Record Summaries: Past, Present, and Future in European Hospitals." *Methods of Information in Medicine*, 1985, *24*, 117–119.

Roger, F. H., Joos, M., and Haxhe, J. J. "An Interhospital Problem-Oriented and Automated Discharge Summary." *Methods of Information in Medicine* (Special issue: *Data, Information, and Knowledge in Medicine: Developments in Medical Informatics in Historical Perspective*), 1988, pp. 44–47.

Roger, F. H. Joos, M., Servais, P., and Legrain, Y. "International Classifications of Disease Extensions: Lessons from Experience in Europe." In R. Salamon and others (eds.), *Proceedings of Medinfo 86*, Vol. 1. Amsterdam: North Holland, 1986, pp. 355–357.

Roger France, F. H., and Santucci, G. (eds.). *Perspectives of Information Processing in Medical Applications: Strategic Issues, Requirements and Options for the European Community.* Heidelberg, Germany: Springer-Verlag, 1991.

Roger France, F. H., and others. "A Survey of Medical Informatics in Belgium." *Medical Informatics*, 1987, *12*(4), 249–262.

Roger France, F. H., and others. "Information System Development for Case-Mix Management in Belgium." In *Proceedings of Medinfo 89*. Amsterdam: North Holland, 1989, pp. 863–865.

Roger France, F. H., and others. "Hospital Comparisons Using a Euro Health Data Base for Resource Management and Strategic Planning." *Health Policy*, 1991, *17*(2), 165–177.

Thayer, C., Boulay, F., and Roger France, F. H. "European Strategies for Training in Health Information Systems." *International Journal of Biomedical Computing*, 1991, *28*, 117–125.

Four

France: The Introduction of Case-based Hospital Management

Gérard de Pouvourville

In June, 1982, the Department of Health's Bureau of Hospital Administration sent public and private hospitals an invitation to participate in a project focusing on a data base recording patient medical data. Experiment objectives were pinpointed as follows: "The project seeks to test the creation of a French hospital data base in a specific number of hospitals within their short-term care section. This data base will facilitate the description of hospital output or medical activities through a range of typical patient cases and medical procedures in order to generate a new management style in hospitals" (Department of Health, 1982). Participating institutions would commit themselves to providing a uniform hospital discharge data set (known as a Résumé de Sortie Standardisé, or RSS), for each hospitalization period. This data set, which was similar to a standardized discharge summary, would assess diagnostic and medical care data. "A new management style in hospitals" meant applying the findings of Robert Fetter of Yale University to French hospitals.

This invitation marked the introduction of diagnosis-

Note: The author wishes to thank Marc Brémond, François Delafosse, Jean de Kervasdoué, André Loth, Robert Maud, Marie-Laure Pibarot, Jean-Marie Rodrigues, Jean Salin, and Gérard Vincent for reviewing this chapter.

related groups (DRGs) in France. Who were the main promoters of the project? In what institutional, political, and technical context did this project evolve? How did the context influence the project and the strategies of the participants? What lies in store for such a project? These are the questions this text will try to answer.

The French Hospital System

The major characteristics of the French hospital system have been stable since 1982. The private sector encompasses both profit and nonprofit institutions. The public system prevails in terms of available beds. Occupancy in public hospitals constitutes two-thirds of short-term occupancy. Private institutions, however, perform over three-fifths of surgical, obstetrics, and gynecology procedures, totaling 50 percent of occupancy. Public hospital-based physicians hold full-time salaried posts, while physicians in the private sector (in profit-oriented hospitals or clinics) are self-employed, are remunerated on a fee-per-service basis, and have a contract with one or more institutions. Table 4.1 provides an overview of the French health care system.

Public sector institutions depend on local government (municipalities). Each hospital's board is chaired by a locally elected politician. The general rules concerning the operations and financing of public sector institutions are defined by legislative or executive guidelines. Thus, these institutions are strictly supervised. For example, a hospital director is appointed by the Department of Social Affairs, acting on the proposal of the chairman of the board. The same director reports to local agencies of the department; to the departmental Office of Social Affairs, and to the Public Health Service. The Department of Social Affairs also plans the supply of hospital care by drawing up a map of health needs. Finally, access to high-tech equipment (such as scanners, MRI machines, or lithotripters) requires administrative approval (such authorization also applies to the private sector). Moreover, the Department of Social Affairs de-

Table 4.1. France: Key Health Care Figures.

General Data
Country area: 547,027 sq. km.
Population: 56,419,675 (1990)
Percent of population over 65 years: 14%
Life expectancy at birth, women: 80.9 years
Life expectancy at birth, men: 72.7 years

Health Expenditures	1980	1990
National health expenditures (in current francs)	226,955 Millions FF	603,488 Millions FF
National health expenditures per capita (in current francs)	4,212 FF	10,696 FF
% Gross national product	8.1	9.4
% Hospital in national health expenditures	44.93	41.20
% Physician services in national health expenditures (excludes public hospital physician salaries)	22.30	25.92
% Medical goods in national health expenditures	16.48	18.10
% Other services to patients in national health expenditures	9.37	7.23
% Other expenditures	6.92	7.55

Health Professionals	1980	1990
Physicians		
Number	104,073	147,949
Number per 100,000 pop.	193.2	262.2
Other health workers	1980	1989
Number	296,663	358,656
Number per 100,000 pop.	550.6	638.6

Hospital Sector (1988)	Public	Private
Number of hospitals	531	1073
Number of beds	370,059	198,846

Beds per 1,000 pop.	1980	1990
Total number	11	9.9
Public sector	7	4
Acute-care	6.2	5.3
Acute-care, public	4	3.3
Acute-care, private	2.2	1.9

Sources: Annuaire des Statistiques Sanitaires et Sociales, Ministère des Affaires
Sociales et de la Solidarité, 1990; Credes, 1991.

fines management and administration techniques used by the public sector.*

Hospital financing is ensured through a national health insurance program called Social Security, which is both mandatory and nationwide. Resources are provided through payroll taxes or (in the case of independent workers) global revenue dues based on income.

Operating budgets of both public sector and private nonprofit institutions are funded by an annual prospective budget allocation. Annual discussions are held between the Department of Social Affairs and the Budget Department to reevaluate the budget in relation to a nationwide growth rate. This rate represents an average that can be marginally adjusted in keeping with the location and the activities of each institution. This mechanism was spelled out in a 1983 decree. Investment outlays are financed either through the institution's eventual operating surplus or through subsidies from the state budget.

In the private sector, doctors are paid per service, and they generally give a percentage of their fees back to the institution where they practice. The institution also receives a per diem for room and board of inpatients and their health care, as well as a lump sum based on the complexity of surgery performed, the use of the operating room, and the medication administered. Radiological and biological exams are also remunerated on the basis of each procedure. The prices of medical procedures are defined by a national fee schedule negotiated between Social Security organizations and the major medical unions. Per diems and other lump sums are negotiated through specific agreements between each institution and local Social Security agencies.

The French hospital system is highly centralized, especially in the public sector. Centralization is omnipresent, be it in the system's administrative procedures or in the use of nation-

*The French public health administration belongs to ministerial departments, the name and scope of which change each time the government changes. For simplicity's sake, in the text, the secretary in charge of this administration will always be called "Secretary of Health." For accuracy's sake, references to official texts quote the name of the department when the text was published.

wide arbitration decisions; for example, with regard to decisions concerning access to equipment. Centralization, however, is kept in check by several factors (Pouvourville 1983b).

First of all, hospital-based physicians — especially those in teaching hospitals — represent a real political force; enforcing an important measure without their support is very difficult, especially when their professional autonomy is at stake. In spite of the diversity of their roles and professional backgrounds, physicians are capable of uniting very quickly. Physicians at teaching hospitals play a key role as technical advisers to the central administration of the Health and Education departments. Well-known professors have direct contacts with national politicians.

The second check on centralization stems from the special status of public hospitals: they are local institutions. Whenever the board is chaired by a politician with a regional or national aura, the director and medical staff have direct access to the national political scene, bypassing the local supervisory body.

The third check lies in the status of the Public Health Administration in France. Not regarded as one of France's most prestigious, the department has little expertise at the highest level. Its territorial administration is understaffed (Moisdon and others, 1987), and its employees are endowed with minimal authority over hospital staff.

The fourth check is a result of the health system's two watchdog bodies. On the one hand, the Public Health Administration is expected to organize the supply of available hospital services. However, it is Social Security that foots the bill. To be sure, as a public institution, Social Security is under the supervision of public authorities. But it is managed by representatives of the insured, in this instance workers' and employers' unions (Pouvourville and Renaud, 1985). Although these bodies have little autonomy, they wield their power in their relations with health care providers. Power play is especially present in their relations with health care providers in urban private practices (Pouvourville, 1988), and it is also manifest in hospitals. This has been especially true since 1983, which was the first year that regional health insurance bodies were asked for their nonbinding opinion on hospitals' provisional budgets.

Finally, the coexistence of both private and public health care sectors acts as a check. Questioning this dual existence is political suicide, and managing such duality requires diplomatic maneuvering. From a legal point of view, the state cannot have the same supervisory power over private and public institutions. Each attempt to harmonize regulations is viewed as threatening by one or the other sector. Ironically, each sector and the central administration would like to see the two sectors harmonized in the name of equal and fair competition.

In spite of the dominating legitimacy of France's central government, a secretary of health encounters great difficulty in trying to change this system. It was in this general context in 1982 that the project to develop patient-related clinical data (known as the Projet de Médicalisation des Systèmes d'Information, or PMSI) was introduced.

Technical and Political Context

In 1982, the technical and political context for PMSI was rather unfriendly. Until this date, French hospitals were not legally obliged to routinely supply data on the medical services provided. The Department of Health evaluates morbidity rates based on multiannual surveys. Hospital-based doctors keep personal records on their patients—but the file contents and descriptions are left to their discretion. As physicians generally rely on a personal coding system or a system developed by their specialty, they are generally ignorant of the codes used by the World Health Organization. In France, the only mandatory epidemiological statistics recorded concern causes of death.

Moreover, French hospitals have no central department to manage and store medical files as in the United States. Central archives do exist, but they serve only for storage purposes. Furthermore, no personnel are trained to handle international coding systems. This deficiency explains why there is no cross-filing system for patient management records (as in the United States), even though health administrators, hospital managers, and researchers may have experienced such a need. It is also why the scope of France's health planning tools is so limited.

Development of PMSI has also been hampered by the lack of an accounting data system to identify patient resource utilization. Using the hospital's present cost accounting system to calculate the cost per DRG would have been difficult. In many institutions, a clear definition of direct consumption of available services per clinical ward was not even possible, and when it was possible, most patient data were not recorded. Calculating the cost of hospitalization for a set patient category required (and still does require) returning to the patient's medical file.

Then there has been the question of financing French hospitals. At the end of the 1970s, the financing debate focused on public hospitals being paid a fixed per diem. Revenue was directly linked to activity. The per diem was set at the beginning of each year and reevaluated every year based on a nationwide rate of increase. The rate was also adjusted as a function of the medical specialty rendering the service. Even though the case mix idea was somehow built into the rates through the specialties, everyone agreed that the underlying breakdown was too coarse. In spite of its prospective nature, this type of financing hardly incited hospitals to increase their productivity. The reason for this was that pricing was based on historical costs rather than on an externally defined standard of good performance. Moreover, as earnings were directly linked to activity, the system did not encourage institutions to limit their global expenses.

In 1978, the Department of Social Affairs launched two experimental systems of alternative financing. One of these alternatives called for a prospective annual budget that hospital administrators were obliged to respect. The system sought to attain two goals: First, to limit hospital expenses and uncouple hospital revenue from activity; second, to make hospital directors and managers more accountable for their budgets.

In 1979, even before this experiment was finished, the first steps were taken nationwide to impose a ceiling on hospital budgets. The per diem system was maintained, but overall hospital expenditures could not surpass the nationally set rate of increase. (This rule could, however, be bent to grant extra subsidies to institutions in deficit.)

When the Socialist government took power in 1981, economic growth spurred by enhanced consumption and new public sector jobs together meant fewer budgetary constraints for public hospitals. In the spring of 1982, however, Secretary of Social Affairs Nicole Questiaux was replaced by Pierre Bérégovoy, who was known as "the budget man," and the clocks were set back on budget rationing. When the secretary issued his new budget plan, its main ideas included a prospective budget (to take effect in 1984) for all public hospitals and the introduction of a room-and-board lump fee to be paid by the patient. At this point, using DRGs as means of payment per patient could not yet be considered. The government's main plan was to put a lid on overflowing hospital expenses, thereby inciting hospital managers to limit unit costs.

What role did DRGs play in such a context? For the director of French hospitals, the issue was simple. On the one hand, limiting the budget was more than a matter of simply rationing hospital expenses. To use a nationwide rate of increase for all institutions regardless of their relative performance or real financial needs would certainly not incite hospital directors to be efficient managers. The director therefore advocated a budget limitation method based on DRGs, facilitating an equitable distribution of resources among institutions. He viewed the GHM (the French acronym for DRG, translatable as homogenous patient groups) as a basis for the annual budget allowance.

The political change occurring in 1981 also produced an overhaul of the Department of Health. Prime Minister Pierre Mauroy's first cabinet included a Health Administration (and health secretary) within a larger Department of Social Affairs. Communist Jack Ralite was named as the first secretary of health and undertook a number of reforms stamped with left-wing ideology. Health care providers greeted the reforms with much opposition. However, the list of reforms is impressive: internal reorganization of public hospitals by restructuring clinical wards into departments headed by an elected doctor who was assisted by a board; an overhaul of specialty training; reforming the status of hospital-based physicians; reforming finances; and abolishing private practice activities in public hospitals. In short, the Bureau of Hospital Administration had a very full work load.

This multifaceted overhaul did not please hospital-based doctors. To begin with, there is a longstanding opposition between left-wing parties and doctors — who are noted for voting for the center and right-wing parties. This ideological opposition is furthered by health care providers' desire to remain independent, therefore opposing state interference in health care organization or state control over medical activity. The appointment of Communist Jack Ralite as health secretary worried doctors, some of whom even viewed it as a provocation. At the end of 1981, a project to abolish private practice in public institutions was issued, unleashing hostile reactions from the most conservative segments of teaching hospital staff. These actions were expressed either as solemn protests in the press, as public demonstrations, or as strikes. The confrontation peaked in the spring of 1983 with teaching hospital strikes. Meanwhile, the first draft of a decree on the transformation of wards into departments was published in December 1982. It was accompanied by a television campaign denigrating the system of medical mandarins, thus rekindling the initial confrontation even though the debate on the private sector had petered out. (The chief physician in a teaching hospital wields unique power stemming from his or her dual roles as a practitioner and a professor. It is for this reason that chief physicians are called mandarins.)

DRGs in the Early Years

Promoting DRGs in France proved, therefore, to be difficult for institutional, political, and technical reasons. The history of DRGs follows the rhythm of the major phases in French politics over the past ten years. The first phase, 1982 through the end of 1986, roughly corresponds to the first Socialist-dominated legislature. Termed "cohabitation," the second era extends from 1987 to 1988, with a right-wing government governing alongside Socialist President François Mitterand. The last era is marked by François Mitterand's reelection in May 1988. Each of these phases brought to power a new director of French Hospitals.

The desire to introduce DRGs in France dates back before 1982, but few people were then aware of the innovation. In the

late 1970s Jean de Kervasdoué played a key role in introducing
the concept into hospitals. He began his career in health administration as head of the economic analysis department of the
Planning Office of Paris Public Hospitals (Assistance Publique).
At the same time he was a researcher at the Management Research Center at l'Ecole Polytechnique. Jean de Kervasdoué was
well known for his work on the diffusion of biomedical innovations, public health policies, organizational sociology, and the
sociology of science. From the time of his doctoral degree
(earned in the United States), he kept in touch with university
researchers in health care services. Especially close ties were
maintained with John Kimberly, who was then a professor at
Yale's School of Management.

The Paris Public Hospitals had commissioned a number
of studies aiming at improving their management information
systems and replacing traditional indicators such as number of
procedures performed or number of days. The studies had
always stumbled because of the difficulties of taking into account case mix. First, the information was not systematically
available in standard form. Second, there was no method of
handling the data. At the time, identifying comparable clinical
cases and calculating their costs was a hospital manager's dream.
The Paris Public Hospitals therefore sought help in introducing
medical data into management control systems. Through his
American contacts, Jean de Kervasdoué learned of the studies
done in this field at Yale. In 1979, a first task force went to the
United States and visited Yale. The group's report proposed that
a number of task forces be set up under the aegis of the Planning
Office to develop management control tools based on case mix.
The first French publication concerning DRGs comes from the
Paris Public Hospital's central administrative analysis committee (Anastasy and others, 1982). Jean de Kervasdoué left the
Paris Public Hospitals to move to a position out of the health
care service field. At the end of 1981, he was appointed director
of French hospitals. Convinced that hospital management and
supervisory institutions needed a major overhaul, he launched
the PMSI. Seeking immediate results, he did not want to waste
time conceiving a new management tool, and he thus based the

project on the work of Yale's Robert Fetter. In April 1982, he organized a research trip to the United States, and two months later the PMSI was under way.

The director of French hospitals assigned project development to a task force within the Bureau of Hospital Administration. The project and a translation of Fetter's seminal article on DRGs in *Medical Care* were the crux of a March 1983 article appearing in the well-circulated journal *Les Cahiers de Gestions Hospitalières* (Rodrigues, 1983). The task force housed several substructures: a scientific committee (including Robert Fetter); a board of executives (entrusted with decision-making powers); technical expertise teams with specific specializations (epidemiology, statistics, accounting, data processing, and organization); a clinical expertise group composed of representatives from professional societies of diverse specialties; and a logistics team called the Application and Development Group.

The Application and Development Group

The Application and Development Group represented the PMSI nucleus. Composed of members from the Bureau of Hospital Administration (a nonhierarchical selection), it was headed by Jean-Marie Rodrigues, a radiologist and public health care specialist. Rodrigues and Jean de Kervasdoué were PMSI's two main advocates in France. Rodrigues called on outside consultants to carry out the four above-mentioned projects. From the beginning of the project, the director of French hospitals called on the resources of the Management Research Center at l'Ecole Polytechnique, as well as the Scientific Management Center at l'Ecole des Mines in Paris. The director knew these two teams personally and placed much confidence in their work. While the Management Research Center was in charge of setting up information systems for discharge summaries, the Scientific Management Center worked on developing a cost model per GHM. Development of data processing tools required for the project was entrusted to the National Center for Hospital Equipment, which had the necessary know-how to develop management information software for public institutions.

The project director had a central role in coordinating the teams, and general communication was ensured by personal contacts that members had established with one another before being appointed to a committee or group. Moreover, communication was facilitated by the small number of people working on the project. The project director and a computer engineer from the National Center for Hospital Equipment made a great many technical choices concerning classification systems and software outputs. The production of medical data was done with the help of an organization expert from the Rodrigues team and researchers from the Management Research Center. The accounting system was first developed by the Scientific Management Center, the technical expertise committee, and another member of the Rodrigues team.

Project participants enlisted on a volunteer basis. A preliminary meeting in September 1982 gathered volunteers at the Department of Health. Twenty-four institutions responded favorably, including three hospital associations. The director of French hospitals stressed the innovative character of the project as well as its importance. He added that the project would be carried out with limited means. Jean-Marie Rodrigues, the project director, presented the project's four phases. The first phase called for a national standardized discharge summary (RSS) for all hospital stays, the goal being to gather 1.5 million summaries as quickly as possible. The second phase was to exploit this national base and form homogenous diagnostic groups (HDGs, later to become homogenous patient groups, or GHMs). The third phase sought to develop information management systems for a nationwide use of the RSS and a fine-tuning of HDGs. The final phase called for a new cost accounting method to calculate costs per HDG. Volunteer institutions were to be operational by January 1983.

The final selection of volunteers was made according to the following criteria. Institutions that had a management information system capable of delivering RSS after minimal changes (two regional teaching hospitals, Caen and Grenoble, and a Marseille public hospital) were automatically enrolled in the project. They were asked to write a specifications report on the

conditions governing the adaptation of their information management systems to RSS. Three community hospitals were
chosen: two without a data processing system (a small and a
medium-sized hospital) and a third with such facilities. Other
hospitals chosen included a private institution and two cancer
treatment centers. Participating institutions were to be assisted
by the Application and Development Group and to serve as
testing grounds for information management systems that
would produce the RSS.

The Rodrigues team launched the four project phases
simultaneously. In May 1983, a report listing the requirements of
the PMSI was submitted to the Department of Social Affairs and
National Solidarity (1983a). A simplified, temporary version of
the ICD9-CM procedure classification to be used by participating volunteers was ready in August 1983 (Department of Social
Affairs and National Solidarity, 1983b). Although planned to
begin in January 1983, PMSI could not be applied in institutions
lacking an adequate data processing infrastructure. This delay
was due to the time needed to produce general documentation.

The Application and Development Group had a very
heavy work load. As the secretary of health did not have the
necessary data processing tools for project management in
Paris, an institution capable of providing the service had to be
found, such as the National Center for Hospital Equipment
(NCHE). Moreover, on-site progress at the pilot center needed to
be followed up and recorded. Specification reports sent by
institutions also needed a coherent program setup and monitoring. Finally, pilot site personnel had to be trained to use the
coding system. This required organizing training sessions for
each pilot site.

A choice had to be made on the type of classification. Was
the grouper to analyze all French data, or would other groupers
be researched and tested? Originally, diverse solutions seemed
possible. Moreover, a new system to code procedures for RSS
application had to be developed and disseminated. The resulting procedure list was to serve the needs of both PMSI and the
global budget product. A new tool to describe medical services
in more precise and exhaustive terms than the existing one was

supposed to be developed. The new classification was to offer two innovations: a code to identify the type of procedure performed and a value scale to measure the relative direct cost of each procedure. To apply the grouper, the new coding system had to be based on the ICD9-CM. Decisions also had to be made concerning the method of cost calculation per GHM and to spell out a cost accounting method for identifying resource consumption per patient.

The project had appeal, answering a great many needs put forward by hospital administrators and other public agents frustrated by simplistic tools or involved in power plays over which they had no control. The idea of establishing a cost per pathology was the Eden they had frequently dreamed of. The need for a system overhaul was even felt by hospital-based physicians, regardless of whether they were for or against the PMSI project. They understood that they would soon have to account for their performances. Existing French research, however, was not developed enough to cover the full range of hospital activities. The absence of pertinent hospital medical data was in fact a vicious circle: with no data, no general tools could be developed; with no such tools, there was no real reason to provide data on health care services.

The decision to impose an existing tool and standard medical data for hospital information systems offered several advantages: the American experience showed that close to a decade is needed to develop a new tool, and that such development requires considerable resources. With the tool in hand, interhospital comparisons could be made on a rational basis. Moreover, a systematic budget revision could be made in order to redistribute resources based on activity. From this standpoint, in 1982, the DRG was the best choice available to the director of French hospitals, even if he knew that this tool was under severe criticism in the United States.

Nevertheless, the decision also entailed important risks. First of all, the basic logic underlying the DRG was at odds with the evolution of the debate on hospital financing and management. Second, it was feared that hospital-based physicians might view the project as an infringement on their professional rights and refuse to provide necessary data. Third, the Department of Health's general overhaul policy did not provide a favorable environment for the PMSI. Fourth, there were risks stemming from the politics of the Social Affairs and Health secretaries and their respective cabinets. Political actors might make decisions for other projects that would entail negative spillover for PMSIs. Moreover, resource allocation for projects is also a political process. Finally, there was uncertainty about the resources that the director of French hospitals could count on. He knew he could rely on only a limited budget and so chose the fast track to implement the project.

Even if France did not need to invest in a new tool, PMSI was nonetheless a very ambitious project. The Department of Health is not one of the wealthiest departments, be it for sub-contracting or for carrying out surveys on its own. In addition, PMSI was not the only ongoing project requiring financing.

Since 1982, the Department of Health's PMSI staff, in addition to the PMSI project manager, has ranged from four to ten people. None of them has ever worked full-time on the PMSI project. Even the project manager played a key role in other reforms. Several outside consultant teams were called in to work on project development, including Fetter's team, which was present from the very start. The project manager had estimated development credits at around $200,000 a year from 1982 to 1984. This jumped to between $330,000 and $500,000 in the project's final years. The cost of software product development is included in these totals and represents between one-third and two-thirds of the budget, depending on the year. Items to be added to the budget for each test site included computer hardware and exceptional personnel positions created in 1984 for RSS coding, especially since these items were not subjected to the national limit on increases in expenditure fixed for hospitals. Excluding job creation and salaries of Rodrigues's team, a realistic budget for 1982 through 1986 falls between $1.25 and $1.7 million.

Although these figures most likely underestimate the sums really spent, the approximation does seem realistic. Two statements can be made concerning the figures. The amount is high compared with the Bureau of Hospital Administration's available resources but low if the scope of the project is considered. Actually, project development was mainly hindered by the Application and Development Group's lack of time. Since no member worked on the project full-time, it advanced in spurts. In addition, much of the development work did not directly concern the test sites but focused on general project infrastructure. The test sites, as a result, would not rapidly receive either general information or specific troubleshooting from the Rodrigues team. For example, the first new sites (other than Caen and Grenoble) sent their RSS to the team in the second quarter of 1984 but only received processed data in April 1985. Another problem was the team's incapacity to handle certain questions when the answer depended on the development of another project facet. For example, the final GHM list, with labeling, was only published in 1986. Moreover, there was no systematic way to communicate progress on the project. This lack of project communication at a national level discouraged the project's local managers as they felt that they were not recognized for their work.

The team's limited size and the need to simultaneously develop various facets of the project did not facilitate training and information activities at test sites. As a result, many test site physicians lost interest in the project, a problem that was reflected in poor data quality. These doctors perceived PMSI as one more administrative survey instead of as a patient management system that could work to their advantage. In some instances, lack of interest increased when computer systems did not accompany PMSI.

Limited resources and the entrepreneurial temper of Jean de Kervasdoué had a major impact on two project decisions. The first was the decision to transpose the American classification system to France, including the grouper. The second was the choice of Fetter's cost modeling system despite objections raised by some members of the technical expertise committee on accounting. In both cases, the decision reveals the concern of the director of French hospitals not to repeat what had already been done elsewhere and to get results as quickly as possible.

At that time, the structure of the DRG classification system was generally accepted. Its validation was coarse. Data from a Grenoble site were sent to Yale; once processed these data showed that the variability for the distribution of hospitalization per DRG was analogous in both countries but that hospitalization was longer in France than in the United States. The findings were reported in an internal department memorandum to justify project feasibility. The results, however, were neither discussed within the Application and Development Group nor circulated outside the group. Even DRG classification quality was not discussed in terms of homogeneity (whether defined in clinical or in economic terms). It was only in 1988 that the Bureau of Hospital Administration began to raise the problem of validating DRGs. At the time, it was considered most important to forge ahead. It is fair to say that the only operational tool available on the market in the early 1980s was Fetter's. Neither disease staging (Gonella, Hornbrook, and Louis, 1984) nor the so-called severity index (Horn and Sharkey, 1983) had yet reached the same stage of development.

Reaction of Doctors

Doctors were violently opposed to reforms undertaken by the Socialist government in 1981. Paradoxically, it is quite likely that PMSI benefited from a three-year period of relative obscurity. Project development was not only far from the test sites but also out of the public eye. Moreover, little had been published in France on the American experience. Medical unions had their hands full with the other reforms, and in the spring of 1983 they were fully absorbed in the new wave of demonstrations (Bedier, Desaulle, and Venencie, 1985). For these reasons, we feel that the project was also less visible for the cabinets of the departments of Social Affairs and Health, which sheltered the PMSI team.

Within hospitals, PMSI could count on some backing from a minority of doctors, a fact that helps to explain the number of volunteer participants. Other motivations, however, also account for volunteer participation. Grenoble, Caen, and Marseille were designated volunteer institutions as they had already developed patient management categories and the data they had already gathered made it likely that a national base could be established within a reasonable time span. Our field work shows that doctors were modestly involved in the project and that an institution's candidacy often reflected the confusion between data processing and information systems (Pouvourville, 1983a; Pouvourville and Jeunemaître, 1983; Pouvourville and Jeunemaître, 1986).

We encountered varying attitudes at the pilot sites. There was strong interest in developing data processing in clinical departments. The main goal here was to improve daily administration (patients, file archives, physician discharge letters) rather than to evaluate medical services and activity. However, there were several obstacles in the way. The only PMSI document doctors had access to at the time was the RSS, which was viewed as providing only gross descriptions of medical activity. Physicians further denounced the RSS as a tool that only accounted for traditional hospitalization cases and ignored outpatient services. PMSI was also seen as a control tool for outside use. Furthermore, its complex features and ambiguous application left doctors with little choice but a priori opposition (because of the perceived threat to the quality of medical care). The hope of acquiring data processing systems or other local incentives could override this opposition. Yet each institution had its hardcore opponents who compromised the exhaustive nature of RSS production or the quality of data input.

Public controversy flared up at the end of 1984 when the details of the PMSI Aquitaine project were specified. In November 1983 the Secretary of Health had announced the launch of PMSI in this region of southwest France for all public institutions. Two community hospital physicians objected publicly to project presentations. The regional project called for centralizing all RSS data at Aquitaine's Regional Administration of Public Health and Social Services. It also planned for an anonymous data base for the region's discharge reports. The two physicians criticized the takeover of medical data by the regional teaching hospital and the Regional Hospitalization Management Center. They also denounced the potential use of PMSI data for automatic calculation of the region's global hospital budget. The Aquitaine experience was finally a failure.

At the end of 1985, the Hospital Medical Union put out a pamphlet criticizing GHMs and DRGs, but project development continued nonetheless. In July 1985, Georgina Dufoix, secretary of social affairs, and Edmond Hervé, assistant health secretary, underlined their determination to carry out PMSI by announcing national use of the RSS within three years. The RSS was to be standard use in regional teaching hospitals by January 1, 1986. They based their decision on a study carried out jointly by the inspectorate of the Social Affairs and Finance departments as well as a private audit firm. A circular published on October 4, 1985 defined the final RSS. Symbolically important, the PMSI became a full-fledged Program for Patient Management Categories.

Could it be that medical opposition actually played a minor role in project development? PMSI sponsors assert that the legal and technical base for a general implementation of the project was ready; they said that the list of hospitals officially or unofficially producing the RSS was growing longer. (Approximately twenty institutions sent RSS data regularly for input into the national data base. Overall, approximately thirty institutions produced the RSS in one way or another.) GHM opponents claimed that this data production remained marginal and that the experiments under way lacked a consensus among hospital-based physicians.

Actually, hospital-based physicians and their representatives were hardly included in project development. Locally, doctors were not told how the RSS or the GHM would be used by supervisory agents or by their own institutional managers. At the end of the first phase, physicians adopted very general positions on information systems or the uses of the PMSI. They used the American experience to reject the GHM as a tariff base or as an automatic means to calculate the global budget. They could not, however, block national progress on information management. The Bureau of Hospital Administration did not need to enlist many institutions for the project, it merely needed a few extra institutions in addition to those already producing

medical data on a detailed and regular basis. Once the Bureau
of Hospital Administration had access to data from Grenoble
and Caen, it held the trump needed to push the project ahead.
From this point on, the Bureau could test the American programs with French data, thereby proving project feasibility in
France. The PMSI team could then rely on hospital heterogeneity and diverse local factors to provoke candidacies,
broadening the data base and showing that PMSI was indeed
worthwhile. In quite a few sites, PMSI worked without strong
participation by medical staff. Due to a lack of national coordination, local teams had to initiate PMSI applications at their
level to promote the project. At the same time, even though
PMSI was not yet accepted by the majority of doctors, some
physicians did see it as a means to personal promotion.

Response of Hospital Managers

In principle, hospital managers should have been ardent supporters of PMSI, as it facilitated a more relevant picture of
medical activity within their institution than traditional indicators. What worried hospital directors and physicians, however,
was how supervisory agents would use the data. The French
Hospital Federation, for example, feared that PMSI was a means
to return to a per-GHM reimbursement basis or a more mechanical method of calculating budget allocations using DRG costs
(Millet, 1985). Thus, PMSI was perceived as a tool that would
reinforce supervisory powers. In interviews with us concerning
analysis of the RSS phase, hospital directors pointed out that
they would never override medical opposition. During this period hospital managers were also mainly preoccupied with new
procedures linked to the global budget.

From this point on a new GHM debate began to unfold. It
pitted proponents of GHMs for internal hospital management
against those who favored GHMs as a tool for external administrative control of the entire public hospital system. This debate,
which continues today, is reminiscent of hospital managers'
criticisms of the pricing system of per diems in 1982. The
pricing system required a cost accounting method to yield a

full cost per diem and per specialty. The same cost and its evolution served as the basis for annual increase rates in discussions carried out between local authorities and hospital directors. Although cost calculations were supposed to help institutions attain better efficiency, they were based on tactics of creative accounting in the negotiation process. Advocates of the prospective budget saw a way to uncouple an institution's internal management tools and finance mechanisms. For them, PMSI represented backtracking. In fact, automatic calculation of a hospital budget based on GHM costs reestablished the link between cost accounting and financing.

This debate also rekindled a long-running argument in French public hospitals over the institution's degree of management autonomy and the state's exercise of power. In the first section, we showed that management of French public hospitals is a subtle combination of centralized hierarchical control and enough local autonomy to ensure institutions some maneuvering room. In this context, any management tool conceived at a national level is assumed to reinforce central authority at the expense of local decision making.

During the first phase, the debate focused on the GHM cost model within the PMSI. Early on, the director of French hospitals and the PMSI project manager assigned the Scientific Management Center to write a report on how to adapt Fetter's management technique to France. The report made several recommendations.

Fetter's model was based on an algebraic method of assigning distinct hospitals' cost centers to the GHM so as to account for reciprocal services between such cost centers (Fetter, Mills, Riedel, and Thompson, 1977). The method is intellectually appealing as it theoretically represents real economic exchanges within a structure. The method does, however, pose problems whenever the task is to retrospectively explain observed deviations from standard costs. Using the algebraic model produces a complex calculation of cost assignment coefficients. Artefactual, these coefficients are an indirect reflection of resource consumption. In short, the method is useful for assigning a hospital's overall expenditures to the GHM and for cal-

culating an overall cost—and thus for calculating a budget. On
the other hand, the tool complicates the use of data for management control, or more precisely for internal management. For
these reasons, the Scientific Management Center strongly recommended developing computation models of costs that were
partial and direct. By using such a model, the only costs that
were assigned to the GHM were those directly linked to the
patient's medical coverage (drugs, consumables, medical procedures, X-ray and laboratory tests, and payment of the relevant
medical personnel). Other costs were assigned to traditional
accounting units such as length of stay or per diem. The decision
was motivated by the desire to give relevant information that
could be exploited for management control.

Another point stressed by the Scientific Management
Center was the sensitivity of hospital budgeting to the various
cost calculation methods used per GHM. The following debate
surfaced. In principle, GHMs should account for case mix differences among institutions in establishing the budget. This was
important for equity's sake. What would happen if the variations
generated by the choice of GHM cost calculation methods were
of the same magnitude as the case mix effect? This implies that
choosing one method instead of another introduces an arbi-
trary element into resource allocation that is of the same magnitude as activity level. In other words, one would not know if the
GHM produced a greater equity in resource allocation. The
Scientific Management Committee proved this point with budget simulations performed at two sites (Moisdon and others,
1987).

These results led to heated discussions within the technical expertise committee on accounting between supporters
and opponents of the American model and between those who
wanted overall expenditures assigned to the GHM and those in
favor of the partial costs model. Most members (accountants)
upheld the Scientific Management Center's viewpoints. The director of French hospitals did not take such a firm stand, while
the PMSI project manager took the opposite view.

Despite these reservations, the principle of the overall
cost calculation method was adopted at the end of 1983. In

addition, the French government asked Yale University's School of Management to demonstrate the model's adaptability to the French context. The school was to use the GHM costs of two hospitals. Meanwhile, the Scientific Management Center pursued its study on distinct budgeting methods. The feasibility test of the American model took place in 1984, and its results prompted adoption of the model. Yale University was commissioned to provide a version that would be compatible with the French hospital accounting system. An outside team was to develop a new cost accounting method compatible with the American cost method. The reasons behind this choice were the same as the ones used to adopt the grouper classification. A software program's capacity to receive data, compile it and generate satisfactory output does not mean that the underlying model is the best; it merely shows that the program runs correctly. Essentially, the director of French hospitals made a practical choice to help the project move on. The new cost accounting guideline was ready for 1985 (Department of Social Affairs and National Solidarity, 1985b), but the adapted software program would not be available until mid 1987.

Political Allies

Handling a project's political risks means avoiding decisions or political stances on subjects that interfere with the current project. It also entails ensuring solid political backing for the project while controlling political initiatives. Political allies of PMSI included the budget secretary's cabinet, the Planning and Programming Budgeting Systems of the Economic Forecasting Division, and finance inspectors. In a 1986 report on management methods used in public institutions, PMSI was cited as an exemplary management tool. From 1982 through 1986 the Finance Inspection was systematically associated with the Social Affairs General Inspection by the director of French hospitals. In so doing, he made his allies more sensitive to the ineptitudes of the hospital system and supervisory management.

As of 1984 another ally joined the force: Europe, followed by the rest of the world. Europe at large started to import DRGs, and tried to formulate an agreement concerning the classification of procedures used and the basis for a standardized discharge abstract (Rodrigues, 1986). In 1986 Yale University organized an international DRG conference in London. At that time, France was considered the leader in the DRG field. Foreign countries sent their teams to study the French model.

In 1985, the director of French hospitals and the PMSI project manager received the results of the GHM cost calculation method carried out in two institutions based on the American model. They presented the results to the cabinet of the Social Affairs Department. Thus, the political level became aware of the notion of cost per pathology, and the differences observed between the two institutions underlined the importance of the notion. The year 1985 was an important one for PMSI as the program became official. At the same time, a report cosigned by the general social affairs and finance inspections and a private audit firm recommended PMSI. In July 1985 the social affairs and health secretaries told hospitals that PMSI would progressively be introduced into regional teaching hospitals starting January 1, 1986, and be used nationwide by all hospitals by 1988 (Marcus, 1985).

If we accept this analysis, we can understand how priority was focused on the development of tools needed at a national level for DRG adoption in France — to the detriment of discussions with hospitals and of on-site training and information programs. We also understand how technical choices were made for safety's sake, guaranteeing results that would show project progress and interest.

In the United States, payers played an important role in the setup of DRGs. In France, however, the payer was never mentioned in the first two phases that we have reviewed. Yet, at the beginning of the project, a certain convergence existed between projects originating from the National Sickness Fund and PMSI. The Sickness Fund was studying new utilization review methods. Utilization review in France is exercised by local carriers and employs three types of control. The first is direct use of the patient file; that is, the medical adviser consults the file on-site. Second are random surveys called transversal studies in which all hospitalization files for a defined period are examined by a medical adviser. Third is a routine control used whenever hospitalization exceeds twenty days.

In any event, if discharge data for each hospitalization had been established regularly, controlling the files would have been much easier. For PMSI the stakes were as follows. The director of French hospitals had told volunteer institutions that RSS was to be implemented without additional financing. He did, however, offer to help institutions simplify administrative procedures, freeing resources for PMSI. (One simplification that had already been tried involved suppression of the request for hospitalization extension. Studies had shown that systematic control of this administrative procedure was not very effective and could be easily replaced with sampling methods.) The Sickness Fund was looking for ways to improve medical control. It recommended that a discharge medical record be established for each patient, similar to the RSS. But hospitalization extension was abolished only in 1986, doing away with an attractive bargaining point for hospitals.

PMSI Under Political Change

When in 1986 the Socialist party lost legislative elections, it seemed impossible to say whether PMSI had reached the point of no return. Everything seemed to hang by a thread. To begin with, the director of French hospitals was expected to resign, as his membership in the Socialist party was public knowledge. Moreover, PMSI project manager Jean-Marie Rodrigues was named Public Health Professor at the Medical School of St-Etienne. As the Bureau of Hospital Administration had expected these changes, the Application and Development Group was reinforced in 1985 by recruitment of two clinicians. Rodrigues was replaced by Jean Salin, who had been a member of the group since 1982.

As this period marked the end of a Socialist legislature, reform projects undertaken by the Department of Social Affairs, like those of many other departments, were put on hold. For political reasons the administration entered a period in which no decisions were made. Many physicians thought that the victorious right wing would immediately undo previous reforms.

In actuality, the outcome was as follows. The PMSI team had worked on a French classification system for medical procedures to group the RSS by GHM (Department of Social Affairs and National Solidarity, 1985b). A catalogue of medical procedures (which also provided hospitals with a value scale of medical procedures for cost accounting) was written up, and development of the French version of the GHM and finalization of the grouper were achieved. At the time about thirty hospitals were regularly producing RSS for patient hospitalizations. Several administrative texts incited hospitals to produce the abstracts, although they were never mandatory. These texts also defined production conditions. Progress reports were presented at a conference organized by the director of French hospitals in February 1986. This conference was the first major public event concerning PMSI (Department of Social Affairs and Employment, 1986).

These positive results did, however, have their shortcomings. Procedure classification had not been validated. The French grouper was still not available on the market, obliging hospitals to develop computer tools needed for RSS production themselves. At the time, with the exception of two Paris public hospitals that developed their own grouper based on Fetter's model, no institution was capable of grouping its own data. Reports on nationally processed data were incomplete and unanalyzed. The information, therefore, could not be used, with a few exceptions, for internal institutional or external review. Furthermore, the cost program software package was not ready. No French translation had been published for the American grouper manual — and only the system's top experts were familiar with it. In terms of experimental data bases, once again Grenoble and the participating institutions in its geographic vicinity served as the main supplier. The pilot hospitals that started from scratch had made little progress. Finally, the training periods for teaching medical information codes lacked professional organization. With the exception of the National Center for Hospital Equipment, no computer service company had included PMSI in its catalogue. Concrete conditions for "industrialization" of the project were definitely lacking.

When newly elected right-wing Prime Minister Jacques Chirac appointed his cabinet members, he kept the large Department of Social Affairs housing a secretary of health: Michèle Barzach. Barzach was new to national politics, and her first statements made no mention of PMSI. After three years of often violent conflicts, the new government sought to appease health care providers. The only known PMSI-related appointment she made was that of a Parisian teaching-hospital–based doctor known for his conservatism and opposition to PMSI. As Jean de Kervasdoué was still the director of French hospitals, he pursued PMSI policies for a few months. During this time, Jean Salin, the new PMSI project manager, pursued his work on technical tools. A new version of the PMSI procedure nomenclature was edited in 1987. The software program to compute costs was finally ready and was tested in four institutions. The Management Research Center was asked to audit the quality of data codes input during the first phase (Minvielle, Pouvourville, and Jeunemaître, 1991) and to validate the scale value of the catalogue of medical procedures for intensive care and anesthesia. Cardiologist F. Boulay, a recent PMSI recruit, provided expert validation of the GHM. At the end of 1986, the National Center for Hospital Equipment marketed its grouper.

The new director of French hospitals was named in October 1986. François Delafosse was a high-ranking civil servant serving as a certified public accountant. His career profile was even more traditional than Jean de Kervasdoué's. He had no experience in public health. His educational and professional background inclined him to be favorable to introducing management tools to rationalize hospital management. He appointed a young hospital director, Christian Anastasy, to his technical committee. Christian Anastasy had worked on the DRGs as administrator of the Paris Public Hospitals. Further, he was active in public health politics (belonging to the same right-wing party as Prime Minister Jacques Chirac). He played a key role in convincing Delafosse to pursue PMSI. In spite of the secretary of health's technical adviser, who was opposed to the project, PMSI remained on the Bureau of Hospital Administration's agenda. A key factor in this decision was the fact that the government had adopted rigorous cost control and rationalization policies. Jean de Kervasdoué's arguments were still compelling: how was one to ensure an equitable and proper use of public funds without precise information on hospital activity? Evaluating medical techniques and acts was becoming ever more important.

While PMSI's continuation was confirmed, its orientation changed slightly to placate physicians. In June 1987, the Bureau of Hospital Administration hosted another national PMSI information day. For the first time, grouped data results (approximately 400,000 records) were presented. The day's proceedings were published in *Informations Hospitalières* (Department of Social Affairs and Employment, 1987–1988). Delafosse, the new director of French hospitals, summed up as follows:

> This information day gathered 330 doctors, including 40 percent hospital-based physicians, giving me the opportunity to remind my audience that PMSI is a government priority. The Prime Minister's recent speech delivered to a Lyons Hospital on March 7, 1987, makes this point: 'I hope that PMSI will be carefully pursued. *It promises to provide spectacular progress as long as it is not implemented hastily or systematically.*' This point is an excellent illustration of the government's decision to pursue PMSI and its pragmatism.
>
> Secondly, I feel it is important to redefine PMSI general objectives as a management tool offering a better analysis of the process of hospital production. *These main goals do not aim to create a new pricing system, but a computerized system that will help us appreciate and evaluate a hospital's activity from an economic point of view.* This information system is representative of hospital activity in both medical and management terms. We hope it will foster a very positive relationship between physicians and man-

agers so that they can together define their institution's policy. *We are not going to copy the American DRG, although the American government chose this pricing system; we are going to use GHM classification as an analysis tool for internal and external use.* We hope PMSI will yield a better evaluation of local operating systems and thus a more accurate planning of health care service structure [translated from French].

This statement demonstrates that PMSI had indeed received high-ranking political support, although this backing was accompanied by a call for prudence and caution. The debate over internal versus external management resurfaced, and this time the accent was placed on internal management. The policy made no reference to a pricing system, apparently closing the door on use of GHMs as a determinant of hospital budgets. This represents a major change from the ideas of the previous director.

New Coalitions

In the same text, François Delafosse also refers to an evaluation of the project. The PMSI team structure has changed. Jean Salin is still the project manager, but he shares responsibilities with Marc Brémond, who was appointed the national PMSI coordinator at the end of 1987. A young doctor practicing in a hospital in west-central France, Marc Brémond used PMSI as a springboard for his career. In 1982, Niort was one of the first hospitals chosen by the Bureau of Hospital Administration to carry out pilot tests for the RSS, and became the program's exemplary student, regularly cited by PMSI members to illustrate ideal project development.

The hospital had another asset: PMSI had been strongly backed by the medical staff, without the hospital director's intervention. Marc Brémond played a key role convincing his colleagues that it was vital that they understood the project and acquired the necessary medical data from the start. Enthusiastic and a good computer technician, he was able to structure an efficient RSS program. He made himself readily available to answer PMSI team members' questions about the unavoidable glitches of this program development phase. Finally, along with colleagues using PMSI at other sites, he launched the French Users' Association of International Health Classifications (AUNIS). The association eventually became a key player for coding training sessions and dissemination of teaching materials on medical classification systems. For example, the association ensured the dissemination of the ICD9-CM French translation done by Francis Roger France.

Brémond reported directly to the director of French hospitals. At the same time, he was appointed a professor at the National School of Public Health. Brémond also organized a task force cofinanced by the Bureau of Hospital Administration and the National School of Public Health, the Medical Information and Hospital Management Commission (IMAGE). It was composed of outside consultants and academics, hospital-based doctors, and hospital directors. Its report was published in December 1989.

A new PMSI Scientific Commission was formed. Although mainly composed of hospital-based physicians and managers, some members came from institutions that had participated in PMSI's experimental phase. Others were named as representatives of hospital-based physicians or hospital directors. Still others were named for their area of expertise.

These appointments and new structures broadened the cast of actors from those directly involved in PMSI development and the gathering of background knowledge to field workers who participated in the project's experimental phase. Thus there emerged a national coalition of actors who were originally isolated from one another. At the same time, an important new organization appeared. Jean de Kervasdoué left the administration and formed a consultant firm, SANESCO, specializing in the health field. He strove to create a range of French software products allowing institutions to develop the GHM. He very quickly developed his own grouper. Jean-Marie Rodrigues served as the agency's scientific adviser. Thus, PMSI was no

longer solely the Bureau of Hospital Administration's baby,
although the bureau continued to play an important role in the
development of necessary project tools and in training agents
on-site. Even at this point, however, the PMSI core group was tiny
compared with the total number involved in the hospital system.
Despite numerous publications describing project tech-
nicalities, many hospital-based physicians were still only familiar with the rudiments of the project. While reassured by the
presence of a group of actors with field experience, many were
waiting for the central administration to precisely define how
GHMs were to be used to regulate hospital management.

Results of IMAGE

The evaluation project that the director of French hospitals
assigned to Marc Brémond covered a number of themes. In
terms of the production and coding of medical data, the group
offered a method to help with the coding (Medical Information
and Hospital Management Commission, 1991). Following the
report's publication, a debate arose as to the definition of the
principal diagnosis.

IMAGE also suggested a way of using GHMs for utilization review. The group thought it was necessary to demystify the
GHM among doctors. Brémond's team wanted to show the system's logic, enabling a physician to recognize his patients behind the labeling of distinct categories. The method was then
applied to gastroenterology and hepatology GHMs. The results
were returned and discussed with the institutions that had contributed data. Such a data return procedure was a first.

The group also suggested an analysis method drawing on
the data base and showing deviations between the length of
hospitalization for one institution and the general average, as
well as for two institutions, paired. Once again, results were
returned and discussed with the participating institutions. We
believe that while hospital-based physicians criticized specific
GHMs during this phase, their attitude changed when they were
given a handbook explaining how to read the information they
had been producing for several years. They now perceived PMSI

as a tool they could use. Yale's Robert Fetter had by this time updated his DRGs, producing refined DRGs that took better account of the relative severity of a case in determining the GHM. The group recommended testing this new product.

Another IMAGE conclusion was the empirical confirmation of the arguments put forth by the Scientific Management Center in 1983 concerning the American cost model. Drawing on an experiment in eastern France, the authors demonstrated that the algebraic algorithm made it difficult to undertake a retrospective analysis of the deviations from the costs per GHM per year and per institution. The survey also showed the rough spots each hospital encountered in setting up a reliable data-gathering system on cost per patient.

A practical guide addressed to institutions and explaining PMSI development procedures for their benefit was also published. The guide evaluated the principal data processing systems producing the RSS and available on the market.

Another IMAGE theme centered on an original planning experiment carried out on the cardiology wards of several institutions in the same geographical region. A methodological study assessed GHM attributes for the experiment. The result showed that the GHM was not by itself a powerful enough tool to plan needs successfully. The problem stemmed from the GHM's inability to accurately describe either the services and know-how within a hospital or the hospital's role in global patient care.

Meanwhile, PMSI training continued. The Scientific Committee also made a vital contribution by defining a new hospital section, the Medical Information Department. The committee laid the groundwork for the management of medical data within a hospital, recommending that a doctor be in charge of this new department under the supervision of the hospital's medical commission. The study also sought to give special status to the doctors who had pioneered PMSI.

Without a doubt, the PMSI project's second phase helped promote the spread of PMSI, partly as a result of greater participation by hospital staff. PMSI was now apparently here to stay, even in the case of a change in political leadership. The director of French hospitals reported the French experience at the Second International DRG Congress in Sydney, Australia, in February 1988. This phase also helped to consolidate technical tools through continuation of studies begun under the previous administration as well as through studies started by IMAGE.

Despite political and technical consolidation, the administration was still taking only exploratory action. The administration offered no precise picture of how GHMs were to be applied in health control. The National Center for Hospital Equipment was slow in marketing its grouper, and hospitals were reluctant to invest in SANESCO's grouper as it provided slightly different results from the administration's.

Institutionalization of PMSI

In May 1988, François Mitterand was reelected president of the French Republic. The National Assembly was dissolved, and elections were held, gaining a slight majority for left-wing parties. Michel Rocard was named prime minister and formed a cabinet. Rocard's arrival heralded yet another transitional phase for PMSI. The Bureau of Hospital Administration used a PMSI-inspired method to assign resources to the various institutions providing health services for AIDS patients. Negotiations were started with Social Security to start a PMSI project in private institutions.

The spring of 1989 brought a new director of French hospitals: Gérard Vincent. Vincent was director of the Hôtel Dieu hospital, one of the two Paris public hospitals that developed PMSI, and president of a major hospital executive union. As director of the Hôtel Dieu, he pleaded for the managerial conception of the role of a hospital director, stressing real responsibility and accountability. He advocated PMSI and its use as an internal management tool, feeling that it would enhance dialogue between doctors and managers. In his hospital, the PMSI team was very critical of the DRG classification. Team members introduced innovations to their own PMSI version, such as the development of a complexity index that took into account the relative complexity and severity of cases. Furthermore, the Hôtel Dieu developed a cost accounting system analyzing direct health costs per GHM, adopting a partial cost approach.

Because of the administration's desire to placate physicians, the PMSI project weathered this latest political storm. Meanwhile, the need for a regulation tool to help public services better allocate budgets among hospitals became increasingly pressing. Hospital nurses staged a spectacular strike at the end of 1988. One of their main complaints was lack of personnel. The Department of Social Affairs and its administration viewed the problem as one of poor resource distribution and not of overall understaffing. Moreover, over the years, reports had pointed to an excess of about 60,000 hospital beds, with unexplainable disparities across institutions. PMSI was the only available tool that could pinpoint activity and performance differences in a less ambiguous way than traditional indicators. If there were still some lingering gray areas concerning precise application of GHMs, their basic utility was no longer questioned. The arrival of Gérard Vincent coincided with the real institutional launch of PMSI in France.

The PMSI unit within the secretary's cabinet became better structured. Until this point, the successive project managers were outsiders, coming neither from the central administration nor pursuing administrative careers. At this juncture, PMSI management within the Health Department was finally entrusted to a high-ranking administrator, André Loth. The team was bolstered by the arrival of a hospital director who concentrated on budget and accounting problems, while a physician honed in on classification and coding problems.

A team of technical consultants formed around the director of French hospitals. Some members were named through PMSI, usually the project's pioneering members. Robert Maud, a public works engineer, was named to the Bureau of Hospital Administration upon the request of the secretary of health's technical adviser. Maud himself served as a technical adviser to the director of French hospitals.

The Scientific Committee metamorphosed once again, the change serving to broaden membership rather than to overhaul structure. The committee became an institution: many presidents and directors of national university and nonuniversity medical commissions were named as members. Two medical advisers representing national health insurance organizations were also named, coming from the National Sickness Fund and the Mutualité Agricole. Both were well known for advocating the evaluation of medical services.

A decade after the initial project launch, these changes symbolized project acceptance by the central administration, even if many PMSI members were not civil servants following a traditional administrative path.

Debate on the Use of DRGs

In late 1989 many people were criticizing the lack of concrete PMSI goals. One group favored PMSI to pay for hospital care, feeling that a strong economic incentive was needed to promote this innovation. In general, the European experience upholds their point of view: the countries that have advanced the most in use of DRGs are those that used DRGs as a hospital financing tool right from the beginning, namely, Portugal, Norway, and Ireland. Jean de Kervasdoué, who made his comeback with the return of the Socialist government, recaptured his political credibility. A renowned and highly respected expert, he was also an excellent player at political football. He continued to support the use of DRGs as an indispensable tool for rational budget allocation.

Others supported the idea of DRGs as a combination of internal management tool and external budget decision aid. Even though this position is vague on concrete uses of DRGs, it was generally upheld by hospital managers. They openly criticized the global budget's perverse effects and the bureaucratic nature of the public agency's authority. At the time, the central administration was beginning to realize that by putting the damper on public hospital's operating and investment budgets, it had involuntarily promoted the development of the private sector. Public hospitals that were both dynamic and appealing had to negotiate every inch of their growth. Under such conditions, GHM financing in a global budget framework was viewed as a tool for reinforcing external control. At the same time, the issue of harmonizing the two sectors' finance modes came back into the picture. Public hospital physicians did not accept a global budget reinforced by GHMs that worked alongside a private sector whose revenues continued to depend on volume of activity.

This grassroots movement had political repercussions. The Department of Social Affairs developed a bill on hospitals. A preliminary report was prepared that advocated implementing new regulation mechanisms for the hospital system based on collective multiyear agreements between a specific facility, the public authorities, and the financing agency. The agreements would be based on each facility's medical plan, a true multiyear strategic plan. The medical plan is part of a regional health care supply plan drawn up by the public authority in agreement with health care providers. This plan would act as a regulation and could be invoked against all regional actors. Finally, the report recommended that medical evaluation be a goal for all public institution plans. As a result, PMSI appeared as a possible instrument to be used for implementing these recommendations.

Some PMSI team members in the Bureau of Hospital Administration advocated the launch of an experiment handling both GHMs and the global budget. André Loth, the new operations manager for the PMSI project, prepared a memorandum. Its purpose was to generalize PMSI to all short-term public hospitals with more than 100 beds. He proposed an agenda with a two-year experimental phase leading to the development of a GHM-based method of evaluating costs to calculate the budget. Among other things, the project involved the determination of cost weights per GHM, with the setup being used as a model.

The draft memorandum was changed by the secretary of health's cabinet. As the method seemed to link a very mechanical budget allocation to GHM-based performance, it came up against the philosophy underlying the new hospital law. This law sought to set up contractual negotiations between institutions and the supervisory agency around objectives. DRG-based prospective budgeting was perceived as reinforcing the weight of external controls on the public sector just when public hospitals were clamoring for *less* external control to be more competitive with the private sector. Finally, some of the hospital director's technical advisers were adamantly opposed to a GHM-based budget. They mainly based their position on results from Paris's Hôtel Dieu hospital, which illustrated that cost variations per GHM were too great to serve as a base for budget calculation.

Little by little the administration built a new logic around PMSI. It emphasized the need to modernize both institutional management and the relationship between the state and the institutions. The administration's message was that although PMSI was an inevitable part of the evolution of hospital management, for the time being it would not be used as a pricing tool.

The administration's position was bolstered by a number of events. First, there was the 1989 circular calling for the generalization of RSS production in public and private nonprofit hospitals over a two-year introductory period (1989–1991). This generalization would be ensured through the creation of Medical Information Departments in the hospitals concerned. Additional budgetary means were allocated to create the necessary human resources to the limit of 0.1 percent of the hospital's overall budget over a two-year period ($30 million in 1990). The circular underlined the introduction of a financial incentive in PMSI development, as well as its institutionalization as a new hospital department.

In the summer of 1989, the Bureau of Hospital Administration set up a task force to study the creation of regional poles of expertise with regard to processing of medical data. This initiative stemmed from several concerns. The new hospital law called for setup of a regional-level structure to map out regional sanitation planning. This structure needed local expertise to analyze medical data stemming from sources other than PMSI. In addition, the hospitals needed a local setup to train personnel to produce, process, and analyze PMSI data. Finally, the regional axis would centralize data sharing between institutions and local state agencies.

This move marked the beginning of a debate on regional

hospital data groups that culminated with the publication of a circular in July 1991. These regional hospital data groups included the Regional Administration of Social Affairs and Public Health and the departmental Office of Social Affairs and Public Health, representatives of institutions producing the RSS in the region, and representatives of local health insurance agencies. This regional task force was bolstered by a national research and training team. The PMSI bureau was aware of the necessity of creating a highly expert pool to analyze and treat medical data. The number of experts was still very limited, with the nucleus still composed of the initial members who joined during the experimental phase from 1982 to 1986. Nonetheless, the IMAGE group helped broaden the membership base between 1987 and 1989, and expertise became more broadly distributed, with teams based in regional teaching hospitals. The administration wanted to draw on this base to create a high-ranking national institute with three objectives: research, training, and consulting. The institute project culminated in 1991 with the Council of Ministers deciding to create a major public health center in the greater Paris area. The hope was to form a French version of the U.S. Center for Disease Control, adding to it a component consisting of an institute for hospital management.

During 1990, the PMSI bureau rekindled the debate on cost accounting in hospitals and GHM cost calculations. At first, a number of meetings sought to review current experiments on cost calculations carried out in six institutions, five of which tested the cost program adapted from the American model. At this point, the debate on the GHM cost model resurfaced. Nevertheless, Robert Maud as PMSI's political leader imposed the PMSI version as an internal management tool. Consequently, the bottom line of the debate on cost accounting was that accounting should primarily serve the concerns of an institution rather than cater to the external control imposed by the state's local agencies. The Bureau of Hospital Administration then entrusted the Scientific Management Center and the Management Research Center with a joint study on a new experimental cost calculation method. Under this method, only direct costs of health care delivered to the patient would be costed in the GHM. These costs include medical procedures, imagery and laboratory exams, medical and nursing care, drugs and various medical products, as well as the depreciation of material used specifically for a particular procedure. Only these expenses were assumed to vary with the type of patient, and consequently with the GHM. Secondly, and if possible, direct care expenses were to be identified per patient so that managers and physicians could have detailed information concerning cost per patient.

Broadening the Infrastructure

PMSI progressively acquired an infrastructure allowing it to maintain and regularly update the various tools required by the program. A new version of the medical procedures catalogue was published in July 1991. A manual was slated to be published by the end of 1991. Ten years after PMSI's beginnings, a detailed description of the French algorithm grouper would finally be available to users. The Bureau of Hospital Administration also commissioned several groups to study the development of classification tools for outpatient care.

Finally, the PMSI team contracted CITI2, a university data center linked to a Parisian medical school, to handle the national public hospital data base (the data base for private institutions is handled by a Social Security organization). CITI2 replaced the National Center for Hospital Equipment, which had developed the first French grouper and the cost software. In 1989, the secretary of health decided to privatize the center. After some tribulations, Cap Gemini Sogeti, one of the world's leading computer service companies, took over the organization's assets, specifically marketing the grouper developed by the center. Moreover, the administration defined the grouper's marketing policy. CITI2 was to provide service maintenance for the core grouper. The core grouper is in the public domain, meaning that a company can get it for free and develop original applications for data processing and analysis around it. For the time being, only the versions developed by the National Center for Hospital Equipment have received public accreditation, but a host of other companies are developing products.

In June 1989, I, together with the IMAGE group and other hospital staffers cohosted a congress with 250 participants. Panelists were mainly American hospital-based physicians giving papers on their practical experience with DRGs in hospital management. Congresses or information sessions of this type have become more and more frequent since 1989. They provide opportunities for the PMSI bureau to present Health Department policy.

The Bureau of Hospital Administration has perfected its communication tools. Since 1990 its major medium has been a communication newsletter entitled *Lettre des Systèmes d'Information Médicalisés*. This newsletter is widely read in French hospitals. In addition, several issues of the magazine *Informations Hospitalières* have featured articles on PMSI and hospital data processing.

The Bureau of Hospital Administration commissioned the National School of Public Health (the IMAGE group) and teaching hospitals based in Montpellier and Nancy to undertake PMSI training. Following publication of the July 1989 circular generalizing PMSI, the three centers had to work quickly. Marie-Laure Pibarot, who organized training at the National School of Public Health, has estimated that since 1989 over 400 people have received basic training on medical data production. Trainees ranged from hospital-based physicians to directors and staff of the departmental Office of Social Affairs and Public Health and the Regional Department of Social Affairs and Public Health. Other organizations have now sponsored training sessions. Today, approximately a thousand professionals have been introduced to PMSI concepts. In the fall of 1991 the Bureau of Hospital Administration was scheduled to offer a PMSI computer tutorial realized by the teaching hospital in Nancy, IMAGE, and AUNIS. Moreover, in the general context of too many doctors and the limited number of appealing positions offered to physicians in hospitals, medical information management offers an attractive new career opportunity for young doctors. Public hospitals (to be later joined by private hospitals) and computer consulting services are starting to hire such doctors.

Beginning in 1989, Social Security started participating in PMSI. The introduction of the payer was the result of several factors. First, the national medical adviser of the National Sickness Fund retired. His opinions against any form of administrative control of medical services were public knowledge. He was replaced by a teaching hospital physician, whose favorable opinion of medical evaluation was well known. At the same time, the government was questioning the fact that the development of the private sector resulted in increasing financial problems for public institutions. The economics of the private hospital became a major political concern. A new general director was named to the National Sickness Fund: Gilles Joahnet, a high-ranking civil servant and a member of the Socialist party.

It was also at this time that Jean Salin, a founding PMSI team member was recruited by the National Sickness Fund and asked to coordinate the launch of a PMSI experiment in the private sector. The experiment was jointly piloted by the three major health insurance organizations, the three professional associations for private hospitals, and the Department of Health (represented by the Social Security Bureau and the Bureau of Hospital Administration). At first, sixteen clinics volunteered to produce the RSS. To finance costs stemming from this new activity, they could charge higher per diems. Depending on the results obtained, the experiment was to be extended to fifty additional institutions.

Launched in the context of a growing Social Security deficit and higher private sector costs, the experiment again sparked off debate on the GHM as a pricing tool. Because of a rapid increase in the operating room lump sum paid out to private clinics, the secretary of health sought a compromise with the private sector: either the lump sum would be arbitrarily reduced by public authorities or clinics would allow their global expenses to be audited. In April 1991, a protocol was directly negotiated between the secretarial cabinet of Social Affairs and a private hospital association. The protocol stipulated that by the end of 1991 both partners must establish prices per case

based on a list of the most frequent and most expensive pathologies. As of January 1, 1992, pricing would be applied to all
private clinics in a specific geographical vicinity. This agreement was then included in a law passed in 1991. It introduced
per-case pricing within a global expense ceiling in the private
sector. A six-month feasibility study was planned and implementation of the agreement was postponed until January 1993. It was
expected to take three to four additional years before the agreement could be extended to the entire private sector.

PMSI Settles In

After nearly ten years, PMSI has succeeded in establishing itself
in the French hospital system. According to the Bureau of Hospital Administration, 135 institutions in the public sector can
regularly produce the RSS, although perhaps not on an exhaustive basis. Political incentives spelled out in the 1989 circular have borne their fruit. The Bureau of Hospital Administration has even said that out of 529 public or for-profit institutions
affected by this circular, 54 percent created a Medical Information Department in 1990, and new departments are still being
formed (Vincent, 1990). The political change that took place in
the summer of 1991 reinforced Health Department policy. The
secretaries of health and social affairs have supported each
other's positions. On several occasions, Health Secretary Bruno
Durieux has defended PMSI as a necessary part of the attempt
to improve distribution of resources within the hospital system.
In September 1991, a new circular stated that public institutions
that had not yet initiated PMSI would have to content themselves
with an overall budget augmented by the national increase rate
for 1992, regardless of any increase in activity.

What accounts for the integration of PMSI into the French
system? First, in France today it would be difficult to contest the
usefulness of medical data for hospital management. Today the
debate has left the question of *whether* to produce medical
information for management purposes to focus on *how* to produce and use such data. Public promoters of PMSI scored when

they succeeded in introducing Medical Information Departments into the hospital system.

It is also true that the government's maneuvering room in
terms of health has shrunk. This is true for both right-wing and
left-wing governments. Health costs have outpaced national
growth, and health insurance revenue has been eaten up by
slower growth and high unemployment rates. To balance the
books there are few choices other than increasing direct taxes
and social contributions. The current government has embarked on a new road: negotiating agreements with health care
professionals based on annual overall budgets. In short, the
logic behind the global budget has extended to all health care
areas. In defense of this general rationing, the government
argues that there is poor allocation of current resources, the
remedy for which is redistribution. To justify redistribution, the
government needs tools to help pinpoint the relative performance of health care providers. GHMs offer such a solution, and
while they could be better, they have the merit of existing and
being already operational in France.

The government's current open promotion of PMSI is
further reinforced by the existence of a structured team within
the central administration, as well as by what one could call a
PMSI lobby. Universities have developed expertise in patient
management categories and have come to rely in part on research credits allocated by the Department of Social Affairs;
doctors have invested in the Medical Information Departments;
industry has developed software for GHM ranking.

Sooner or later GHMs will be used as a finance tool in
France—but it is hard to say exactly how. At the end of 1991,
France was once again weathering political turbulence. The
government was pursuing a strict budget policy and dealing
with a wave of economic and social problems, including unemployment and immigration. In the fall of 1991, the nurses took
to the streets again, demonstrating mainly because of understaffing. It seemed highly unlikely that the government would
yield by creating a significant number of jobs when the current objective was to *reduce* the hospital sector and redistribute
resources. Negotiations with physicians in private practice con-

cerning installation of global expense caps proved to be difficult. Moreover, between 1983 and 1986, following the application of new regulations, hospital-based doctors showed extraordinary inertia once they felt the government was losing legitimacy. It is difficult to predict if a similar scenario will be repeated in the years to come. For many hospital-based physicians, GHM classification is still a very coarse medical description tool and has an unpleasant taste of bureaucracy. Furthermore, even if a large number of Medical Information Departments are launched or being formed, we will have to wait at least two years before all public institutions produce high-quality and plentiful data.

Thus, much will depend on the strategy of health care providers — particularly hospital-based physicians — in the years to come. Will they seek to take advantage of a political context in which the government is frail? Or are most of them convinced that the French hospital system needs reshuffling, and that it is wiser to take part than to sit out when the new hand is dealt? In any event, it appears that PMSI has sparked off two irreversible trends in France. The first is the trend toward routine use of the new medical data. The second is the progressive installation of information systems pinpointing per-case costs. In France, doctors have even asked to have more precise information concerning patient costs. In other words, doctors are demanding that managers apply the same intellectual rigor and attentiveness that they claim to apply to their own profession. In the long run, they will also seek out more efficient medical classifications.

Epilogue

Six months after this chapter was finished, events show that the French government is firmly determined to put a cap on total health expenditures. Moreover, the GHM-based rate-setting regulation in the private sector has (as predicted) created a strong incentive for the public sector to move toward case mix–based prospective budgeting in order to avoid unfavorable comparisons with the private sector. Administrators in favor of a hard line with DRGs have taken over at the Department of Social Affairs, with strong political support.

   Another new experiment was launched at the beginning of 1992. The objective is to build a data base to calculate reference costs per GHM and to test different models of prospective budget setting based on case mix. Over 120 hospitals have volunteered to participate, among which 30 or 40 should be selected on the basis of the quality of data. Even though this initiative may still be sensitive to political turmoil, as has always been the case since 1982, there seems to be enough momentum to keep the ball rolling until costs per GHM are finally available. If it turns out to reveal important differences among hospitals, this experiment may prove a turning point in the history of case mix in France. What precise use will be made of such information is unpredictable, however, the main variable being the evolution of overall health and hospital expenditures in France.

References

Anastasy, C., and others. "Professor Fetter's 'Analogous Diagnostic Groups': A Cost Endoscopy." *Les Cahiers de Gestions Hospitalières*, June–July 1982, *28*(217).

Bedier, P., Desaulle, S., and Venencie, I. "Hospital Medical Staff and the Hospital: A Changing Profession." Master's thesis, National School of Public Health, Rennes, France, 1985.

Credes. *Eco-Sante*, vers. 2.5 (Computer Software). Paris, Credes, 1991.

Department of Health. "Memorandum to the General Directors of Regional Hospital Centers and to the Directors of Hospital Centers." Paris: Department of Health, Bureau of Hospital Administration, June 1982.

Department of Social Affairs and Employment. "Medical Information Systems in Hospitals." *Informations Hospitalières*, May–June 1986 (Special issue).

Department of Social Affairs and Employment. "Medical Information Systems: Experiment Highlights." *Informations Hospitalières*, Dec. 1987–Jan. 1988.

Department of Social Affairs and National Solidarity. "PMSI: Standardized Data Summary." Roneograph document, May 1983a.

Department of Social Affairs and National Solidarity. "Appendix H: Nomenclature of Medical Procedures." Roneograph document, Bureau of Hospital Administration, August 1983b.

Department of Social Affairs and National Solidarity. *Catalogue of Medical Procedures* (Special issue B.O. 85-9b) Paris: Department of Social Affairs and National Solidarity, 1985a.

Department of Social Affairs and National Solidarity. *Methodological Guide for Cost Accounting in Hospitals.* (2 vols., special issues 85-4b and 85-26b) Paris: Department of Social Affairs and National Solidarity, 1985b.

Department of Social Affairs and National Solidarity. *PMSI: Homogeneous Patient Groups.* (B.O. 86-30 bis) Paris: Department of Social Affairs and National Solidarity, 1986.

Department of Social Affairs and National Solidarity. *PMSI Circular 303.* Paris: Department of Social Affairs and National Solidarity, Bureau of Hospital Administration, July 24, 1989.

Descamps, J. M., Loirat, P., and Pouvourville, G. de. "Evaluation of the Medical Procedure Catalogue: OMEGA (Intensive Care)." In research proposal 308606, Department of Social Affairs and National Solidarity, Paris, 1989.

Fetter, R. B., Mills, R. E., Riedel, D. C., and Thompson, J. D. "The Application of Diagnosis Specific Cost Profiles to Cost and Reimbursement Control in Hospitals." *Journal of Medical Systems*, 1977, *1*(2).

Gonella, J. S., Hornbrook, M. C., and Louis, M. S. "Staging of Disease: A Case-Mix Measurement." *Journal of the American Medical Association*, 1984, *251*(5), 637–644.

Hatchuel, A., Moisdon, J. C., and Molet, H. "The Global Hospital Budget and Homogenous Patient Groups." In *Regulation of Health Systems in France and West Germany*. Paris: La Maison des Sciences de l'Homme, 1988.

Horn, S. D., and Sharkey, P. D. "Severity of Illness to Predict Patient Resource Use Within DRGs." *Inquiry*, 1983, *20*, 314–321.

Marcus, F. "PMSI's Long March." *Le Quotidien du Médecin,* July 17, 1985 (3457).

Medical Information and Hospital Management Commission. *Medical Information Systems: Production and Coding.* (IMAGE guide 2) Rennes, France: Editions de L'ENSP, 1991.

Millet, A. "The Public Hospital — Reforming Management Methods: Future Projects?" *La Revue Hospitalière de France,* Nov. 1985 (385).

Ministère des Affaires Sociales et de la Solidarité. *Annuaire des Statistiques Sanitaires et Sociales.* Paris: La Documentation Française, 1990.

Minvielle, E., Pouvourville, G. de, and Jeunemaître, A. "PMSI: Ensuring Quality Coding." *Les Cahiers de Gestions Hospitalières,* 1991, *302,* 17–22.

Moisdon, J. C., and others. "Local Supervisory Power on Hospitals: Tools and Impediments." *Revue Française d'Administration Publique,* 1987, *43,* 59–70.

"PMSI Spreads Its Reach." *La Lettre d'Information Hospitalières, Lettre des Systèmes d'Information Médicalisés,* 1991, *5.*

Pouvourville, G. de. "Introducing a New Information System in Hospitals: PMSI." Paris: l'Ecole Polytechnique Management Research Center, 1983a.

Pouvourville, G. de. "Should the Health System Be Centralized?" *Projet,* 1983b (179–180), 1082–1097.

Pouvourville, G. de. "What Purpose Does Nomenclature Serve?" *Prospective et Santé,* 1988, *47–48,* 91–98.

Pouvourville, G. de, and Jeunemaître, A. "Producing Standardized Data Summaries for PMSI: Analysis of Four Volunteer Institutions." Report for the Department of Social Affairs and National Solidarity, Bureau of Hospital Administration, Paris, 1983.

Pouvourville, G. de, and Juenemaître, A. "PMSI Hospital Reforms: Reviewing the SDS Phase." Report for the Department of Social Affairs and National Solidarity, Bureau of Hospital Administration, Paris, 1986.

Pouvourville, G. de, Pontone-Liverneaux, S., and Finkel, S. "Evaluation of ICR-Beta (Anesthesia) of the Medical Procedure

Catalogue." In research proposal 308606, Department of Social Affairs and National Solidarity, Paris, 1990.

Pouvourville, G. de, and Renaud, M. "Hospital System Management in France and Canada: National Pluralism and Provincial Centralism." *Social Science and Medicine*, 1985, *20*(2), 153–164.

Rodrigues, J. M. "PMSI: Method, Definition, Organization." *Les Cahiers de Gestions Hospitalières*, Mar. 1983 (Supplement to *Gestions Hospitalières*), 224.

Rodrigues, J. M. "How Medical Data Systems Are Used Throughout the World and in Europe." *Informations Hospitalières*, May–June 1986 (Special issue).

Vincent, G. "Editorial." *La Lettre d'Informations Hospitalières*. Paris: Department of Solidarity, Health, and Social Protection, Apr. 1, 1990.

Five

Sweden: A Health Care Model in Transition

Eric M. Paulson

Sweden is situated in northern Europe and in 1991 had a population of 8.6 million. Despite a rather small population, the country is fourth in surface area in Europe. It is consequently sparsely populated in many areas, with an average population density of 19 inhabitants per square kilometer. The demographic transition to an aged population is most accentuated in Sweden compared to all other countries in the world. In 1991 the proportion of citizens 65 years or older was 18 percent.

Health care is regarded as an important part of the Swedish welfare system. A general description of the health care sector was recently published by the Swedish Institute (1990). General statistics on the area are reported annually by Statistics Sweden (1990a) and the Federation of County Councils (1990).

Structure of Health Care

According to the Health and Medical Service Act, county councils are required to promote the health of residents in their

Note: The author wishes to thank Leni Björklund, Stefan Håkansson, Åke Lindgren, Björn Ljungqvist, Anders Lönnberg, and Carl-Axel Nilsson for reviewing this chapter.

areas. They are also responsible for offering their inhabitants equal access to good medical care. The act requires county councils to plan the organization of health care with reference to the aggregate needs of the county population. This planning must also include health care provided by other organizations than the county councils, such as private practitioners, industrial health services, and so on.

Sweden is divided into twenty-three county council areas and three municipalities (the city of Gothenburg, the city of Malmö, and the island of Gotland), which also have responsibilities as county councils. The populations of these twenty-six units range from some 60,000 to 1.6 million inhabitants (about 300,000 on average in 1991).

County council members are directly elected by county residents for three-year terms. Among their other tasks, these representatives must decide the financial resources available for health care in their area and the size of the county council income tax. However, a temporary law prevented the county councils from raising taxes during 1991 and 1992.

The county councils are affiliated with the Federation of County Councils, which provides services to its members and represents their interests. It also serves as a central negotiating body for concluding financial agreements with the national government and for resolving pay issues.

The state is responsible for ensuring that the health care system develops efficiently and that it is in keeping with overall objectives, based on the goals and the constraints of social welfare policy and macroeconomic factors.

Central government administration of health care below Parliament and Cabinet is divided into two levels: The Ministry of Health and Social Affairs and relatively independent administrative agencies, chiefly the National Board of Health and Welfare. The Ministry of Health and Social Affairs prepares Cabinet business and draws up general guidelines in fields such as health care, social welfare services, and health insurance. The National Board of Health and Welfare is a central administrative agency for matters concerning health care and social welfare services. Its tasks include supervision and evaluation of developments in all areas of social policy, including health and medical care. All health and medical personnel, whether employed in private practice or by the county councils, come under the supervision of this organization.

The Swedish Council on Technology Assessment in Health Care is a new governmental organization founded in 1987. It aims to synthesize scientific knowledge on medical technologies as a basis for decision making at different levels of health care.

The Swedish Planning and Rationalization Institute of Health and Social Services (Spri) is jointly owned and financed by the central government and the Federation of County Councils. Spri works on planning and efficiency measures, undertakes special investigations, and supports research and development work in health care administration. An important task is the development of improved methods of health care management.

Most Swedish health care is financed and organized by the county councils. Private providers are responsible for only a minor part of health care. About 5 percent of physicians worked full time in private practice in 1989. A limited number of private medical institutions provide chiefly long-term nursing care and elective surgery. Private health insurance represents a new but infrequent source of financing for health care in Sweden. The number of people covered by such schemes was estimated in 1991 at 25,000, which corresponds to 0.3 percent of the population (Federation of County Councils, 1991a).

The traditional public Swedish health care system is structured in three levels. The primary care level is normally organized into districts that are primarily responsible for the health of the population in their areas. Each district includes one or more health care centers and at least one nursing home. At the health centers, general practitioners (and sometimes also specialists) provide medical treatment, advisory services, and preventive care. The primary care system includes district nurses and midwives and also runs clinics for child and maternity health care.

When primary care resources are insufficient for diagnosis or treatment, the patient will be referred to the county or regional medical care levels. The county hospitals provide both outpatient and inpatient services. Normally there are a few short-term somatic hospitals in each county area. These hospitals are divided, according to their size and degree of specialization, into two types: district county hospitals with at least four specialties (internal medicine, surgery, radiology, and anesthesiology) and central county hospitals with fifteen to twenty specialties. Ordinarily there is one central county hospital in each county council area.

The regional medical care level is responsible for those patients whose problems require the collaboration of a large number of specialists and perhaps also special equipment. Sweden is divided into six medical care regions, each serving a population of 1–2 million. Each region has one (or sometimes two) regional hospitals. These hospitals are also involved in teaching and research, as they are affiliated with medical schools.

The three-level health care structure does not prevent any patient from seeking treatment in any health care institution in case of an emergency or acute illness. The number of hospital beds is relatively high, some 13.3 per 1,000 inhabitants in 1990, while the number of visits to physicians is comparatively low— about 3.2 visits per inhabitant per year in 1988 (see Table 5.1).

In 1989 there were 25,000 physicians in Sweden, or about one doctor per 340 inhabitants. Physicians working in public hospitals or primary care are salaried and have no remuneration based on the fee-for-service principle.

The increase in the numbers of health care personnel has been very great during the past few decades. In 1989, about 460,000 people worked in the health sector, while the comparable figure for 1960 was 115,000. The rapid growth in the number of employees in the health care sector is to some extent due to a growing proportion of part-time employees.

In 1988 Sweden spent SKr 94 billion on health care (investments are included in this figure). Health care costs have increased rapidly in recent decades. Up to 1982 the health care cost share of gross domestic product also increased, with a peak

Table 5.1. Key Health Care Figures for Sweden.

Country area	450,000 sq. km.
Population, 1990	8.5 million
Average population density	19 per sq. km.
% of population over 65, 1989	18%
Health care expenditures, 1988	SKr 94 billion
% spent on somatic short-term care	48%
% spent on somatic long-term care	23%
% spent on outpatient primary care	17%
% spent on psychiatric care	12%
% of GDP devoted to health care, 1982	9.7%
% of GDP devoted to health care, 1988	9.1%
% of GDP devoted to health care, excluding care of	
mentally retarded, 1988	8.5%
Number of short-term somatic hospitals (est.)	100
Number of local health care centers (est.)	800
Number of hospital beds per 1,000 population	13.3
General hospital beds per 1,000 population	4.1
Psychiatric hospital beds per 1,000 population	2.4
Long-term hospital beds per 1,000 population	6.2
Number of beds in municipal homes for the elderly per	
1,000 population	5
Visits for health care, per capita, 1988	
to physicians	3.2
for paramedical care (incl. nurses, midwives, and	
physiotherapists)	2.7
Locus of visits to physicians, 1988	
Hospitals	38%
Primary care institutions	39%
Private practices	15%
Total number of health care workers, 1989	460,000
Health care workers as % of population, 1989	10%
Total number of health care workers, 1960	115,000
Health care workers as % of population, 1960	3%
Number of physicians, 1989	25,000
Ratio of physicians to population, 1989	1 per 340
Number of physicians, 2000 (est.)	28,000

Source: Data from the Swedish Institute, 1990.

value of 9.7 percent. Since that year there has been a slow decrease (see Table 5.1).

The distribution of total health care costs by main sectors in 1988 is shown in Table 5.1. Somatic short-term care accounts for nearly half of the total costs. By contrast, outpatient primary care adds up to only 17 percent.

In 1987 about 90 percent of the health care expenditure was publicly financed. The sources of income for the county councils in 1988 were county council income taxes (62 percent), national health insurance (11 percent), state subsidies (9 percent), patient fees (3 percent), and other (15 percent).

About 80 percent of the expenditures of county councils is for health care. Each year the county council decides on the total sum available for the following year's publicly financed health care in the area. The resources within a county are allocated to hospitals and health care centers through a budget negotiation process. The hospital budget is then further divided into each hospital department. There is normally no direct connection between the activity level and the amount of resources available at a unit level.

Clinical and administrative information on each patient discharged from a public hospital is collected and processed by the counties. Both somatic and psychiatric inpatient care are included. The first counties started to register activity data by patient in 1964, and in 1985 all collected such data. The information is also reported by the counties to a national discharge data base organized by the National Board of Health and Welfare. The national data base has mainly been used for planning purposes and epidemiological studies. For 1989 the data base contained records on about 1.6 million discharges.

Costs are generally known at the functional departmental level (for example, clinical chemistry). However, information on costs for treatment of individual patients or patient groups is almost entirely lacking in Sweden today. This is due to the fact that health care is almost exclusively financed by budgets allocated at the departmental level. In the traditional Swedish health care system, cost control is achieved through fixed budgets and not through cost accounting.

There is one main exception to the general principle to integrate financing and provision of health care within the same organization. When a patient is referred for highly specialized care to a regional hospital outside the county, the county referring the patient will pay for the treatment. According to the agreements for regional care, the actual cost of such treatment should be reimbursed. This has created an incentive to develop patient-related cost accounting in some regional hospitals.

Introduction of DRGs

Late 1984 or perhaps early 1985 could be considered a starting point for a more general awareness of the DRG concept in Sweden. At this time a number of articles on DRGs were published in *Läkartidningen*, the journal of the Swedish Medical Association. A brief description of the authors and their messages will give some insight into the early thinking and development of DRGs in Sweden. The first Swedish conference on DRGs was also organized during this period.

The first article in *Läkartidningen* was written by Stefan Håkansson (1984), a health economist working at Spri. He described the DRG system as well as the application of DRGs for reimbursement to hospitals of Medicare inpatient costs in the United States. At the end of the paper he concluded that it would be interesting to calculate Swedish DRG cost weights to obtain a better basis for comparisons between different health care units. He also suggested that perhaps the costs for patients referred to regional hospitals could be reimbursed according to DRGs.

The next article on the subject appeared two issues later and was written by a physician, Carl-Axel Nilsson (1984). He was a consultant in gynecology and obstetrics and also a board member of the senior medical staff section of the Swedish Medical Association. Carl-Axel Nilsson also commented on DRG applications in the United States. He concluded that comparisons of productivity and costs between departments and hospitals would probably be unavoidable in Sweden in the future due to the situation of the general economy. However, he stressed that comparisons must be done using an appropriate method and that DRGs might be useful in this context.

One week later an editorial in *Läkartidningen* ("Betalning per diagnos?," 1984) commented on the situation of Swedish and U.S. health care in relation to DRGs in rather general terms. It stated that even if DRGs did not represent any general solution of efficiency problems, it would certainly be possible to make use of the experiences from the United States in this field.

There was no connection between the two early papers by Stefan Håkansson and Carl-Axel Nilsson, as the articles were written independently. Stefan Håkansson had, as a researcher, followed the general developments in the field of case mix measures. In late 1984 he met Yale University professor Robert Fetter at a seminar organized by the CASPE institute in London. At that time Fetter declared his willingness to visit Stockholm to present his work on DRGs and to discuss possibilities for research cooperation.

Carl-Axel Nilsson noticed the DRG concept for the first time in the late 1970s in a scientific journal of health economics. In 1979 he participated in a European senior medical staff meeting in the Netherlands, as a representative for the Swedish Medical Association. At this meeting the DRG concept was discussed.

Many of the Swedish DRG activities have converged at Spri. In early 1985 Spri organized the first Swedish conference on DRGs. Altogether 150 people, representing a broad spectrum of the Swedish health care field, attended the meeting. The Medicare prospective payment system application of DRGs was presented, and possible uses of the new case mix measure in Sweden were discussed. At this time there was already a substantial knowledge of DRGs among some central actors and researchers in Sweden. This was reflected in the comments from the audience during the meeting.

The director of Spri at that time, Torsten Thor, concluded at the end of the conference that DRGs seemed to be an innovative approach to measuring health care productivity. He also promised that Spri would put effort into investigating the possibilities of the DRG instrument in Sweden. It was also announced that a policy working group would be constituted. An important task for the group was to analyze possible applications of DRGs in Sweden. Each county council was also given the opportunity to elect two contact people (one administrator and one physician) to follow the DRG project to come.

The First DRG Project

Spri decided at the beginning of 1985 to formally launch a DRG project. The aim was to investigate the possibilities for using DRGs in the Swedish health care system. Stefan Håkansson at Spri was the person responsible for the first phase of the project. When I presented the general outlines of the project at a Spri board meeting, the plan met with a positive response. The board members represented several important central actors in Swedish health care. Participants in the meeting included individuals from the Ministry of Finance, the Ministry of Health and Social Affairs, the Board of Health and Welfare, and the Federation of County Councils, as well as politicians from different county councils.

Early DRG activities at Spri developed along two main lines. One was more technically oriented and aimed at making a DRG classification of Swedish inpatients possible. An important task for that part of the project was to validate the properties of the DRG measure with respect to available Swedish data.

The other main line of DRG activities was to formulate a policy on how a DRG instrument could fit into the Swedish health care system. This policy discussion was partly dependent on how well the DRG measure was able to describe patient groups in Sweden, so in practice the work could be characterized as an interactive process between the two main lines.

A DRG policy working group connected to Spri was constituted in 1985. A well-known professor of surgery, Tore Scherstén, was appointed chairman of the group. The other members represented administrators, physicians, and researchers from different parts of Sweden. Stefan Håkansson, Carl-Axel Nilsson, and I were part of the policy group.

The group worked as an advisory body for DRG activities at Spri. It also produced the first policy statement on possible uses of DRGs in Sweden. The draft of this statement was prepared by Johan Calltorp, a physician in social medicine at Uppsala University. It circulated in the working group. After some rewriting, the policy statement was distributed by Spri in

early 1988. This document stated in part, "At the clinical department level, DRGs can primarily constitute a means of assisting
in the work load analysis. The task of management is, among
other things, to optimize the use of resources. Simple and
satisfactory measures are needed for the follow-up of both the
medical and economic aspects of care. Cost and production
accounts based on DRGs can be an important means of assistance for hospital departments.

"...The present decentralization of budget responsibility and authority decision demands a development of a practical
follow-up system that is both administratively and medically
meaningful. These shall constitute an important information
channel between the responsible physicians, administrators,
and politicians. DRG information should constitute a central
ingredient in these new systems" (Spri, 1988, pp. 10–11; my
translation).

Another area of use for DRGs at the national level is
comparisons between different care units. Up to now such comparisons (for example, frequency of different procedures or
lengths of stay) were rather rough and could be questioned
from a methodological viewpoint. DRGs provide the possibility
to carry out more exact comparisons. Likewise, DRG information makes it possible to include resource components in
comparisons.

In parallel with the policy discussions quoted above, considerable work involving more technical aspects of DRGs was
carried on. These activities were facilitated by the fact that a
number of data items were already recorded for every patient
discharged from a public hospital in Sweden. The correspondence between the data set available and the requirements of
input data for a Medicare DRG grouper is described in Table 5.2.

As shown in this table all data items needed for a DRG
classification were already collected in Sweden. However, for
diagnoses, procedures, and discharge status, different classifications were used in Sweden compared to the United States. Even
if there was considerable similarity in the basic structure of the
classifications, the coding was to a large extent different.

A DRG classification of Swedish discharge data is

Table 5.2. Prerequisites for DRG Assignment of Swedish Discharge Data.

Data Item	Included in Swedish Discharge Record?	Same Classification as Used by Medicare Groups?	Number of Codes in the Swedish Classification
Diagnosis	Yes	No	Approx. 5,600
Procedure	Yes	No	Approx. 2,200
Sex	Yes	Yes	2
Age	Yes	Yes	Approx. 100
Discharge status	Yes	No	4

achieved by a two-step process. The Swedish codes for diagnoses, procedures, and discharge status are first converted to the corresponding U.S. codes. Thereafter a commercially available DRG grouper may be applied. By using this strategy one can avoid the extensive work of developing a national Swedish DRG grouper program. Furthermore, one can more easily benefit from the extensive developmental work carried out in the United States to improve the DRG classification.

A research contract along this line was established between Spri and the Health Systems Management Group headed by Robert Fetter at Yale University. The agreement involved setting up preliminary conversion tables for Swedish procedure and diagnostic (ICD-8) codes as well as DRG assignment of a Swedish discharge data set to test the conversion tables. Some results from the early work included in the research contract were presented by Fetter and Jean Freeman at a Spri conference in Stockholm in December 1985. An analytic DRG study based partly on results from this work has also been published (Håkansson, Paulson, and Kogeus, 1988).

However, it was clear to Spri that Sweden was going to adopt a new classification of diseases (ICD-9) in 1987. A new conversion table for diagnoses therefore had to be produced. The DRG policy working group also advised Spri to build up the practical competence in Sweden in DRG classification and analysis of large discharge data sets. However, a validation study of DRGs based on Swedish hospitalizations had to wait until discharge registers with ICD-9 diagnosis codes were available in the latter part of 1988.

Widening the Scope of DRG Work

At this time there was a growing interest in Sweden in DRGs, especially among politicians and hospital administrators. The DRGs were still mainly seen as a tool to improve information systems for internal management and to make possible better comparisons of productivity between different clinical departments. To facilitate the developments in this area it was decided to start prospective investigations in a number of clinical departments. It was also realized that the hospital accounting systems must be improved before costs by DRG could be compared. The scope of the DRG work was now extended, and Spri activities were reorganized into four main projects.

One project focused on the DRG tool itself. The aim of this project was to create conversion tables for the new ICD-9 diagnosis and the modified Swedish procedure classifications. The DRG system would also need to be validated with respect to Swedish discharge register data. The first set of DRG cost weights was to be calculated based on the patient-related cost accounting available from one Swedish university hospital. The second project was set up as a clinical department study. The objective of this study was to use DRGs in a number of clinical departments of gynecology and obstetrics as an information system for internal management. The third project focused on DRG costing. The initial goal of this project was to test the DRG cost model developed by Fetter in a joint project with six university hospitals. This work was expected to produce Swedish costs by DRG. The aim of the fourth project was to increase efforts to disseminate information on the DRG concept and DRG activities in Sweden.

The following sections detail the course of these projects up through June 1991.

The DRG Tool

Conversion tables from Swedish to U.S. diagnostic and procedure codes have been jointly published by Spri and the National Board of Health and Welfare (Spri, 1990a). I coordinated the work and also wrote the introductory section in the report. The new conversion tables were based on the Swedish version of the ICD-9 classification of diseases and on the revised and extended Swedish classification of procedures.

Preliminary conversion tables were developed in cooperation with the Health Systems Management Group (HSMG) in the United States. Robert Fetter was the principal investigator at HSMG and director Robert Mullin, who was associated with HSMG, made important contributions in producing the preliminary conversion tables. The material was then reviewed by me in cooperation with Swedish medical experts in health care classifications.

In some cases a precise translation was not possible because of differences in the structure or precision of the two classifications involved. These differences were usually of no importance for the DRG assignment. However, sometimes the conversion problems resulted in Swedish DRGs not corresponding to the original definitions. This problem affected mainly some DRGs in orthopedics and obstetrics.

A software company in Sweden, Medisys (formerly Norrdata), had in 1990 produced the first Swedish DRG grouper package for personal computers. It was based on the Spri conversion tables and a DRG grouper program from Health System International/3M in the United States. According to Medisys, about a hundred such program packages were licensed on the Swedish market in the beginning of 1991. Conversion tables were also available from Spri for those who preferred to construct their own Swedish computer system for DRG assignment. At least two independent software companies offered Swedish DRG classification programs on the Swedish market in June 1991.

Well-planned prospective studies would from a theoretical standpoint be the best way to carry out assessments of DRGs in Sweden. In such studies information is collected for a given purpose in a carefully prepared way. This methodology reduces the risks of inadequate data. However, a limitation of prospective studies is that they often require a long time and consume resources. This is especially the case when extensive amounts of data need to be collected.

An alternative possibility is to utilize previously collected data. All the variables necessary for DRG classification were already recorded on a routine basis. The Swedish validation studies of DRGs started as soon as discharge registers with the new ICD-9 diagnosis coding (used from 1987 on) were available—that is, during the latter part of 1988. All data processing was done at Spri. Length-of-stay statistics were investigated for a sample of twenty-six hospitals, and cost statistics were calculated for one university hospital.

Discharge registers from 1987 were obtained directly from individual counties or hospitals. All short-stay hospitals within four counties and two additional regional hospitals were included. The material consisted of about 550,000 discharge records. The conversion tables previously described in combination with a Medicare grouper program (second revision) were used for the DRG assignment.

A small number of DRGs accounted for a large proportion of all discharges. The twenty most common DRGs corresponded to about 30 percent of the total activities measured both as discharges and as days of care. A considerable proportion (six out of twenty) of the most frequent DRGs were unspecific rest groups and therefore contained rather different kinds of patients.

There was a considerable difference in the variability of length of stay within different DRGs. The variation depended to a large extent on how similar patients were within single DRGs. The variation in length of stay was also influenced by medical care practices, availability of follow-up care, and data quality. Examples from the study showing small variation (DRG 39, lens procedures) and considerable variation (DRG 14, specific cerebrovascular disorders except transient ischemic attack) are shown in Figures 5.1 and 5.2.

The importance of trimming (exclusion of outlier cases) to improve the statistical power of the DRG measure was clearly demonstrated in the study (Table 5.2). All DRGs analyzed had a

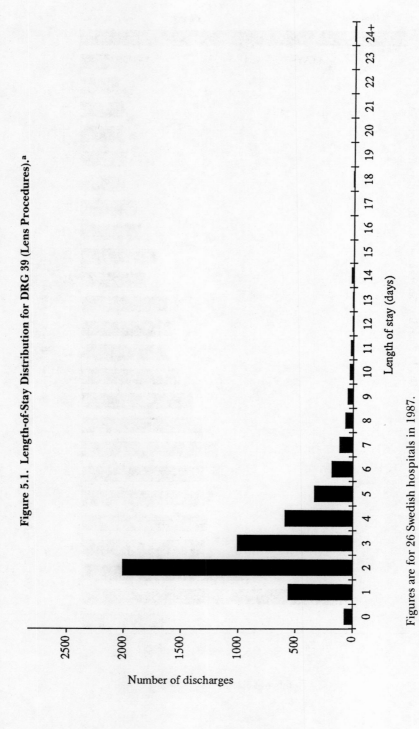

Figure 5.1. Length-of-Stay Distribution for DRG 39 (Lens Procedures).[a]

Figures are for 26 Swedish hospitals in 1987.

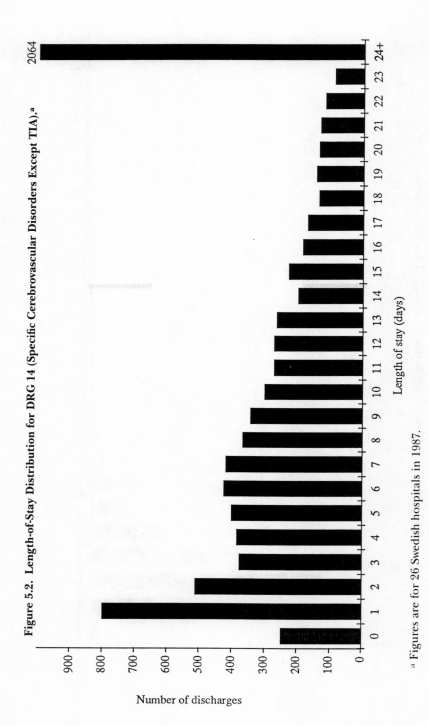

Figure 5.2. Length-of-Stay Distribution for DRG 14 (Specific Cerebrovascular Disorders Except TIA).[a]

[a] Figures are for 26 Swedish hospitals in 1987.

Table 5.3. Coefficient of Variation for Length of Stay per DRG.[a]

Coefficient of Variation	No. of DRGs	
	Untrimmed	Trimmed[b]
0.00–0.24	0	3
0.25–0.49	10	67
0.50–0.74	49	148
0.75–0.99	77	181
1.00–1.49	184	22
1.50–1.99	75	0
2.00–2.99	23	0
3.00–	3	0
Total	421	421

[a] Discharges from 26 Swedish hospitals in 1987; DRGs with at least 30 discharges.

[b] Discharges with a length of stay exceeding $Q_3 + 1.5(Q_3 - Q_1)$ excluded. Q_1 = first quartile, Q_3 = third quartile.

coefficient of variation below 1.5 after trimming. (The formula used for trimming is also given in Table 5.3.)

The Sahlgrenska University Hospital was the Swedish health care provider that had the most developed patient-related cost accounting when the project started. The material studied from this hospital included information on 44,400 discharges from 1987. The basic information needed for DRG assignment and cost calculations was initially in different registers. The first step therefore became to link clinical and resource data for every hospitalization.

A total cost was then calculated for each patient discharged. The total cost for a hospitalization consisted of a patient-specific component and a basic cost component. On average 33 percent of the total cost was patient-specific. This proportion varied from 3 percent in dermatology to 66 percent in thoracic surgery. The basic cost was allocated to patients by length of stay. The cost of a bed day was differentiated between the clinical wards.

The average cost for all hospitalizations amounted to SKr 20,200. When the 240 DRGs with at least thirty discharges were analyzed, average costs for the single DRGs varied between SKr 3,759 and SKr 85,227. In other words, the most resource-consuming DRGs averaged out at twenty-three times the cost of the least resource-consuming DRGs. The average cost per DRG may also be expressed as a relative value (cost weight). About 70 percent of the DRGs analyzed had cost weights in the interval 0.50–1.99. (A detailed presentation of results from this project is given in Paulson, 1990.)

Clinical Department Studies

The first DRG project on the clinical departmental level was started in 1987 and involved some ten departments in gynecology and obstetrics. The aim was to investigate the possibility of using DRGs as an information system for internal management. Carl-Axel Nilsson was chairman of the study group of clinicians from all the departments involved. The prospective study design included extensive training in DRG classification and handling of personal computers.

All the initial processing of discharge information, including DRG classification, was done on a personal computer in each clinical department. This method of collecting data improved the quality of the basic information compared to already existing central discharge registers. Meetings with representatives from all departments in the study were held on a regular basis. On the agenda were discussions of methodological issues and interpretation of DRG-based statistics. Spri has supported the project with DRG know-how, financial resources, and administrative services.

Similar projects involving other medical specialties have been initiated by Spri during the last few years. In June 1991 these activities involved more than a hundred clinical departments all over Sweden, representing eight specialties in more than fifty hospitals (Table 5.4).

Understanding of the DRG concept among physicians will be facilitated by the broad number of departments participating in the these projects. Project results will clarify how well suited the original DRGs are to describing inpatient production within various specialties in Sweden. The first edition of

Table 5.4. Clinical Departments Participating in Studies of DRGs as an Information System for Internal Management.

Type of Department	No. of Departments
Obstetrics/gynecology	39
General surgery	15
Urology	5
Internal medicine	22
Eye disease	3
Ear, nose, and throat	8
Orthopedic surgery	13
Infectious diseases	13
Total number of departments	118

the Swedish conversion tables will also be scrutinized and improved by the specialists in these projects. Results from the first specialty started (gynecology) were scheduled to be reported during the autumn of 1991.

For some of the departmental studies the scope of activities has been extended since the projects started. Initially all projects were mainly focused on the potential use of DRGs as a way to describe hospital inpatient work loads for the purposes of internal management. In the extended projects of gynecology and general surgery, outpatient activities are also covered. Ambulatory patients undergoing surgery are classified by the DRG system. Other classifications will be adopted or developed for nonsurgical outpatients. In addition, the perspective of quality assurance will be added to the original project plan for general surgery. It has not yet been decided how much emphasis will be put on the development of new measures of quality.

Considerable efforts have been made to develop cost accounting at the clinical departmental level. This work will be described in the following section on DRG costing. The cost of physicians is included in the calculations, as Swedish physicians in public hospitals are salaried. Measurements of nursing care will also be studied in some of the projects.

DRG Costing

Improvements in cost accounting are another important part of DRG-related activities. In principle there are two methods to bring costs down to a DRG level: bottom-up individualized patient costing and top-down cost modeling. It is possible to combine the two approaches.

First the DRG cost model developed at Yale University was studied in cooperation with representatives from some regional hospitals. Interest in testing the model was not great enough to justify the rather extensive work needed in each hospital for it to participate in such a study. However, the work on DRG costing was carried on in the following years, and DRG costing concepts were integrated into some of the departmental studies mentioned before. Staff with skills and training in economics were added to the projects at both the central and local level.

It was decided to use a top-down approach and to start with the function-oriented information on costs already available. All costs for inpatients and ambulatory surgery patients listed in the traditional budget of a clinical department were to be included in the analysis. The total consumption of medical and technical services by the same patients would also be estimated.

Costs by DRG would then be calculated using DRG allocation keys. The keys would be based on patient care consumption statistics when available, otherwise on clinical judgment. The first results from this study were scheduled to be produced during 1991.

Another brand of developments in DRG costing in Sweden is more centrally oriented. In 1990 the computer software company Medisys launched a project in cooperation with ten county councils and Spri. The aim was to increase knowledge about DRGs and to make possible a comparison of costs by DRG in different clinical departments.

Discharge data covering 1989 were collected from eighteen hospitals in the ten counties participating in the project. The material, which consisted of about 300,000 discharge records, was first checked for errors, and then DRGs were assigned by Medisys.

DRG cost weights from Medicare (1990) and Norway were used to calculate the number of DRG points produced by each clinical department in the material. Those figures were com-

pared with extended budgets calculated for the same departments. The extended budget is the traditional budget for the
inpatients in a clinical department plus the estimated total costs
for services consumed by those patients in different service
departments of the hospital. A considerable effort was done to
standardize the cost accounting to make the extended budgets
comparable.

The cost for a DRG point was calculated for each clinical
department. The average cost for a given DRG in a clinical
department was then estimated by multiplying the department-
specific cost for a DRG point with the general DRG cost weight
for the DRG in question. The analysis of extended budgets in
relation to DRG production was set to be reported in the autumn of 1991. It has been stressed by the investigators that the
results must be interpreted with caution.

Information Activities

Spri has been rather active in marketing the DRG concept
through various channels. The organization has also put a lot of
effort into disseminating information about the results of the
ongoing DRG activities. Several articles on DRGs have appeared
in the monthly Spri magazine *Spri News*. This publication is
distributed to a large number of central actors and also to
personnel in administrative positions in Swedish health care.
Oral presentations of the DRG concept were also given to politicians and managers in health care at various meetings and
seminars by Stefan Håkansson and other members of the Spri
staff.

A DRG symposium was held at the annual scientific meeting of the Swedish Society of Medicine in 1989. The symposium
attracted a large audience, and the speakers included economists, physicians, and a politician from the Ministry of Health
and Social Affairs. Several of the speakers had experience of the
Spri-related DRG projects. The DRG concept was presented
together with results from the DRG demonstration project in
gynecology. All the speakers conveyed a positive attitude to the

use of DRGs in Swedish health care. The presentations from the meeting were published as a report by Spri (1990b).

Besides the national activities already presented, the project managers at Spri developed close contacts with the international network of researchers involved in the development of DRGs and other case mix measures. Personnel from Spri attended various meetings on DRGs organized by the Health Systems Management Group and the Patient Classification Systems–Europe. I also participated with Stefan Håkansson in the Yale Executive Summer Program in New Haven, Conn., in 1987.

All of the Nordic countries except Iceland have public institutes similar to Spri for development activities in health care. These institutions are all involved in projects with a focus on DRGs or case mix management in hospitals. During the late 1980s, each of the Nordic countries had developed the capacity to make a DRG classification of national discharge records. Regular meetings have been held since 1987 among DRG researchers from the institutes to discuss results and future plans for DRG activities and related projects.

In the spring of 1990 France's Jean-Marie Rodrigues was invited by the Delegation for Social Research (an arm of the Swedish Ministry of Health and Social Affairs) as a visiting professor to Linköping University in Sweden. During his stay in Sweden, Rodrigues presented the DRG concept at seminars both in Stockholm and in Linköping. He also investigated the possibility of running a study in Sweden on DRGs as a tool for quality assessment.

The international contacts have supported DRG activities in Sweden in two main ways. The first is the development of the capacity to make a DRG classification of Swedish discharge records. This process was facilitated by the transfer of know-how from the United States and the United Kingdom. However, some momentum was lost when Sweden adopted a new classification of diseases in 1987. The second is related to the diffusion of the DRG concept in Sweden. As mentioned earlier, Robert Fetter and coworkers visited the country at the beginning of the DRG project at Spri. They gave some excellent presentations for various audiences involved in health care management. Those presentations increased the awareness and also the positive interest in the DRG concept in Sweden.

The DRG activities at Spri have received considerable support from the Federation of County Councils and the Ministry of Health and Social Affairs. These organizations were both represented on the board of Spri and were also kept informed through various informal consultations as well as through the DRG working and reference groups connected to Spri.

The so-called Dagmar 50 initiative was organized in 1989 to support development projects in health care. An important objective was to increase the capacity and productivity of the system. Altogether SKr 60 million has been reserved for this purpose from the national health insurance remuneration to health care. The project applications from health care providers were reviewed by representatives of the government, the Federation of County Councils, and Spri.

The DRG-related activities mentioned before in connection with Spri have received considerable financial support from the Dagmar 50 initiative. More than a hundred clinical departments and ten county councils have shared SKr 9 million for DRG development projects.

Anders Lönnberg, a political adviser in the Ministry of Health and Social Affairs, early identified the need for improved information as a strategic issue in order to increase efficiency in the health care sector. In early 1987 he was the chairman of a national commission (INFHOS) with the task of investigating the information structure in Swedish health care. Both the Federation of County Councils and Spri were represented in the commission.

Lönnberg continued to support different initiatives in the information field after he was appointed undersecretary at the Ministry of Health and Social Affairs in 1987. He was succeeded as chairman of the INFHOS commission by S. Åke Lindgren. The commission presented a white paper in May 1991 (Ministry of Health and Social Affairs, 1991). This document gives a detailed description of the information already available and also suggests a number of important areas to develop. The following extract sums up the paper's position on DRGs (my translation):

> Grouping of patients by diagnosis-related groups (DRGs) may be used for the description and comparison of work load within individual departments and between different departments over time in inpatient short-term care. At the central level DRGs may make it possible to follow the evolution of Swedish health care in a summary fashion.
>
> *The extensive trial at present being carried out under the guidance of Spri should be given continued support.*
>
> In the opinion of the commission, results so far indicate that the DRG is a classification method well suited as a brief description of what health services do, at least with regard to surgical specialties. In the field of, for instance, internal medicine and related specialties, there is at present insufficient information for a decision to be made concerning the use of DRGs. An independent analysis of results from the trials already in progress should be conducted in cooperation with sections of the Swedish Society of Medicine. Notwithstanding this reservation, it is important to give continued support to work with DRGs, with an aim to providing a standardized description of inpatient health care. Systems corresponding to DRGs should be developed and tested in ambulatory care, long-term care, and possibly also in psychiatric care.
>
> The use of DRGs on a broad basis in Swedish health care presupposes that the system is followed up and evaluated. In the United States a special organization, the Prospective Payment Assessment Commission (ProPAC), has been established in order to provide a continuous follow-up of experiences gained in the use of DRG. . . . The ap-

propriate structure and localization of a Swedish institution of this type should be a matter for consideration. *During the initial phase of development the responsibility for follow-up and evaluation should rest with Spri in collaboration with the National Board of Health and Welfare.*

Response of Professional Groups

Physicians have been involved from the beginning in the DRG project supported by Spri, first as members of the policy group and later also in demonstration projects for internal management based on clinical specialty. Before any large-scale application of DRGs, the concept is tested and (if necessary) modified by the clinical specialty involved.

There has been no visible criticism from Swedish physicians for using DRGs in systems for better internal management in hospitals. However, some concern has been articulated when it comes to an application involving payment in internal medicine. It has been argued that the complexity of many patients in this discipline may not be caught within the case mix systems available today. Furthermore, a focus on the individual hospital stay may not be optimal for patients needing multiple stays in a hospital each year.

The first Swedish application of DRGs for payment took place in one department of gynecology. The change to a new system of financing the unit was done on a consensus basis. The head physician in this department is a former chairman of the Association of Gynecology. He also participated in the first Swedish demonstration project using DRGs as a tool for internal management in some departments of gynecology.

Up to now, there has been no official reaction from the Swedish Medical Association concerning the use of DRGs. However, a policy group within the association is now preparing a document on the future organization of hospital care. Since about 95 percent of all gainfully employed physicians are members of the organization, the Medical Association may be considered representative for Swedish physicians.

The labor union that organizes nurses (SHSTF) has published a policy paper on DRGs (SHSTF, 1991). According to the union, it is obvious that the health care system and the personnel working therein would benefit if its activities could be described and related to the goals decided on. The DRG system is one of several tools that should be tested and assessed in this context. The importance of finding good tools for economic planning, distribution of resources, and management is of concern to the union. For this reason, the union feels that attention in the investigations should be focused on any negative effects that appear and on the possible limitations of the DRG system. Quality of care must be considered and cost weights must better reflect the nursing component of care.

As yet, the DRG activities organized by or connected with Spri have been rather uncontroversial and (at least on the surface) characterized by consensus among the important actors. A part of the explanation may be the position of Spri in the health care field. The organization has close links to the central administrative bodies of the health care sector. Spri also has put a lot of effort into establishing good contacts in the research community and the medical profession.

Another factor making consensus easier to achieve is that Spri has avoided making any definite statement on the usefulness of DRGs for reimbursement. When this chapter was written in June 1991, DRGs were not (except for the one clinical department in gynecology mentioned earlier) used anywhere in Sweden in any live application, as a tool in the budget process, or for case-based reimbursement.

In sum, the DRG projects at Spri have been rather process oriented. Finding acceptance with important actors in the health care field has sometimes had priority over focus and speed in the project activities. By June 1991 the DRG concept was well known among central actors and was also known to many professionals working in hospitals. Software packages were available for DRG assignment of Swedish discharge records.

The validation studies of Swedish discharge registers were reported in 1990. Prospective studies, evaluating DRGs as a tool for internal management, are now in progress in cooperation with physicians representing eight different specialties. However, much is still to be achieved when it comes to costing of DRGs. In June 1991, DRGs were used for payment in one clinical department only.

Spri is an institute that, among other things, develops new methods for management of health services. It is up to other organizations like the county councils and the national government to decide about changes in the traditional Swedish health care model and the application of new information technologies. The basic work on DRGs will be relevant regardless of its final application. However, future DRG activities at Spri will be influenced and guided by decisions made by the county councils on the use of DRGs in Sweden.

Development Trends

The traditional Swedish health care model is the subject of considerable discussion today. Behind the debate are a number of perceived problems in the health care sector. One of the most urgent problems is the economic situation of the county councils. In 1990, their total costs exceeded revenues by SKr 7 billion. Not even the running costs could be covered, resulting in the need to borrow money on a short-term basis. The deficit in running costs corresponded to 3 percent of the total turnover of about SKr 120 billion in 1990.

Problems in the economic balance are related to several factors. The central government has decided to control the economic expansion of county councils and local municipalities. According to the 1991 Finance Plan from the Ministry of Finance, the yearly expansion in volume of the local government sector must be restricted to no more than 1 percent. It is concluded in the same document that rationalization and reconsideration of the present activities will be necessary.

As part of the effort to control costs, county councils were by law not allowed to increase the taxation level in 1991 and 1992. Maximum patient charges were previously decided in detail by the national government. Today, the restriction on patient fees set by the government has an upper limit of SKr 1,500 per patient per year.

About 20 percent of the revenues of county councils come from the national health insurance and state subsidies. The principles for payouts from the social insurance system were changed in 1985 (the so-called Dagmar reform). The change was from an activity-based reimbursement to a fixed sum of money for each county council (based mainly on capitation). The amount of resources transferred from the national government to the county council level has from 1984 to 1988 decreased by about 15 percent in fixed prices.

Salaries and wages in the health care sector increased more than expected in 1989 and 1990. This was partly a consequence of health sector wages lagging behind other sectors during the preceding years

Additional pressure is being put on the system because the need for health care is expected to increase in the years to come. In a recent governmental committee for long-term economic forecast it was estimated by the Federation of County Councils that a yearly expansion in volume of about 2 percent will be needed in the 1990s. The increase in volume is to compensate for the aging of the population and for the demand to adopt new and effective developments in medical technology (Ministry of Finance, 1990).

A number of useful new medical technologies such as hip replacement, eye lens implants, and coronary bypass surgery have evolved during the last decades. In spite of a substantial increase in operation capacity for these procedures, waiting lists are still often too long. The waiting time also differs considerably between counties, which is incompatible with the emphasis on equal access to care in the national health care act.

A considerable number of long-term patients in short-term hospitals is also a problem. Even when an acute illness episode has been treated and controlled, it may not be possible to discharge the patient due to lack of capacity in other institutions.

Another important force suggesting structural changes to come is the demand for consumer choice within health care.

The traditional and well-defined catchment areas of health centers and hospitals are being questioned by the general public to an increasing extent. The younger urban generation especially creates pressure for political action in this area.

Despite the problems listed above, there are many positive aspects of the present Swedish health situation and the health care model. The total expenditure on health care is not especially high in relation to other member countries of the Organization for Economic Cooperation and Development when the age structure and low population density in Sweden are taken into account. In 1988, life expectancy at birth was longest in Sweden compared to all other countries except Iceland and Japan (Statistics Sweden, 1990b). Infant mortality in the first year of life in 1989 was among the lowest in the world (Organization for Economic Cooperation and Development, 1991). The health status of the population is affected by actions in many sectors of the society. However, present figures are compatible with a well-functioning health care sector.

A New Health Care Model

Structural changes in health care are on the political agenda in Sweden today. It is suggested in the debate that several of the problems mentioned above could be solved by structural reforms. One of the main themes in the political discussion is a separation between the financing and the production of health care. The idea behind this change is to increase productivity by competition and also to make consumer choice possible. Consumer preference is also considered to be one important mechanism for allocating resources to effective providers.

There are many areas of interaction between health care and other sectors of the Swedish welfare state, such as the national health insurance and the social services provided by the local municipalities. The question of whether the present administrative structure in Sweden has created artificial barriers between sectors, thus preventing an efficient use of resources, is at present also being widely debated.

Starting in 1992, the municipalities will have an overall

responsibility for care and services in local nursing homes and other specific accommodations for the elderly and handicapped. Some 40,000 employees and SKr 20 billion will be transferred by this reform from the county councils to the municipalities.

Local nursing homes as well as medical care (except physician services) in specific accommodations for the elderly will in principle be organized by the municipalities after the reform. This level of local government will also be responsible for financing somatic long-term care provided by the county councils. In long-term care is included the care of "bedblockers"—that is, long-term patients who have already been treated for their acute illness episode but are still stuck in short-term hospitals.

Some other aspects of coordination between the present sectors of the welfare system will be tested on a limited scale starting in 1992. Thus, the responsibility for primary care for the entire population in some municipalities will in trial projects be transferred from the county council to the local municipal level. It is also planned to initiate local projects with the aim of improving the coordination between the health care sector and the national health insurance system.

Substantial changes in organization are taking place not only between the sectors of the welfare system but also within the county councils. Several counties have decided or are in the process of deciding about profound changes in the organization of health care. The principles behind the changes have much in common. The developments in one county will be described here to illustrate the general trends in the structural changes taking place in many counties today.

The county council of Dalarna was the first in Sweden to take the formal decision about implementing a new health care model. The overall aim of the structural changes was to produce more health care with the limited resources available. Dalarna, which is located in the middle of Sweden, has a population of 290,000 and has four short-term hospitals within its borders.

A blueprint for a new organization was suggested in 1990 by the Scandinavian Institute of Administrative Research, a management consultant company. A basic principle behind the changes was a separation of the financing and production of health care.

The implementation process of the new health care structure in Dalarna started in January 1991. The county was to be divided into fifteen health care districts, each with a board of politicians. Financial resources will be allocated to a health care district in relation to the need of the population living in the area. The district boards are then responsible for financing the health care of the population.

There is at least one health care center with several general practitioners in each district. A "population contract" is established between each health care center and the district board. In the contract is specified the population to be covered by the health care center and the corresponding amount of resources available for health care. The health care center is then responsible for financing all health services necessary to the population. These services may be primary care produced by the health center itself or specialist or hospital care that is bought from other providers.

The four short-term hospitals in Dalarna were to be merged into one organization under the leadership of a board of politicians. (This move actually departs from the consultants' recommendation that the hospital board include professionals only.) Clinical departments within the hospital group will not have a yearly budget as before. They will be financed by income from selling services to the primary health care centers. The agreements ("care contracts") between individual health care centers and clinical departments are signed by the district board and the board of the hospital group. Those care contracts define the kind of care delivered by the clinical department together with the general conditions and the costs. No general decision has been taken on how clinical activities will be described in the care contracts.

Internal Markets in Hospitals

Many interesting developments in the organization of hospitals are also taking place within the framework of the present health care model. A broad consensus seems to exist on the need to make an effective use of the limited resources available for health care.

From a functional perspective a hospital can be divided into three different kinds of units: clinical departments (such as general surgery), medical service departments (such as diagnostic radiology), and general service departments (such as maintenance of buildings). By tradition each department in a hospital has its own budget. This structure creates a weak connection between authority and accountability when it comes to resources. A radiology investigation ordered for a patient in the department of surgery will be a cost within the budget of the department of diagnostic radiology. It has been shown that only part of the costs generated by the decisions of a surgeon will consume resources within the budget of his own department. The other part of the costs will be ascribed to budgets of medical and general service departments.

As a result, there is a growing tendency to create internal markets within hospitals. There should be no free services available to physicians. In this new situation, service departments are financed by an income instead of a budget. The income is generated by selling services to other departments. According to a recent survey, more than 80 percent of the counties had at least one service unit financed mainly by selling services (Federation of County Councils, 1991b). The developments along this line have been most pronounced for general service departments.

Much development work on internal hospital markets and the case mix management concept in Sweden has been done by researchers at the Swedish Institute of Health Economics in Lund and the Department of Health and Society at Linköping University.

The Clinical Manager

The importance of physicians as triggers of resource consumption is widely recognized today. Case mix management per se in a system operated by fixed budgets is therefore not much of a controversial issue. However, the crude measures of productivity used today (cost per bed day or case) have been widely criticized by physicians for not taking into account the huge variation in resource needs among different patients.

The understanding of the central role of physician decisions for resource consumption is reflected in an addendum to the Health and Medical Service Act that came into effect July 1991. It stated that the head of a department, who is responsible for both medical care and administration including the budget, must always be a physician in those units where it is required to guarantee the safety of the patients.

The health care units where a physician should be the department manager have been defined by the National Board of Health and Welfare. The units specified included most clinical as well as many medical service departments. Combining responsibility for clinical practice and resources in one person creates a suitable structure for introducing the clinical manager and the case mix management concepts into Swedish hospitals.

There is no similar restriction on the formal background of a hospital director. Only a few of the hundred people holding this position in short-term hospitals in Sweden today have a medical background. However, the hospital director is supported by a chief physician who acts as a medical adviser at the hospital level.

Applications of Case Mix Measures

Much of the power for organizing the health care system in Sweden is decentralized to the county councils. Therefore, it is not probable that the use of the DRG classification during the next five years will be exactly the same or initiated at the same time all over Sweden.

Most of the development work on DRGs has until now been done in cooperation with Spri. However, as DRG groupers adapted to Swedish classifications are now commercially available, it is rather easy for any actor in health care to make a DRG classification of Swedish discharge data. The developments in the DRG classification technology will thus also decentralize DRG activities in Sweden.

DRG statistics will certainly be used at different levels of Swedish health care as an information system to compare important aspects of short-term somatic health care. Comparisons by DRG may include admission rates, length of stay, and costs. Such comparisons could be one of several inputs in a negotiation process setting global budgets. The new case mix measures also have considerable potential in systems for internal management.

The first Swedish demonstration project using DRGs instead of a yearly budget to pay a public health care provider was started in 1990. The project involves one clinical department (gynecology/obstetrics) at the county hospital in Helsingborg in southern Sweden. Since the project started, the department has been financed by an income that is directly related to the activity level of the unit. Costs for all inpatients are reimbursed according to a list of fixed prices based on DRGs. Nonsurgical outpatients are paid for per visit by a relative value classification. The implementation of a system for quality assessment is also part of the demonstration project.

The unit described was part of the Spri project investigating DRGs as a departmental tool for internal management. However, many practical aspects of the new system for reimbursement have been worked out in cooperation with the Swedish Institute of Health Economics.

It is too early to draw any general conclusions about the consequences of the new arrangement, as the model was introduced rather recently. However, the head physician of the department involved, Stig Gårdmark, has publicly expressed his positive attitude toward the new method of financing the unit.

The Stockholm County Council has also decided to use DRGs as a tool for reimbursement of inpatient care in several clinical departments starting in January 1991. All clinical departments of general surgery, orthopedic surgery, urology, and gynecology in the eleven short-term hospitals in the county will be involved.

In one other county council (Bohus), patients from all

specialties in short-term somatic hospitals will be reimbursed according to DRGs. Information systems needed for patient-related cost accounting have already been developed. According to the plans, the new method of financing hospital care was to be tested as a shadow system in parallel with the still operational budget-based system during 1992. The DRG-based reimbursement would then take effect from the beginning of 1993.

In some medical care regions there are plans to introduce DRGs for reimbursement of cross-boarder county council referrals. Today such patients are reimbursed according to the principle of actual costs. Cross-boarder referrals may increase if it becomes more common for patients to choose their own hospitals.

The future use of DRGs for reimbursement depends much on the experiences gained in these first applications in combination with the general development trends in Swedish health care.

DRGs are the only case mix measure in short-term somatic care that has received some general attention in the Swedish health care sector. This is to a great extent due to the strong focus on DRGs in the development projects organized and supported by Spri. Although the DRG classification covers one important sector of health care (short-term somatic in-patient care), there is a need for improved methods of measuring patient case mix in other areas of health care. Extensive research in this field has resulted in several published methods.

Resource utilization groups are one such a patient classification system for long-term care. This method is being studied by Gunnar Ljunggren in a number of geriatric departments under the Stockholm County Council.

There is also considerable interest in exploring the possibilities of case mix systems for ambulatory care and psychiatry. As far as I know, in June 1991 there were no projects testing such classifications on a broad basis in Swedish health care.

Many actors see a considerable potential in market mechanisms for solving several of the present problems in Swedish health care. The traditional budget-based system has been criticized for a rigid structure preventing an efficient use of resources. However, some conditions must be fulfilled to make market mechanisms useful within health care.

Cheap health care is not a goal in itself. It is more important to have value for money; that is, to maximize health benefits in relation to resources spent on health care. From a theoretical perspective, it would be more relevant in a market system to pay for results obtained than for such products of health care as hospitalizations, days of care, visits, and so on. However, due to practical considerations, market systems often to a large extent focus on the price of such products. If inpatient care is reimbursed with a fixed price per DRG, it will be necessary to include quality of care in the steering mechanisms.

It is important to select a case mix measure with a small variation in costs within each group of patients. Homogeneous groups will prevent the risk of patient selection within a given group of a case mix system. Heterogeneous groups, on the other hand, may result in an involuntary selection of specific patients, giving an unfair reimbursement to some providers. Such heterogeneous groups also open up the possibilities for intentional selection of profitable patients and dumping of other cases.

New administrative routines will be necessary if a more market-oriented model is implemented. It is important that costs for new routines be less than the savings realized by an increased efficiency of the health care system.

The traditional budget-based health care system in Sweden has been successful from a cost containment perspective. However, demand for health care seems to be unlimited. In a more market-oriented system with a third-party payer, it will thus be necessary to implement some restrictions on health care utilization to prevent a loss of overall cost control.

The decentralized structure of the Swedish health care system creates the opportunity to test new approaches to health care organization on a limited scale. It also makes it possible to adjust the health care model to local circumstances. This is an important advantage as the conditions for health care are rather different in a densely populated urban area like Stockholm compared to a sparsely populated county in northern Sweden.

The nature of medical specialties varies to a considerable

extent (for example, thoracic surgery versus psychiatry). It is important to adjust the management strategy in relation to the specific circumstances in different kinds of health services.

Carefully evaluated demonstration projects would be a valuable way to learn about how the new concepts of health care organization work in practice. By a stepwise implementation of new concepts, it will be possible to learn from the experiences gained and to make necessary adjustments in the health care structure.

Epilogue

The Swedish case study covers the time period up to July 1991. The subsequent twelve-month period has been characterized by changes within the framework of the traditional county council health care system. The trend to make a division between purchasing and provider functions has continued in many county councils. The financial agreements vary from block contracts to reimbursement per case and fee-for-service arrangements.

The debate on more profound change possibilities in the Swedish health care model has also continued. Several reviews of the present system and options for change have been published (Calltorp, Ham, and Rosenthal, 1992; Culyer, 1991; Federation of County Councils, 1991a).

The most recent review was by a group of foreign health economists. The study was organized by Studieförbundet Näringsliv och Samhälle (SNS), the Center of Business and Policy Studies. The summarizing report concluded, "What Sweden has is a set of problems — whose solution is admittedly by no means easy — that are shared with nearly every other country in the developed world. Moreover, Sweden has these in a form that is often less severe than can be found elsewhere and is already containing them in ways that seem superior to the ways adopted in at least some other developed countries" (Culyer, 1991, p. 3).

A national governmental committee on financing and organization of health care was set up in March 1992. The committee will review different models for a Swedish health care system. The following three models will receive particular attention:

1. *The reformed county council model.* This is close to the present model. County councils will still be responsible for the financing and the supply of health care. However, market mechanisms will be used within the framework of the present system. Public and private providers should compete from a basis of equality.
2. *The primary-care-based model.* Health care resources will be allocated to the primary care level. Each Swedish citizen will be given the opportunity to choose a family practitioner. The practitioner will be responsible for all health care costs of the listed patients. The model has some resemblance to the GP fund holding concept introduced in Great Britain.
3. *Compulsory health care insurance.* The financing of health care will be by one or several insurance organizations and the present authority to tax will be removed from the county councils.

The committee on financing and organization of health care will publish the final report by March 1994.

Publicly financed and organized primary care is a part of the traditional Swedish health care model. Primary care physicians are salaried and organized in health care centers. Each such center is responsible for primary care in a well-defined geographic area.

The Ministry of Health and Social Affairs has recently published a white paper on a new structure for primary care. The proposed new model is based on family practitioners. The primary care physician will assume responsibility for listed patients instead of the population in a geographic area. The practitioner will be payed by a capitation system.

A substantial number of county councils have already started to implement some kind of family practitioner model in advance of the recommended national plan. A common planning target is a maximum of two thousand persons listed to each family practitioner. The present number of general practitioners (a medical specialty in Sweden) is presently not sufficient to achieve this target.

In Sweden, as in several other European countries, there have been considerable waiting lists for some elective procedures. A *vårdgaranti* (guarantee for health care) was introduced in January 1992 to reduce waiting times for treatment. The reform covers some well-defined conditions requiring surgery and gives a patient the right, in principle, to treatment within three months.

The Swedish National Board of Health and Welfare is introducing a national reporting system on ambulatory visits to physicians in public settings. Administrative and medical information will be collected. This reporting system is a practical result of the INFHOS commission described earlier in this chapter. A similar reporting system for inpatient care is already in operation.

Since July 1991 DRG-related activities have continued to evolve along the lines previously described in this chapter.

Reports from several of the medical specialty working groups on DRGs connected to Spri (see Table 5.4) will be published at the end of 1992. These will include an assessment of the clinical usefulness of DRGs together with estimates of DRG cost weights based on best available Swedish costing data.

Preliminary results from some surgical specialties were presented at a national Spri conference in January 1992. It was concluded that DRGs represent an improved measure of production compared to number of discharges or number of bed days. However, it was also mentioned that the DRG measure had limitations. A similar conference on DRGs in internal medicine took place in October 1992.

DRG-based financing of four kinds of medical specialties was introduced in the Stockholm county council in January 1992 as planned. The new financing scheme involves about twenty clinical specialties, such as general surgery, obstetrics/gynecology, orthopedic surgery, and urology. Some costs (research, development, and teaching) are still financed by a fixed yearly budget. Most of the remaining activities are payed for up to 100 percent based on production described in DRGs.

Modified Medicare and Norwegian DRG cost weights are used. The standard amount (payment for cost weight 1.00) is related to historical costs. However, the calculated historical costs are reduced by 10 percent.

Outpatient care is also financed according to activity level. Ambulatory surgery production is described in DRGs. However, the price level is 60 percent higher than corresponding inpatient DRGs. Other outpatients are reimbursed based on a locally constructed classification of patient visits (KÖKS). Prices in the system are renegotiated if total production increases more than 10 percent. Each medical specialty must develop some indicators of quality to be followed in the new system.

The Stockholm county council has decided to extend the financing model to all kinds of somatic clinical departments in short-term hospitals in 1993. An evaluation will be made of the new health care model in Stockholm. It is obviously too early to have any firm conclusions on the effects of the new model. Preliminary data on the first six months indicate a considerable increase in production and also an increase in total costs as well as a decrease in the number of patients waiting for medical treatment.

The county councils in the northern health care region have priced regional specialty care at the University hospital in Umeå by DRGs since the beginning of 1992. Medicare cost weights are used in this DRG application. The agreement involves inpatients referred from outside county councils only. Most of the patient load at the Umeå hospital is made up of patients from the local county council. Care for those patients is still paid for on a fixed budget basis. It has been decided to introduce similar DRG-based payment for referred regional inpatients in several other health care regions in 1993.

References

"Betalning per diagnos?" (Reimbursement by diagnosis?). *Läkartidningen*, 1984, *81*(45), 4125–4126.

Calltorp, J., Ham, C., and Rosenthal, M. (eds.). "Special Issue: Swedish Health Services at the Crossroads." *Health Policy*, 1992, *21*, 95–186.

Culyer, A. J. *Health Care and Health Care Finance in Sweden: The Crisis That Never Was; the Tension That Ever Will Be.* Occasional Paper No. 33. Stockholm: Swedish Center for Business and Policy Studies, 1991.

Federation of County Councils. *Statistisk årsbok för landsting 1990/91* (Statistical yearbook for county councils 1990/91). Stockholm: Federation of County Councils, 1990.

Federation of County Councils. *Crossroads: Future Options for Swedish Health Care.* Stockholm: Federation of County Councils, 1991a.

Federation of County Councils. *Enkät om ekonomistyrning i landstingen 1991. Redovisning av enkätsvaren* (Survey on economic planning and management in the county councils 1991: presentation of the survey answers). Stockholm: Federation of County Councils, 1991b.

Håkansson, S. "DRG—recept mot höga sjukvårdskostnader?" (DRG: a prescription against high cost of health care?). *Läkartidningen*, 1984, *81*(42), 3783–3790.

Håkansson, S., Paulson, E., and Kogeus, K. "Prospects for Using DRGs in Swedish Hospitals." *Health Policy*, 1988, *9*, 177–192.

Ministry of Finance. *Landsting för välfärd. Bilaga 14 till långtidsutrdningen 1990* (County councils for welfare: Appendix 14 to the committee on long-term economic forecast 1990). SOU 1990(14) (Appendix 14). Stockholm: Ministry of Finance, 1990.

Ministry of Health and Social Affairs. *Informationsstruktur för hälso- och sjukvården—en utveclingsprocess. Betänkande av utredningen om informationsstrukturen för hälso- och sjukvården* (The structure of information in health care—a process of development: a white paper from the committee on the structure of information in health care). SOU 1991(18). Stockholm: Ministry of Health and Social Affairs, 1991.

Nilsson, C.-A. "Diagnosrelaterad ersättning—djärvt experiment med en teknik som kan användas i Sverige" (Diagnosis-related reimbursement: a bold experiment with a technique that could be used in Sweden). *Läkartidningen*, 1984, *81*(44), 4000–4005.

Organization for Economic Cooperation and Development. *OECD in Figures*. (1991 ed.) Paris: Organization for Economic Cooperation and Development, 1991.

Paulson, E. *DRGs in Sweden: Adaptation and Applications on Patient Discharge Data*. Stockholm: Swedish Planning and Rationalization Institute of Health and Social Services, 1990.

SHSTF. *SHSTFs syn på DRG inom vården* (The views of SHSTF on DRGs used in health care). Stockholm: SHSTF, 1991.

Statistics Sweden. *Hälsan i Sverige. Hälsostatistisk årsbok 1990* (Health in Sweden: statistical yearbook on health 1990). Stockholm: Statistics Sweden, 1990a.

Statistics Sweden. *Statistisk årsbok 1991* (Statistical abstract of Sweden 1991). Stockholm: Statistics Sweden, 1990b.

Swedish Institute. *Fact Sheets on Sweden: Health and Medical Care in Sweden*. Stockholm: Swedish Institute, July 1990.

Swedish Planning and Rationalization Institute of Health and Social Services. *DRG—ett sätt att sätta värde på vården* (DRGs: a way of valuing health care). (Print 165) Stockholm: Swedish Planning and Rationalization Institute of Health and Social Services, 1988.

Swedish Planning and Rationalization Institute of Health and Social Services. *DRG-gruppering. Omvandlingstabeller för diagnos- och operationskoder* (DRG assignment: conversion tables for diagnostic and procedure codes). (Report 276) Stockholm: Swedish Planning and Rationalization Institute of Health and Social Services, 1990a.

Swedish Planning and Rationalization Institute of Health and Social Services. *DRG i startgroparna* (DRG in the starting blocks). (Report 288) Stockholm: Swedish Planning and Rationalization Institute of Health and Social Services, 1990b.

Six

Switzerland: Diffusion and the Canton System

Bernard J. Güntert
Fred Paccaud
Markus Sagmeister
Andreas Frei

Switzerland has an area of around 41,000 square kilometers and a population of between 6 and 7 million (see Table 6.1). Its political structure is based on a confederation of twenty-six states, called cantons. The Swiss health care system is decentralized and is mostly under the jurisdiction of the cantons. The cantonal authorities have the responsibility for most aspects of their health care systems. The federal government has only a few tasks. This set-up is different from most other European countries, whose health care is generally more centrally governed.

Outline of the Health Care System

The federal Department of the Interior is responsible for health services at the national level. It is in charge of the control of communicable diseases, radiation protection, and food and drug regulation, for example. The federal government is also responsible for the control of most of the health care professions (including physicians, pharmacists, and nurses) and subsidizes

Note: The authors wish to thank Dr. Gerhard Kocher for reviewing this chapter.

174

Table 6.1. Key Health Care Figures for Switzerland.

Country area	41,293 sq. km.
Population, 1988–89	6.673 million
% of population over 75	6.8%
Average life expectancy, men, 1988–89	74 years
Average life expectancy, women, 1988–89	80.9 years
Gross national product, 1988–89	SFr 305.22 million
% of GNP spent on health care, 1988	7.4%
% of GNP spent on health care, 1990 (est.)	7.8%
Average income per capita, 1988	SFr 35,912
Total spent on health care, 1980	SFr 12.4 billion
Total spent on health care, 1988	SFr 20.9 billion
% spent on hospitals	49%
% spent on physicians	19%
% spent on other suppliers	32%
Number of hospitals	833
Number of acute-care hospitals	279
Number of short-term hospital beds	42,600
Number of physicians, 1988	10,300
Number of physicians per 10,000 inhabitants	16
Number of dentists, 1988	4,170
Number of dentists per 10,000 inhabitants	5.2
Increase in no. of physicians, 1980 to 1988	+4.6%
Sources of financing for health care	
Sickness funds	43%
Cantons (taxpayers)	25%
Private insurers and other private payers	32%

Source: Data from Bundesamt für Sozialversicherung, 1990; Frei and Hill, 1990; and Vereinigung Schweizerischer Krankenhäuser, 1990.

social health insurance through authorized sickness funds (*Krankenkassen*). The federal Social Security Agency controls the activities of these sickness funds, especially the handling of compulsory coverage.

However, supervision of the health care system, especially the organization of hospitals, is mainly managed by the cantons themselves. In particular, the cantonal health administrations are attached to one of the departments with cantonal executive authority. These health departments play an important part in running the hospitals.

At the same time, the influence of the cantonal health administration on the ambulatory health care sector is limited, in part because the ambulatory health care sector is privately organized. The cantonal health departments, however, control the tariffs and the price structure negotiated between the cantonal sickness funds association and the cantonal medical association.

In some cantons, the communities are also involved in the provision of hospital care. However, their main responsibility is the provision of home care and extramural nursing care (called *Spitex-Dienste*).

The cantonal directors of health affairs (the *Sanitaetsdirektoren*) together form a conference (*Sanitaetsdirektoren-Konferenz*) that tries to coordinate the health care system and puts out recommendations for the entire country. These recommendations are not legally binding.

Switzerland has a highly diversified hospital system with a total of 88,660 hospital beds in 833 institutions. For short-term care (or acute care), 42,600 beds are available in 279 acute-care hospitals. In 1988 the acute-care hospitals accounted for 13.3 million patient days. The main characteristics of the hospitals in Switzerland are shown in Table 6.2 (Vereinigung Schweizerischer Krankenhäuser, 1990).

The regional or community hospitals for acute care are the backbone of the Swiss hospital system. A typical regional or community hospital has 100–200 beds and is usually organized into three departments: internal medicine, general surgery, and gynecology and obstetrics. These hospitals provide basic (or extended basic) hospital and emergency care.

Above these hospitals are the large regional or cantonal hospitals, which function as referral hospitals, providing specialized hospital care. Finally, the six university hospitals provide highly specialized hospital care for the whole country.

Eighty-five percent of all beds available are provided by public hospitals owned by the cantons or by communities. The rest belong either to private nonprofit organizations or to for-

Table 6.2. Use of Hospital Beds in Switzerland, 1988.

Institution	Bed density (beds per 10,000 pop.)	Average length of stay (days)	Utilization rate (% of beds occupied)
Hospitals for short-term care (<30 days)	64	13.7	81%
Hospitals for long-term care (somatic illnesses)	42	233	95
Psychiatric hospitals	22	153	86
Others	5.5	293	76
All institutions	133	27	86

Source: Frei and Hill, 1990.

profit hospital chains. About 30 percent of all beds in public general hospitals are private beds that the head physician of the department and the chief residents can use for privately insured patients.

Physicians working in hospitals get a monthly salary for the treatment of patients in ordinary wards. The heads of department and some of the chief residents have the right to treat private patients, in which case they are entitled to directly charge patients who have additional insurance coverage. Thus, physicians' earnings in hospitals depend to a large extent on the number of private patients treated, on the specialty of the physicians, and on their contract with the hospital.

The hospital board normally consists of a doctor, an administrator, and a nurse. In some cantons, nursing is not represented on the board; in others, all head physicians (or a delegation of physicians) are included among the directors. In public hospitals the managerial responsibilities of the hospital board are rather limited. The board is responsible for budgeting, project management, and operations management. Strategic management decisions, however, are usually made on the superior political level, normally by the cantonal health department. Hospital board physicians have little responsibility for costs, mainly because there are no limitations on or standards for the quantity of services per case.

Ambulatory care in Switzerland is privately organized. There are about 10,300 physicians and 4,170 dentists in free practice (Frei and Hill, 1990). The number of practicing physicians increased by 37 percent in the years from 1980 to 1988, a trend that was expected to last for several more years.

In all cantons, patients have free access to both individual doctors and hospitals within the canton. If they do not go directly to a hospital or its resident physicians for ambulatory or hospital care, they can freely choose any doctor or specialist, who may then refer them for hospital treatment. When a physician decides to refer a patient for hospital treatment, he or she can choose any hospital within the canton. In practice, about 75 percent of referrals go to the regional hospital. There the patient will be treated either as an ordinary patient or (for those who have additional insurance to cover the extra cost) as a private patient. Referral to a hospital outside the canton is generally allowed for patients with additional private insurance and for special medical conditions not treated in the local hospital, such as open heart surgery.

Financing Health Care

Total expenditures for the Swiss health care system have risen from SFr 12.4 billion in 1980 to SFr 20.9 billion in 1988, with a growth rate of about 8.6 percent a year (Frei and Hill, 1990). Health care expenditures increased from 7 to 7.4 percent of the gross national product (GNP) in the same period. In other words, health expenditures are increasing at a higher rate than the GNP.

Expenditures by hospitals have amounted to almost half of all health expenditures (see Table 6.1). Practicing physicians accounted for close to a fifth of expenditures, and all other suppliers (pharmacists, dentists, and so on) for the remainder.

Financing is provided by the sickness funds, the cantons (that is, their taxpayers), private insurers, and private payers (see Table 6.1). The private component makes up one-third of health financing, which is a relatively large proportion compared with health systems in some other European countries.

Today over 99 percent of the population is insured against

the costs of disease and injury through 195 authorized sickness funds (Bundesamt für Sozialversicherung, 1992). These sickness funds get subsidies from the central government, the cantons, and the communities, but their main source of income is premiums paid by the insured. More than 20 percent of the population has some sort of private or supplementary insurance coverage. The premiums are paid fully by individuals themselves and are priced by age groups. Income situation or family size are not relevant for the computation of premiums. Employers are not normally involved in health insurance.

The number of sickness funds has dropped sharply—by 38 percent from 1978 to 1988 (Bundesamt für Sozialversicherung, 1990) and by another 46 percent from 1988 to 1991 (Bundesamt für Sozialversicherung, 1992). This concentration of the health insurance market will—according to all predictions—continue over the next few years.

The costs paid by the sickness funds are dependent on the tariff and price structure negotiated with the cantonal medical associations (for ambulatory care) and with the cantonal health department (for hospital care). As can be seen in Figure 6.1, the prices and the sum of services are negotiated on different levels. In this system it is very difficult to control costs (Güntert, 1986).

The authorized sickness funds work on two different systems of reimbursement. In the *tiers-garant* system used in some cantons, the patient gets the bill and is reimbursed by the insurance company (usually with a deduction of 10 percent). In the *tiers-payant* system used in the other cantons, the sickness fund gets the bill and pays the physician directly (see Figure 6.1). In the case of referral to a hospital, the insurer gives a guarantee to pay the bill, either as a lump sum per diem for treatment in ordinary wards (in which case diagnostic and therapeutic procedures are included) or as a fee to cover the service if the patient has private insurance.

The authorized sickness funds are represented by the Association of Swiss Sickness Funds (*Konkordat Schweizerischer Krankenkassen*), based in Solothurn. This association coordinates the efforts of the sickness funds in the different cantons,

Figure 6.1. Typical Structure of Cantonal Outpatient Health Care in Switzerland.

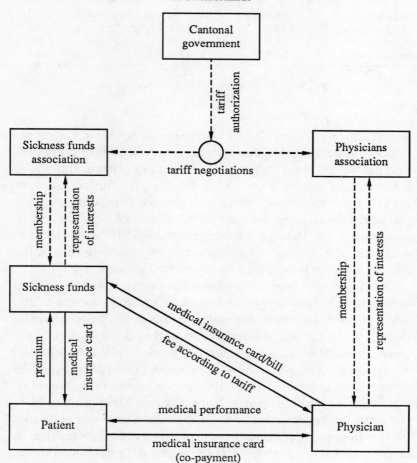

deals with the federal Social Insurance Agency, and tries to influence health policy in Switzerland.

The sickness funds are supplemented by private health insurance companies, which normally base their coverage in part on what the sickness funds do. However, they also provide

Table 6.3. Composition of Swiss Hospital Costs, 1989.

Salaries	72.8%	Energy and water supply	1.5%
Medical supply	10.5	Capital interest	4.7
Hotel supply	4.6	Administration	2.1
Equipment	2.6	Other	1.0

Source: Vereinigung Schweizerischer Krankenhaüser, 1990.

additional coverage. The Swiss National Accident Insurance Fund (*Schweizerische Unfallversicherungsanstalt*, or SUVA) and several private accident insurers also play an important role in the financing of health care. SUVA used to be the compulsory accident insurer for industrial firms and construction and transportation companies. Because SUVA provides insurance in all cantons and has to negotiate with the Swiss Medical Association and with hospitals in all cantons, it plays a leading role in the development of health care tariffs in Switzerland.

Hospital expenditures for acute care account for 77 percent of total hospital expenditures in Switzerland. Between 1980 and 1988, total hospital expenditures increased by 80 percent; that is, by 10 percent annually (Frei and Hill, 1990). The composition of hospital costs (1989) is given in Table 6.3. When analyzing the composition of the running costs of hospitals in Switzerland, one has to know that amortization of investments is not included in these figures. Normally, investments are paid by the cantonal government and—up to now—have not appeared in the hospitals' cost accounting. However, this situation is changing with the new cost accounting model introduced by the Swiss Hospital Association (VESKA) in the summer of 1992.

The sickness funds in most cantons pay a flat rate per patient day, the amount of which is negotiated between the sickness funds and the cantonal governments and is updated every two to three years. This rate covers, on the average, about 48 percent of the operating costs of public acute-care hospitals (Frei and Hill, 1990). The rest is paid with tax money from the cantonal or local government, according to the ownership of the hospital. This system has the disadvantage that neither the cantonal and local governments nor the sickness funds are genuinely interested in cost containment because there is no single agency responsible for covering the entire costs. The government always has the possibility of reducing its share by increasing the flat rate per day for health insurance; the sickness funds, in turn, try to reduce their share through successful negotiations.

In most cantons, the sickness funds have to pay costly procedures such as computer tomography, renal dialysis, and intensive care in addition to the day charges. Diagnostic and therapeutic procedures not included in the daily rate are reimbursed according to a so-called hospital tariff developed by SUVA and the Swiss Hospital Association (*Vereinigung Schweizerischer Krankenhäuser*, or VESKA). The tariff catalogue used in most cantons lists over 1,500 medical procedures and attributes a certain number of points (Taxpunkte) to each of them. In the treatment of ordinary patients, benefits are paid on the basis of negotiated monetary values attached to the points. For private patients, the monetary value for the tariff points for the different procedures is higher. From time to time the point system for a group of diagnostic or therapeutic procedures is reassessed on the basis of cost analysis in about fifteen reference hospitals. To do this, a special commission (Medizinal-Tarif-Kommission) was established in 1976, with representatives from sickness funds, SUVA, private insurers, hospitals, and cantons. This commission is especially active in evaluating new technologies such as computer tomography, MRI, ultrasonography, and so on. It finds it difficult, however, to agree on an average cost level as a basis to compute the points, because the hospitals vary greatly from one to the other. Most procedures, including all surgical procedures, have never been analyzed or measured. All costs are therefore at best good estimates.

Private patients pay a higher daily rate and an extra charge for certain diagnostic and therapeutic procedures. They normally are treated by the head physicians or the chief residents and get a little bit more luxury in the form of single or double rooms.

In most cantons the government (mainly cantonal) covers

the subsidies and deficits of the hospitals. This sum amounts to 30 percent of the total operating budget and is met by the taxpayer. The cantonal government also usually finances all or a large part of the investment costs. This is how the infrastructure is coordinated, and with it the supply of hospital services in the cantonal hospital system.

In recent years activities in the area of outpatient care have started in some cantons. The goal is to care for the ill in their own homes at a reasonable price. The amount of money flowing into this domain increased by 45 percent from 1986 to 1988. However, the financing mechanisms for extramural nursing care have not yet been clearly defined. In particular, there is no uniform regulation of the share contributed by the sickness funds. The cantons contribute from 30 to 80 percent, depending on their health care policy.

Physicians in private practice are reimbursed by a fee-for-service system. The fees are fixed by negotiation between the cantonal medical associations and the cantonal sickness fund associations. The private physicians are financed by the sickness funds (64 percent), by private insurers and patients paying directly (32 percent), and by other health insurers (4 percent) (Frei and Hill, 1990).

For a long time health care costs did not seem to be a substantial problem in Switzerland. The stable economic situation (the statistics showed a steady increase in the GNP) was overriding the health care cost explosion on the macro level. However, in the last few years, the health care sector has consumed an increasing share of the GNP (see Table 6.1), and the competition for funds between health care and other sectors has been increasing. Initially, the strategy of most cantonal governments was to stabilize or even to reduce the proportion of health care costs in their total expenditure. Depending on the involvement of the communities in financing investments in health care and hospital operating costs, this proportion varies between 17 and 22 percent of the total cantonal budget (Güntert and others, 1988). However, stabilizing public funding of health care has led to an increase in the financial involvement of the sickness funds. Insurance premiums have increased at a higher-than-average rate over the last few years. Since 1990, these premiums have exploded: the increase for 1990–1991 averaged 12 to 13 percent, and the increase for 1991–1992 was estimated at 15 to 20 percent (Bundesamt für Sozialversicherung, 1991). This situation has led to massive public criticism of health care and its financing system. The federal government is now intervening for the first time and intends to establish urgent new regulations on health care financing. However, these new regulations will not include changes in the structure of the system. Instead, they will focus on regulated price and cost development (Bundesamt für Sozialversicherung, 1991).

Controlling Health Care Expenditures

In Switzerland, a routine hospital statistics system was implemented in the early 1970s. This system was developed and is still run by VESKA. Basically, participation in the statistics is voluntary and paid by the participating hospital; between 30 and 40 percent of acute-care hospital stays are currently covered by the VESKA statistics. However, since the mid 1970s, four cantons (Zurich, Ticino, Vaud, and Valais) have made these statistics mandatory for the publicly funded hospitals.

The content of the VESKA statistics was strongly influenced by the hospital discharge survey in the United States and is very close to the minimum data base set developed in Europe since 1982 within the framework of the Biomedical Information Systems of the European Study Group on Advanced Informatics in Medicine (BICEPS-EUROAIM) (Lambert and Roger, 1982). The hospital *stay* is the basic unit for sampling and collecting information on demographic features of the patient, the diagnosis, and the procedures performed during the stay. The hospital *department* is the unit considered for data collection; therefore all data, such as length of stay, diagnosis, procedures, and provenance of the patient, refer to a single hospital department and not to the hospital as a whole.

There are two other major features of the VESKA system that deserve specific comment. First, data collection is highly decentralized: all statistical information is coded within each

department of each hospital, including diagnostic and pro-
cedural codes; only a minimal control is performed in Bern,
where the files are centralized. Second, specific VESKA codes
have been used for diagnostic and surgical procedures from
the beginning. The diagnostic coding scheme (Vereinigung
Schweizerischer Krankenhäuser, 1987) has been strongly supported by the World Health Organization. There are, however,
several embarrassing differences when mapping this code with
others (Eggli, Grimm, and Paccaud, 1987b, p. 104). The procedures coding scheme is specific to Switzerland and is regularly
updated (Vereinigung Schweizerischer Krankenhäuser, 1986);
the problem of mapping with other codes is, of course, still more
important than the problem of mapping with diagnosis codes
(Eggli, Grimm, and Paccaud, 1987b, p. 104; 1987a, p. 53).

For many years, the main use of the VESKA statistics has
been as a computerized file of hospital cases by the participating
hospital departments for internal purposes only. The first systematic use of the VESKA files was made in the early 1980s by a
research team led by T. Abelin (Abelin and others, 1984). Several
epidemiological topics were addressed in that study, such as
trends in hospitalization for myocardial infarction (Berweger,
Küng, and Abelin, 1987), hepatitis B, or chronic lung diseases
(Abelin, 1989). One remarkable result of this study has been an
assessment of the quality of these routine hospital statistics
(Berweger and Fahrni, 1985; Berweger and others, 1985). Other
health services topics were considered by this research project
(Fahrni, Patil, and Abelin, 1984; Minder and Abelin, 1986),
although it was not a major line of investigation. At the same
time, other researchers used these routine statistics for specific
epidemiological ends; for example, as a quality control tool for
death statistics (Paccaud, 1984).

The uncurbed development of costs is gradually becoming worrisome for politicians, the sickness funds, and the general public. Expenditures on health by each of these sectors are
increasing rapidly. Therefore strategies to control costs must be
sought on different levels.

The fee-for-service system in the ambulatory health care
sector has been strongly criticized because of the risk of an

increase in the demand for physicians' services, which would lead to high costs. It would also boost the number of practitioners because doctors have an attractive position in the health care market and high social status (Sommer, 1983). Basic reforms in the structure of the ambulatory care system can, however, scarcely be realized. For political reasons, free choice of a doctor or specialist and private organization of the ambulatory services cannot be done away with. In the ambulatory health care sector, one strategy is to move toward an increase in copayments by the insured. Another is to improve the ability of the sickness funds to ensure that high standards of care are maintained. Both proposals are part of the current attempt to revise the health insurance law, which dates back to 1918.

The introduction of global budgets is being discussed in some limited areas of the ambulatory health care sector (for example, for the medication prescribed by doctors in the canton of Solothurn). A first attempt was made at a health maintenance organization (*HMO*) in 1989 in Zürich on the initiative of a group of sickness funds and health economists. They formed a study group for alternative health insurance systems, and this study group prepared the ground for HMOs. Further attempts with HMOs have been started in Zürich and Basel; more are planned in other cities, some of which will be realized in the next few years. The study group is evaluating the model projects together with the federal Social Insurance Agency (*Bundesamt für Sozialversicherung*).

Reduction of costs in the nonambulatory health care sector is proving to be far more difficult. Since the running costs of the public hospitals are financed partly by the sickness funds and partly by the cantons, no party has a particular interest in tackling the overall costs. For a long time each party has limited itself to reducing or stabilizing its own proportion of costs. The cantons and other owners of public hospitals, for instance communities, then began to influence not only the investment costs but increasingly the running costs as well through a rigid budget system. With the control of investment costs an attempt has been made to control the potential supply of health care services through a graded care system (that is, hospitals with differing care levels). Since an exact definition of care levels is difficult, most cantonal hospital planning boards are content with a general description and a definition of bed capacities (Staatskanzlei St. Gallen, 1986). In its recent hospital planning the canton of Zürich has tried to relate epidemiological data according to VESKA codes to capacity data (Direktion des Gesundheitswesens..., 1990). However, there are problems with assigning VESKA codes for predicted developments to specific hospital departments or services. The VESKA coding system (a variation of ICD9) simply does not suffice as a basis for planning investments in new capacities and technology.

In order to come to grips with hospital running costs, most cantons have introduced a more or less rigid budgeting scheme. As Figure 6.2 shows, cost containment on this basis has not been very successful.

In contrast to the cantons, the sickness funds cannot directly influence the supply of and demand for hospital services or the standard of care in the hospital. The contractual reimbursements have to be paid. The funds only have the possibility of exercising pressure for cost containment on a political level.

On the hospital level there has likewise not been much reason to control cost development for a long time. On account of the rigid budget mechanisms and the many handicaps set by higher authorities, no active hospital management has been able to develop. The biggest handicaps have been the strong influence of the political system on strategic management decision making and the insufficiency of hospital management information systems, mostly due to lack of responsibility for costs (Güntert, 1990b). Administrative and medical data can scarcely be related to each other, cost accounting based on cost centers is not related to patients, quality cannot be recorded in a routine manner, and environmental data are normally missing. The poor data situation is hampered by the lack of standardization possibilities (Ulrich, 1987). New financing models have only just recently been applied in some cantons (Zweifel and Pedroni, 1987), and these do make new demands on hospital management with regard to cost containment. Besides the academic interest in using patient classification models for planning,

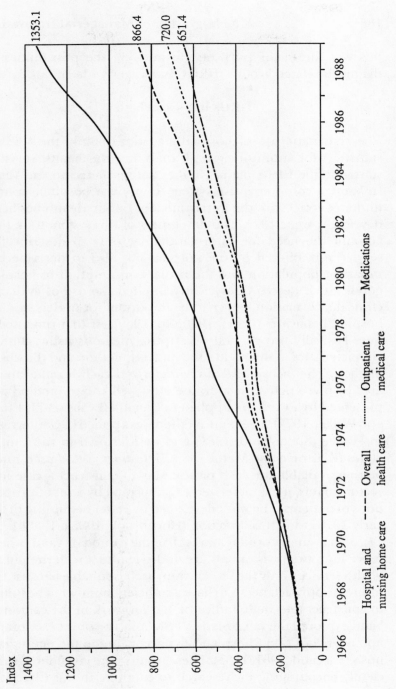

Figure 6.2. Rises in Health Care Costs per Insured Party, 1966–1989.

this was the major purpose for studying the possibilities of diagnosis-related groups (DRGs) in Switzerland.

DRGs in Switzerland

The systematic use of hospital statistics (mainly the VESKA statistics) for monitoring and analyzing the health services started in the 1980s, mainly in the cantons of Ticino and Vaud. In Vaud, a comprehensive system to monitor hospital services under contract with the Department of Public Health has been developed since 1975. The developers of this system took into account the need for information not only to describe the service mix offered by the hospital but also to describe the inpatient population and the actual consumption of hospital goods. Such descriptions clearly implied the use of available clinical information known to be important for understanding hospital behaviors (Berry, 1970; Ro, 1969). At that time, there were basically two general descriptive methods using clinical characteristics of inpatients: the indirect method and the direct method. The *indirect method* characterized each hospital in an area by one single indicator; the most well-known method was presented by Evans and applied to Canada (Evans, 1971; Evans and Walker, 1972). The same method was applied by Souteyrand in France (Souteyrand, 1981) and by Klastorin in the United States (Klastorin and Watts, 1980). The *direct method* used information available for each patient stay to construct a case mix vector; that is, it characterized each hospital by a set of proportions of patients. The work developed by Fetter beginning in the early 1970s took this direction (Hornbrook, 1982a, 1982b).

In a small hospital market like the canton of Vaud (where fewer than twenty hospitals are under contract with the public health service), only the second approach is suitable because the indirect approach needs to have a sufficient number of hospitals to construct the single indicator. Earlier work in the canton of Vaud explored the value of the VESKA statistics for describing a homogeneous set of hospital stays according to the main diagnosis (Paccaud, 1981, 1983). These results were considered sufficiently encouraging for research to continue in this direction.

The Case Mix Study in Lausanne

In 1980, the publication by Robert Fetter and his group presenting the first DRG scheme (Fetter and others, 1980) provided firm
evidence that routine hospital statistics combining most of the
available information (including all the diagnosis and procedures codes) could describe the variety of situations present in
acute-care hospitals. The adoption of DRGs by several health
administrations in the United States for prospective reimbursement schemes and the emerging interest in some European
countries, especially the United Kingdom (Sanderson and Andrews, 1984) were important indications that case mix schemes
were coming of age. Despite the fact that several case mix
systems were available—some of which are currently under investigation in Europe (Leidl, Potthoff, and Schwefel, 1990)—the
DRG scheme was rapidly identified as the most promising way
to carry out investigations in Switzerland.

In 1983, several health administrations (mainly those in
the Italian- and French-speaking parts of Switzerland) agreed to
undertake a study of DRGs. This study, set up by nine cantons
and conducted by the Division of Health Services Research of
the Institute of Social and Preventive Medicine of the University
of Lausanne, started in 1984 and ended in 1988. The aim of this
study was to establish how DRGs could be used within the Swiss
context. More specifically, the purpose of the study was to test
the applicability of the U.S. DRG scheme to Swiss hospital
statistics, to clarify the conditions of use of DRGs, and to develop some examples of DRG use.

This study provided substantial information on the use of
DRGs in Swiss hospitals, more specifically on the practical problems posed by the use of DRGs as a tool for the monitoring and
analysis of the health services. The study results have been
published in summary (Etude Casemix, 1989), and complete
results can be found in Paccaud and Schenker (1989, 1990).
Specific recommendations have been made to the participating
cantons and to communities running hospitals (Paccaud and
Schenker, 1989; Gutzwiller, 1989).

The data base for the study was provided by VESKA,

although other hospital statistics were also used. Information on about 100,000 hospital stays per year was available for the study. From the beginning, specific VESKA codes were used for Swiss diagnosis and surgical procedures. The first step of the study was to transform these codes into U.S. codes (ICD9-CM codes), allowing direct use of the Yale grouper for DRGs. It was decided to carry out the code transformation before using the Yale grouper (see Figure 6.3). This procedure allowed the large majority of hospital stays to be classified: only 3 percent of stays were not attributed, half of which, however, were on account of the lack of precision in the Swiss codes.

The second step showed that overall performance of the DRG scheme was similar to what had been observed in the United States. More specifically, the variability of the length of stay within DRGs was found to be similar in Switzerland and the United States despite the fact that mean length-of-stay values are substantially higher in Switzerland. Figure 6.4 shows the distribution of DRGs according to the length of stay in Switzerland and the United States; Figure 6.5 shows the distribution of DRGs according to the coefficient of variation in Switzerland.

Similar observations have been made when comparing DRGs in Australia and Switzerland: lengths of stay in Australia are substantially longer than in Switzerland, but the coefficient of variation follows the same distribution, being even somewhat lower in Switzerland than in Australia.

A further analysis undertaken in Switzerland shows that DRGs are able to reduce about 29 percent of the overall variability of length of stay, although this proportion varies among hospitals. Analyses of other aspects of homogeneity were either less favorable (homogeneity of medico-technical procedures, hierarchy of surgical procedures) or simply ignored certain items (clinical homogeneity of DRGs); however, this exercise provided evidence that there is a remarkable stability in the performance of DRGs independent of local length-of-stay values. This was taken as an argument that a DRG scheme has some general capacity to describe the inpatient case mix.

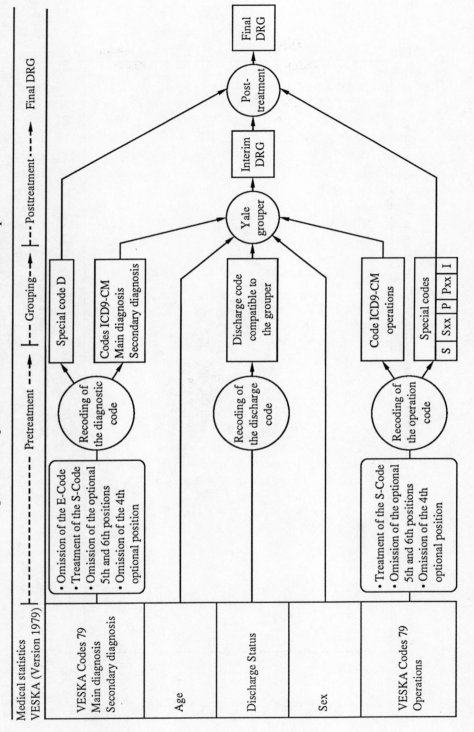

Figure 6.3. Adaptation of VESKA Data to the Yale Grouper.

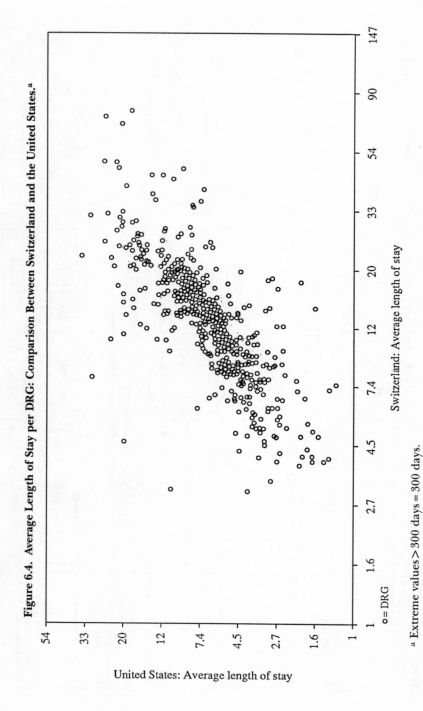

Figure 6.4. Average Length of Stay per DRG: Comparison Between Switzerland and the United States.[a]

Switzerland: Average length of stay

United States: Average length of stay

o = DRG

[a] Extreme values > 300 days = 300 days.

Figure 6.5. Distribution of DRGs by Coefficient of Variation: Switzerland and the United States.

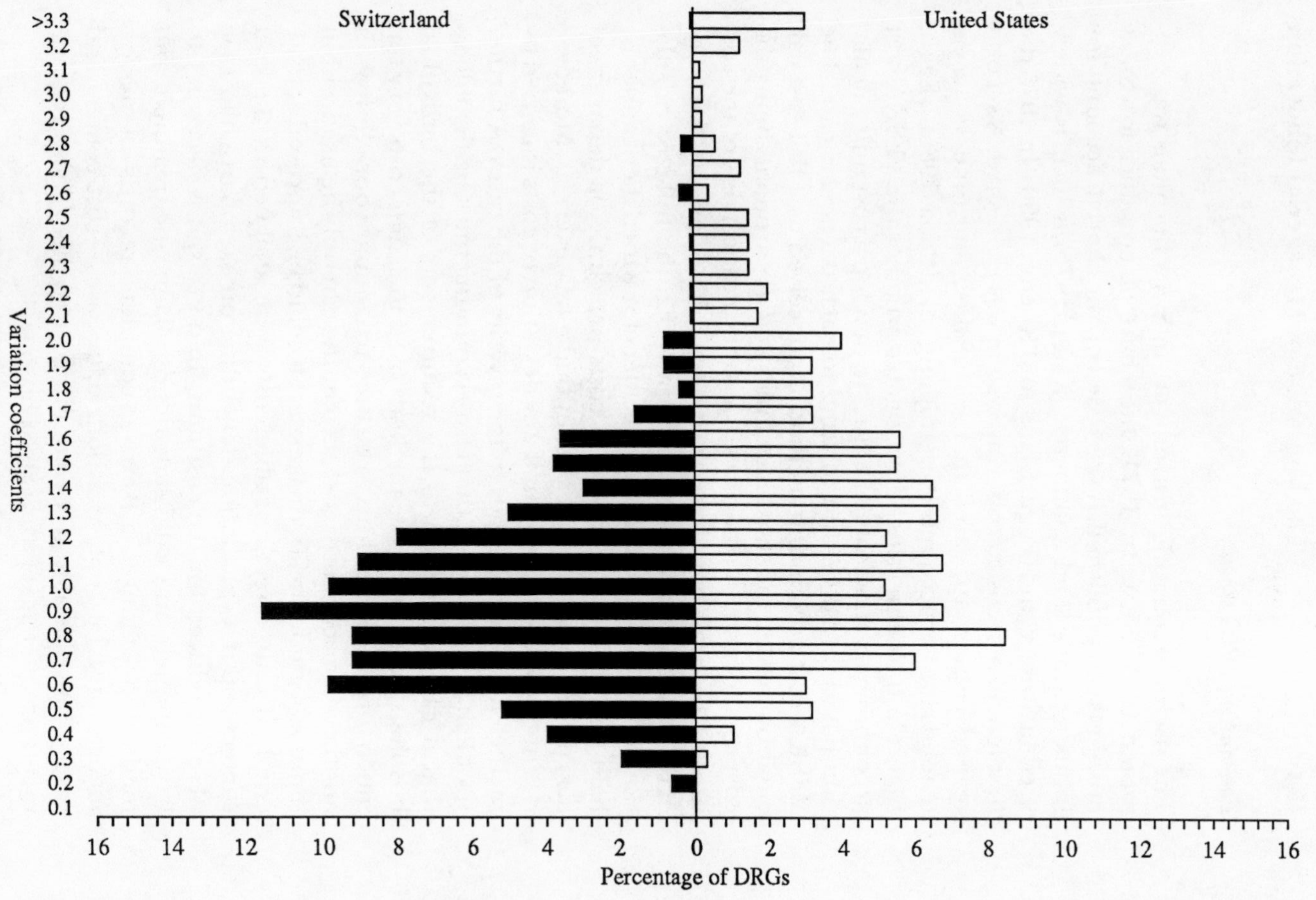

Estimating DRG Costs

The use of accounting instruments in Swiss hospitals was promoted by VESKA. In 1971, the chart of accounts for Swiss hospitals was published. It was based on the chart of accounts for industry, trade, and commerce (Käfer, 1975), which is widely used in Switzerland (Eggli, Blanc, and Koehn, 1990). In 1975 the first model of a cost accounting system was published. A second revised edition appeared in 1985 at the same time as an extended chart of accounts (Vereinigung. . . , 1985a, 1985b). Eggli, Blanc, and Koehn (1990) investigated whether the VESKA cost accounting method could be used to develop a cost unit calculation based on DRGs and relating to each particular case. The VESKA cost accounting method is conceived as a full-cost calculation model, with hospital clinics and departments being the cost centers and, in some cases, also the cost centers of the cost units. Cost unit accounting with regard to patients does not exist. One criticism of this concept is that the full-cost calculation model assigns costs to cost centers for which they cannot be held responsible. Average case costs per clinic or department also do not show the causes of any budgetary excesses. Moreover, it is not possible to find out if any deviation of costs is caused by inefficiency or by changes in the severity of the cases. A further problem lies in the fact that cost accounting must be flexible so that it can be adapted to the requirements of the individual hospitals. At present, the methods used to assign costs vary too much for the calculations to be used to compare one clinic with another. Consequently, cost accounting can only be used within limits as a guideline. In this respect it could be improved considerably if only direct, variable costs were assigned to the cost centers and if a calculation depending on each particular case were introduced for the cost unit. To do this, it is necessary to have complete and valid statistics on diagnostic treatment and medical procedures. Likewise, complete records of performance must be kept, and both data bases — cost centers and cases — must be able to be combined together. These requirements are met at very few Swiss hospitals.

Statistics on diagnoses and operations are usually not

kept on a standardized basis by the different departments. Only approximately 40 percent of all departments are taking part in the VESKA statistics program (Vereinigung. . . , 1986, 1987). In particular, there are large gaps in the statistics on surgical procedures performed since many surgical departments only keep statistics on the diagnoses. It is also rare to come across hospitals with integral records on performance since this is not required in the general departmental statistics on patients.

The choice of case groups presents a further problem. The DRG system with 472 patient categories is only applicable in university hospitals or large cantonal hospitals. It is already necessary for hospitals with 5,000–8,000 patients a year to reduce the number of categories as otherwise too few cases would be recorded for each category. In smaller hospitals, which make up the large majority in Switzerland, a reduction of 100–150 groups would be required. For the further development of hospital cost accounting, a minimal standardization of rules in the area of defining and splitting up the costs should be striven for.

In an exploratory study (Morraz and Patel, 1990), the researchers attempted to determine the total costs for patients with specific illnesses, using data already in existence. In doing so, large difficulties became evident in obtaining and processing the necessary data. The authors, therefore, had to limit themselves to three pathologies (appendectomy, hernia recovery, and transurethral prostate resection). The way labor costs were recorded turned out to present a special problem.

As a necessary basis for cost allocation to procedures or diagnosis, primary data have to be obtained systematically and on a regular basis. According to the authors, keeping such records on a regular basis is not common in hospitals. The ratio obtained by analyzing work and machine hours needed and splitting costs between cost centers and procedures can only be regarded as stable on a short- or medium-term basis. Therefore it is necessary to update such cost studies periodically, which is very time-consuming and expensive.

Koehn, Schenker, and Patel (1990), in addition to undertaking the calculation of overall costs, also investigated use of the American DRG evaluation, of estimation by means of regressions, and of DRG evaluations specific to cost centers as further ways to determine DRG charges. The American evaluation did not turn out to be usable. Regressions are indeed methodologically possible but require a data base that cannot be realized in Switzerland, and theoretical problems in interpretation would be expected. Foreign evaluations of the DRG per cost center, similar to those being used in France, the United Kingdom, and the United States, seemed to be the only possible usable method. These evaluations could be adapted to Swiss conditions, at least until a cost accounting model based on the individual cases is introduced.

Financing and Management of Hospitals

The use of DRGs to finance hospitals by set rates, as practiced in the United States, has not been recommended for Switzerland (Eggli, Koehn, and Schenker, 1990; Schenker and Paccaud, 1990). The reasons for this include the differences in the organization of the public hospital services, the still insufficient data base (in terms of both quality and quantity), the difficulties of defining charges for DRGs, and reservations with regard to the clinical homogeneity of DRGs. However, the use of DRGs has been recommended for consideration when calculating the level of prospective global hospital budgets (Eggli, Koehn, and Schenker, 1990).

In the area of hospital management, DRGs serve to incorporate the medical dimension into management. Through a DRG-oriented accounting system, physicians can be shown their responsibility for hospital costs. Such a system forces physicians to play an active role in cost containment and in the management of hospitals (Sagmeister, 1991). Since DRGs can be interpreted as products of the hospital work, they offer a good basis for the introduction of a matrix organization (Eggli, Blanc, and Schenker, 1990). DRGs are also a good indicator of hospital performance. They are an excellent way to improve a hospital's management information system, to connect medical data with administrative data, and to develop management-oriented indicators (Güntert, 1990b). Used in cost management, the DRG system allows the causes of budgetary deviations (cost deviation, changed spectrum of efficiency, changes in the case mix) to be investigated (Eggli, Blanc, and Schenker, 1990).

In a further study, the tools for an inter-institutional case mix comparison were presented, and such a comparison was made of three hospitals. In doing so, summarized indicators of different aspects of the clientele were used (number of DRGs at a hospital; number of DRGs that cover half of all cases), and analyses were made according to the most frequent DRGs and the DRGs that showed the greatest number of hospitalization days (Eggli, Koehn, and Paccaud, 1990).

Koehn, Paccaud, and Eggli (1990) discussed standardization methods based on DRGs and drew standardized comparisons of the lengths of stay. They investigated differences between the average length of stay in individual hospitals and standard lengths of stay. Their analyses enabled them to judge to what extent the hospital itself was responsible for the length of stay through its treatment and care pattern and the influence of its case mix and to what extent the length of stay was influenced by circumstances.

Koehn, Eggli, and Paccaud (1990) made a comparison of the lengths of stay for selected DRGs in Australia, Belgium, Finland, Norway, Sweden, Switzerland, and the United States. The lengths of stay varied considerably in almost every respect, with the United States having the shortest and Switzerland the longest average lengths of stay. It is important to note that the validity of such comparisons may be reduced by national characteristics in the coding system and by the quality of the coding. Yet differences certainly exist, although nothing can be said yet as to how far these differences can be traced back to economic, social, or medical causes. Also missing in this comparison were countries such as Austria or Germany, which would compare better with Switzerland than some of the others. Nevertheless, the authors of this study are justified in concluding that there is still considerable potential in Switzerland for a reduction in the duration of stays.

The use of DRGs to simulate scenarios for hospital planning is furthest developed in Switzerland. A simulation model called SIMULIT (Grimm and Paccaud, 1986, 1987) has been developed for this purpose. To simulate activities in acute-care hospitals, the model draws on certain basic characteristics of patients' movements and the population the hospital is serving. It allows different working hypotheses to be investigated and the effects of demographic, epidemiological, and health-related political scenarios to be studied. The model was used for hospital planning in the canton of Vaud to investigate how the hospitalization rate, lengths of stay, and occupancy rate would develop in relation to population development (migration, demographic aging, and changes in different clinical groups formed by DRG merging). Changes in hospitalization rates, lengths of stay, and treatment patterns have also been analyzed for how they affect the need for planning. The model allows the inclusion of daily and seasonal fluctuations, which enables much more realistic planning than mere annual averages. For example, the daily occupancy rate fluctuates approximately 40 percent on average. This indicates possibilities for improvements in the area of patient admission (Paccaud, Grimm, and Koehn, 1990).

DRGs do not contribute only to planning nonambulatory acute care. They can also be useful as a basis for planning long-term care in conjunction with data on demographic development. This allows for greater accuracy in terms of supply matching demand (Sagmeister, 1991).

Diffusion of DRGs

The Lausanne case mix study played an important role in the academic field for diffusion of the DRG concept. Health economists, planners, and managers are now discussing the DRG concept and its possible implications for the Swiss health care system. Although all the conceptual work has been done, a major breakthrough in the implementation of the DRG concept at the federal level cannot be expected in the near future. There are several reasons for this.

In the first place, federal action is inhibited by cantonal responsibilities for the health care sector. In the second place, there has been no direct support of the concept by the sickness funds up to now. They find the DRG concept very complicated and the efforts required for its implementation too demanding. In the third place, physicians have expressed major concerns regarding the structure and the homogeneity of DRGs. They are using their political power to hinder the implementation of DRGs.

Up to now, the political pressures for structural changes — such as the introduction of a prospective payment system based on patient classification — have simply not been strong enough. However, this is beginning to change. Besides the Lausanne case mix study and the related projects in the canton of Vaud, there have been some efforts in other places to promote the DRG model.

The health department of the canton of Valais intends to introduce a DRG system, primarily for allocation of medical services and for analyses of the lengths of stay of the different patient groups. Prior to a definite introduction, pilot projects will be launched in order to define information needs, to test information systems and their application possibilities, and to provide thorough training for the people in charge. An agreement that introduction of a comprehensive hospital information system was an essential requirement for the implementation of the DRG model was first obtained from the different partners, in particular the hospitals.

In the canton of Zürich there has been a parliamentary enquiry into the use of the DRG model instead of daily flat rates as a basis for financing hospitals. The Interdisciplinary Research Center for Public Health in St. Gallen was commissioned to develop a methodology for calculating DRG costs based on the Swiss hospital cost accounting system (Güntert and Sagmeister, 1989). A task force of hospital administrators under the leadership of the secretary of the Zürich Hospital Association, Hermann Plüss, is working on a methodology for estimating DRG costs. The problem the task force faces is the structure of the cost accounting model used in Swiss hospitals. This model is cost-center–oriented, not patient-oriented. Computing the costs for individual patients is not possible with the present cost accounting system. More clarity is needed (Plüss, 1992).

In the canton of Ticino, the hospital association, which represents all hospitals of the canton, has been commissioned to examine the possibilities DRGs offer for cost containment. In addition, interest in the DRG concept has been shown by the public health administration of the canton of Geneva, which is watching very closely all developments in this field (Rey, 1991).

These efforts to further the diffusion of DRGs are being made difficult by the fact that most of the hospitals and the sickness funds do not have appropriate information systems yet to generate and combine the medical and administrative data as needed. Hospitals and sickness funds are often critical of DRGs because of their complexity, and they therefore prefer to stay with the status quo, the simple system of flat rates per hospital day.

Further efforts to spread the DRG concept are being made by the Swiss Study Group on DRGs, founded in 1989. Some of its members are opinion leaders of the Swiss health system, some are involved to a greater extent with DRG projects, and some hold important positions in the Swiss health care system. The aim of the study group is to exchange information on current projects and results as well as to coordinate activities promoting the use of DRGs in Switzerland. The study group also keeps itself informed on DRG-related developments in other European countries.

Another task of the Swiss Study Group on DRGs is to argue for the necessity of patient classification systems in Switzerland and for a standardized basis for management of the health system. For this purpose the study group meets three or four times a year, publishes the widely distributed *DRG Newsletter*, and organizes conferences and meetings on DRG topics.

The Future of DRGs in Switzerland

Neither the federal Agency for Public Health nor the federal Agency of Social Security have forced fundamental changes in the health care system. Several attempts have been made in the last few years to revise the health insurance system (Güntert, 1990a, 1991). However, they all failed in the political process. A prospective payment system based on patient classification has not been proposed yet, and there are no known official statements by federal agencies on this topic. The agencies' interest in the Lausanne case mix study and other studies has been low, and they have offered no substantial financial support for studies conducted in this field.

There is considerably more interest being shown at the cantonal level. In addition to the DRG projects conducted in the canton of Vaud and the projects in the cantons of Zürich and Valais, the cantons of Geneva and Bern are now showing a particular interest in the DRG concept.

There are no concrete projects being planned in Geneva at the moment. The main reason why Geneva cannot work on the planned implementation yet is that the current, very sophisticated management information system (DIOGENE) at the university hospital, the major hospital in the canton, works with a unique coding system for diagnosis. Unfortunately, the patient classification system used is based on an older version of the ICD code and is not compatible with the VESKA code or with ICD9. Therefore the transcoder and grouper developed in the Lausanne case mix study cannot be used.

In the canton of Bern, on the other hand, experiments with three different financing models for hospitals are to be carried out and evaluated in the next five years. The financing models will have to support both the economic and the daily management of hospitals. The first model allows for a modest daily flat rate for infrastructure costs and all services that cannot be allocated to individual patients, a nursing supplementary charge, and a fee-for-service reimbursement for services that can be allocated. A strict budgeting approach is being planned in the second model. The hospital will be responsible for keeping the costs within the budget, and the government will subsidize the hospital according to the planned budget. In the third model, a modified prospective payment system is finally to form a basis of reimbursement for the patients in general wards. This model bears a similarity to the DRG model. The actual costs of a

DRG will be the starting point for reimbursement. However, imposing such a system could raise problems because the cost accounting model used is not oriented toward the patient but toward the cost centers. The implementation of the DRG model is also thought to be very demanding. However, the expectations of the cantonal health department for this model are indeed very high (Fehr and Joder, 1991).

In September 1991, the legal basis for these experiments was set up in the canton of Bern. Participation in the experimental stage is voluntary for the hospitals. The whole attempt was scheduled to begin in 1993, to last for three years, and to be periodically evaluated. It will apply to regularly insured patients only, not to patients with additional private insurance coverage. It is planned to incorporate at least two hospitals per model. If other suggestions arise, the experiment can be expanded to other models (Jaggi, 1992).

Recent developments in this experiment have revealed some problems. The regional hospital in Thun is willing to take part and to test the modified DRG approach. However, the modifications needed for the cost accounting and information system are significant. At the beginning of the experiment, the hospital will only be able to define one patient group (such as general surgery, orthopedic surgery, or internal medicine) for each cost center or medical clinic. More detailed information is not yet available, but the system will be improved step by step during the experiment. Although the sophisticated Yale system with 477 DRGs will not be introduced, for the first time in public hospitals in Switzerland a prospective payment system will be implemented.

Activities in the Insurance Sector

The concordat of the Swiss sickness funds has up to now shown little interest in changing the financial setup to a prospective payment system. Great reserve has been shown with regard to both health maintenance organizations and DRGs. Some individual sickness funds, however, have shown themselves to be more eager to experiment. At present, at least two of the major sickness funds are striving for concrete projects with patient classification systems. An earlier attempt by one of the sickness funds to set up such a project with a private hospital in the canton of Zürich fell through in 1990 following the objection of the cantonal health insurance funds association. Just recently (May 1992), however, the health insurance association of the French part of Switzerland signed a contract with two privately owned hospitals that specialized in cardiac surgery but also provided other services like obstetrics. This contract is still opposed by the cantonal medical associations of Vaud and Geneva, but the two hospitals and the health insurance association want to implement it for their major patient categories (Audétat, 1992).

It is also known that the Swiss Accident Insurance Company (SUVA) is studying the implementation of a prospective payment system. With regard to this approach, SUVA hopes to get answers to the following questions (Bapst, 1992):

- Is a given hospitalization really necessary?
- Is a given hospitalization in the appropriate institutional setting?
- Is the length of stay in an appropriate relation to the diagnosis?
- Do the costs follow the objectives of efficiency and appropriateness of treatment?

Together with the private chain of acute-care hospitals called Hirslanden/AMI, SUVA is working on a pilot project to implement a patient classification system and on prospective payment. However, this model will only be available for patient groups related to accidents, and it is still not clear whether the DRG model or another patient classification system will be applied. SUVA is fully in favor of using the DRG model, but a complete DRG system will not be needed. Fifty percent of their patients' hospital days can be accounted for with 14 DRGs, while an additional 27 percent of SUVA cases can be accounted for with 20 DRGs. The private hospital chain is more suited for this experiment than public hospitals because its collection of data for its management information and accounting systems is patient oriented, very detailed, and much more developed than the information systems in most public hospitals.

Activities on the Hospital Level

In the regional hospital of Morges in the canton of Vaud, an information system is presently being introduced that allows DRG applications and more extensive case groupings and analyses (Jacot, 1990). The medical description of patients is made easier by means of a clear text facility and coding help. The main element of this system is a thesaurus containing approximately 28,000 expressions in actual use, which are recoded into different classifications (for example, ICD9, ICD9-CM). Further modifications are used that allow the degree of development and certainty of the diagnosis to be described as well as the treatment to be registered. The effort involved on the part of the doctor for clarification and treatment is directly recorded. A simple system for recording the nursing data completes the medical dimension. On the strength of this data base, the information system is in the position of directly grouping the cases into DRGs and thereby carrying out cost analyses. Additionally, a number of analyses can be made that are more adaptable to the requirements of information and management within the hospital.

On a general note, it can be observed that hospital information systems are being improved. The collection of data is increasingly being carried out with reference to individual patients, and the diagnoses are forming a more and more integral part of the patients' records. Thus, the requirements for the application of the DRG concept are set. We do not know of any concrete plans for its introduction and application apart from the above-mentioned examples. However, the modern hospital information systems will allow more accurate information to be collected on a patient basis. Thus, many of the present reservations against DRGs will disappear. Therefore, it can be expected that the more the hospitals are pressured to work on cost containment, the more they will move toward alternative financing systems.

All these activities show that there is a wide interest in the DRG concept. There are people in different fields interested in using this model, either as a base for a prospective payment system, as a planning tool, or just as a way to improve information on hospital performance. However, because of the strongly differentiated structure of the Swiss health care system, all these attempts remain at the cantonal level. For cantonal authorities, it is very costly and risky to conduct their own projects in this field: the matter is very complicated, there are too few skilled people in Switzerland, and the resources are scarce. Therefore, many cantons, health insurance organizations, and hospitals remain rather passive at present. On the political level there has not been much attempt at fundamental changes in the system. However, this could change dramatically given the cost increases expected in the near future and the growing political pressure for changes in the Swiss health care system.

Epilogue

The most recent developments in the Swiss health care system are dominated by significant cuts in public budgets on all levels (federal, cantonal, and community). The worldwide economic recession is affecting the financial situation of the public sector and private households. Therefore, the pressure for cost containment in hospitals, as well as in the ambulatory health care sector, has increased substantially since 1991. In response, the federal government has proposed an update of the urgent regulations on health care financing for 1993. The main idea of this proposal, which still has to pass the parliament, is to freeze the health insurance premiums on the one hand, and the rates for hospital care and the tariffs for outpatient services on the other. Sickness funds and the providers of health services are opposing this new regulation. However, they do not provide better alternatives.

Interestingly enough, the actual pressure for cost containment does not stimulate experiments with alternative health

206 The Migration of Managerial Innovation

care financing models. Even a planned experiment with a rather simple prospective payment system has been postponed and it is not clear yet when or if at all it will be implemented. The present public discussion shows that within the tighter economic frame, cantons, health insurance, and providers prefer traditional instruments of cost containment, such as restrictive budgeting and controlling. The new model for hospital cost accounting, introduced by VESKA in the summer of 1992, is bearing out this tendency, rather than a patient categories-oriented costing and reimbursment system.

Also, the Swiss Study Group on DRGs seems to have put more of its effort into the development of a sophisticated system (for instance, severity index, including nursing care) than into its implementation. Even the name of its newsletter was recently changed to *PCS News*; the newsletter now covers patient category systems more broadly.

The proposal for the new health insurance law, which should replace the present law dating from 1919, however, includes a lot of possibilities for alternative financing systems. The proposal will be discussed in parliament in 1993. It is very likely (and our hope) that prospective payment will get more attention than in the second half of 1992, and that there will be some progress in implementing such a system.

References

Abelin, T. "L'utilisation des statistiques hospitalières en santé publique" (The use of hospital statistics in public health). In F. Paccaud and L. Schenker (eds.), *Diagnosis Related Groups: Perspectives d'utilisation*, Paris: Lacassagne-Masson, 1989, 27–38.
Abelin, T., and others. *Interdisziplinäre Auswertung der VESKA — Spitaldiagnosen- und Operationsstatistik 1980–1984* (Interdisciplinary evaluation of the VESKA statistics on hospital diagnoses and procedures 1980–1984). (Schlussbericht des NF—Projektes 872–79) Bern: Institut für Sozial- und Präventivmedizin der Universität Bern, 1984.
Audétat, D. "Deux cliniques et les caisses maladie attaquent le cartel des médecins" (Two clinics and the sickness funds chal-

lenge the cartel of the doctors). *Le Nouveau Quotidien*, May 21, 1992, p. 23.

Bapst, L. "Plädoyer für einen baldigen Pilotversuch" (Plea for a quick pilot project). In Institut Suisse de la Santé Publique et des Hopitaux (ed.), *PCS-DRG: Tools for What?* Proceedings of a conference Sept. 18, 1991. Lausanne, Switzerland: Institut Swisse de la Santé Publique et des Hopitaux, 1992, 66–74.

Berry, R. "Product Heterogeneity and Hospital Cost Analysis." *Inquiry*, 1970, 7, 67–75.

Berweger, P., and Fahrni, U. *Datenqualitätsprüfung der Medizinischen Statistik VESKA: Eine Untersuchung von Datenblättern des Jahres 1981* (Evaluation of the data quality of the VESKA medical statistics: An analysis of the data sheets of 1981). Bern: Institut für Sozial- und Präventivmedizin, 1985.

Berweger, P., Küng, P., and Abelin, T. "Spitaleintritte wegen akutem Myokard-Infarkt—Eine Trendanalyse" (Hospital admissions due to acute myocardial infarction—a trend analysis). *Sozial- und Präventivmedizin*, 1987, *32*, 217–218.

Berweger, P., and others. "Zur Datenqualität der medizinischen Statistik VESKA" (The data quality of the VESKA medical statistics). *Sozial- und Präventivmedizin*, 1985, *30*, 233–234.

Bundesamt für Sozialversicherung (ed.). *Statistik über die Krankenversicherung 1988* (Health insurance statistics, 1988). Bern: Eidgenössische Drucksachen- und Materialzentrale, 1990.

Bundesamt für Sozialversicherung. *Dringliche Massnahmen gegen die Kostensteigerung und die Prämiensteigerung in der Krankenversicherung* (Urgent measures against the increase of costs and premiums in health insurance). Bern: Pressemitteilung, October 1991.

Bundesamt für Sozialversicherung (ed.). *Verzeichnis der vom Bund anerkannten Krankenkassen* (Register of the sickness funds recognized by the federal government). Bern: Eidgenössische Drucksachen- und Materialzentrale, 1992.

Direktion des Gesundheitswesens des Kantons Zürich (ed.). *Zürcher Krankenhausplanung 1990* (Hospital planning in Zürich, 1990). Zürich, 1990.

Eggli, Y., Blanc, T., and Koehn, V. "DRG-gestützte Kostenrechnung" (DRG-based cost accounting). In F. Paccaud and L. Schenker (eds.), *Diagnosis Related Groups: Gültigkeit, Brauchbarkeit, Anwendungsmöglichkeiten* (pp. 114–125). Bern: Huber, 1990.

Eggli, Y., Blanc, T., and Schenker, L. "Spitalführung und DRG" (Hospital management and DRG). In F. Paccaud and L. Schenker (eds.), *Diagnosis Related Groups: Gültigkeit, Brauchbarkeit, Anwendungsmöglichkeiten* (pp. 145–150). Bern: Huber, 1990.

Eggli, Y., Grimm, R., and Paccaud, F. "Table de transcodage des diagnostics: VESKA (version 1979)—ICD-9-CM" (Transcoding table of the diagnoses: VESKA [1979 version]—ICD-9-CM). (Cahiers de Recherche Doc IUMSP, no. 20) Lausanne, Switzerland: Institut universitaire de médecine sociale et préventive, 1987a.

Eggli, Y., Grimm, R., and Paccaud, F. "Table de transcodage des opérations: VESKA (version 1979)—ICD-9-CM" (Transcoding table of the operations: VESKA [1979 version]—ICD-9-CM). (Cahiers de Recherche Doc IUMSP, no. 21) Lausanne, Switzerland: Institut universitaire de médecine sociale et préventive, 1987b.

Eggli, Y., Grimm, R., and Paccaud, F. "Transcodage des codes opératoires et diagnostiques VESKA (version 1979) en codes ICD-9-CM" (Transcoding of the VESKA operational and diagnostic codes [1979 version] into codes ICD-9-CM). (Cahiers de Recherche Doc IUMSP, no. 14) Lausanne, Switzerland: Institut universitaire de médecine sociale et préventive, 1987c.

Eggli, Y., Koehn, V., and Paccaud, F. "Der Casemix—Vergleich zwischen Spitälern" (Case mix comparison between hospitals). In F. Paccaud and L. Schenker (eds.), *Diagnosis Related Groups: Gültigkeit, Brauchbarkeit, Anwendungsmöglichkeiten* (pp. 155–159). Bern: Huber, 1990.

Eggli, Y., Koehn, V., and Schenker, L. "Finanzierung der Spitäler mit DRG" (Financing of hospitals with DRG). In F. Paccaud and L. Schenker (eds.), *Diagnosis Related Groups: Gültigkeit, Brauchbarkeit, Anwendungsmöglichkeiten* (pp. 138–144). Bern: Huber, 1990.

Switzerland 209

Etude Casemix. "Principaux résultats de l'étude suisse sur les DRG's" (Main results of the Swiss study on DRGs). *Sozial- und Präventivmedizin*, 1989, *34*, 156–166.

Evans, R. "'Behavioural' Cost Functions for Hospitals." *Canadian Journal of Economics*, 1971, *4*, 198–215.

Evans, R., and Walker, H. "Information Theory and the Analysis of Hospital Cost Structure." *Canadian Journal of Economics*, 1972, *5*, 398–418.

Fahrni, U., Patil, S., and Abelin, T. "Hochrechnungen von Hospitalisationen aufgrund der VESKA—Diagnosenstatistik 1984" (Hospitalization estimates on the basis of the VESKA diagnostic statistics, 1982). *Sozial- und Präventivmedizin*, 1984, *29*, 174–175.

Fehr, H., and Joder, R. "Mit neuen Modellen die Spitalkosten senken" (New models to reduce hospital costs). *Bieler Tagblatt*, Aug. 30, 1991, p. 9.

Fetter, R., and others. "Casemix definition by Diagnosis Related Groups." *Medical Care*, 1980, *18* (Supplement), 1–53.

Frei, A., and Hill, S. "Das schweizerische Gesundheitswesen" (The Swiss health care system). Basel, Switzerland: Verlag G. Krebs AG, 1990.

Grimm, R., and Paccaud, F. "SIMULIT: un modèle de simulation pour l'analyse et la planification de l'activité hospitalière, Institut universitaire de médecine sociale et préventive" (SIMULIT: A simulation model for the analysis and planning of hospital activities). A working paper of the Institute of Preventive and Social Medicine, University of Lausanne, 1986. (Cahiers de Recherche doc IUMSP, no. 1 S. 4).

Grimm, R., and Pacaud, F. "SIMULIT—un modèle de simulation pour la planification hospitalière" (SIMULIT: A simulation model for hospital planning). *Sozial- und Präventivmedizin*, 1987, *32*, 201–204.

Güntert, B. "Gesundheitswesen zwischen Plan und Markt" (Health services between planning and market). *GDI impuls*, 1986, *1*, 53–71.

Güntert, B. "Das Gesundheitswesen im Dilemma—Strategien zur Reform" (The health service in a dilemma: strategies for reform). *Dokumentation zur Wirtschaftskunde*, 1990a, *5/6*, 21.

Güntert, B. "Managementorientierte Informations- und Kenn zahlensysteme für Krankenhäuser" (Management-oriented information and indicator systems for hospitals). Heidelberg, Germany: Springer-Verlag, 1990b.

Güntert, B. "Der Einfluss der Entschädigungssysteme auf die Kostenentwicklung" (The influence of reimbursement systems on cost development). In M. Künzi and G. Kocher (eds.), *Neue Entschädigungs-systeme im Gesundheitswesen. Schriftenreiche der Schweizerische Gesellschaft für Gesundheitspolitik*, no. 20, Horgen, Switzerland, 1991.

Güntert, B., and Sagmeister, M. "Pilotstudie zur Einführung eines DRG-Systems im Kanton Zürich" (Pilot study for the introduction of a DRG system in the canton of Zürich). Unpublished report for VZK, Zürich Hospital Association, St. Gallen, Switzerland, 1989, p. 48.

Güntert, B., and others. "Kostenentwicklung im st. gallischen Krankenhauswesen" (Cost development in the St. Gallen hospital service). Unpublished paper prepared for Gesundheitsdepartement des Kantons St. Gallen, St. Gallen, Switzerland, 1988.

Gutzwiller, F. "Empfehlungen zur Verwendung der Spitalstatistiken für Spitalplanung- und -management" (Recommendations for the use of hospital statistics in hospital planning and management). *Sozial- und Präventivmedizin*, 1989, *34*, 192–196.

Hornbrook, M. "Hospital Casemix: Its Definition, Measurement and Use. Part I: The Conceptual Framework." *Medical Care Review*, 1982a, *39*, 1–43.

Hornbrook, M. "Hospital Casemix: Its Definition, Measurement and Use. Part II: Review of Alternative Measures." *Medical Care Review*, 1982b, *39*, 73–123.

Jacot, F. "Un outil pour mieux connaître l'hôpital" (A tool for better hospital information). *DRG News*, 1990, *1*, 14–16.

Jaggi, K. "Neue Finanzierungsmodelle im Kanton Bern" (New financing models in the canton of Bern). *DRG News*, April 1992, 7, 3–6.

Käfer, K. *Plan comptable général pour entreprises artisanales, industrielles et commerciales* (General accounting plan for technical, industrial, and commercial businesses). Bern: Cosmos SA, 1975.

Klastorin, T., and Watts, C. "On the Measurement of Hospital Casemix." *Medical Care Review*, 1980, *18*, 675–685.

Koehn, V., Eggli, Y., and Paccaud, F. "Internationale Vergleiche" (International comparisons). In F. Paccaud and L. Schenker (eds.), *Diagnosis Related Groups: Gültigkeit, Brauchbarkeit, Anwendungsmöglichkeiten* (pp. 168–171). Bern: Huber, 1990.

Koehn, V., Paccaud, F., and Eggli, Y. "Standardisierte Vergleiche der Aufenthaltsdauer" (Standardized comparisons of duration of stay). In F. Paccaud and L. Schenker (eds.), *Diagnosis Related Groups: Gültigkeit, Brauchbarkeit, Anwendungsmöglichkeiten* (pp. 160–167). Bern: Huber, 1990.

Koehn, V., Schenker, L., and Patel, M. "Methoden zur Bestimmung eines Preises pro DRG" (Methods of determining the price of DRGs). In F. Paccaud and L. Schenker (eds.), *Diagnosis Related Groups: Gültigkeit, Brauchbarkeit, Anwendungsmöglichkeiten* (pp. 129–133). Bern: Huber, 1990.

Lambert, P. M., and Roger, F. H. (eds.). "Hospital Statistics in Europe." Amsterdam: North Holland, 1982.

Leidl, R., Potthoff, P., and Schwefel, D. (eds.). "European Approaches to Patient Classification Systems." Berlin: Springer-Verlag, 1990.

Minder, C., and Abelin, T. "Projection of Needs, Impairments and Morbidity of the Elderly in Switzerland." In World Health Organization, Regional Office for Europe, *Health Projections in Europe: Methods and applications*. Copenhagen: World Health Organization, 1986.

Morraz, A., and Patel, M. "Eine Schätzung der Gesamtkosten von drei chirurgischen Erkankungen" (An estimate of the total costs of three surgical illnesses). In F. Paccaud and L. Schenker (eds.), *Diagnosis Related Groups: Gültigkeit, Brauchbarkeit, Anwendungsmöglichkeiten* (pp. 126–128). Bern: Huber, 1990.

Paccaud, F. "Effects de certaines caractéristiques des patients sur la durée du séjour hospitalier et application aux comparaisons entre hôpitaux" (Effects of certain patient characteristics on the length of stay and their use in comparing hospitals). Doctoral dissertation, Faculté de médecine de Lausanne, Switzerland, 1981.

Paccaud, F. "Comparaisons entre hôpitaux et caractéristiques des clientèles: méthodologie et évaluation du casemix" (Comparisons between hospitals and patient characteristics: Methodology and evaluation of the case mix). In J. Martin, C. Klelber, and G. Tinturier (eds.), *Schriftenreihe der SGGP*, Vol. 6: *Maîtrise des coûts dans l'économie hospitalière*. Horgen, Switzerland: 1983.

Paccaud, F. (ed.). "Krebssterblichkeit: Qualität der Daten in der Schweiz/Mortalité cancéreuse: qualité des données en Suisse" (Cancer mortality: Data quality in Switzerland). Vol. 125: *Beiträge zur schweizerischen Statistik*. Bern: Bundesamt für Statistik, 1984.

Paccaud, F., Grimm, R., and Koehn, V. "SIMULIT — Ein Simulationsprogramm für die Spitalplanung mit Benutzung der DRG" (SIMULIT: A simulation program for hospital planning with the use of the DRG). In F. Paccaud and L. Schenker (eds.), *Diagnosis Related Groups: Gültigkeit, Brauchbarkeit, Anwendungsmöglichkeiten* (pp. 172–180). Bern: Huber, 1990.

Paccaud, F., and Schenker, L. (eds.). "DRG (Diagnosis Related Groups) — Quelle perspective d'utilisation en Suisse" (DRG [diagnosis-related groups]: What are the prospects of using them in Switzerland?) Paris: Lacassagne-Masson, 1989.

Paccaud, F., and Schenker, L. (eds.). *Diagnosis Related Groups: Gültigkeit, Brauchbarkeit, Anwendungsmöglichkeiten* (Diagnosis-related groups: Validity, workability, application possibilities). (von A. Frei, trans. and ed.) Bern: Huber, 1990.

Plüss, H. "Frustration mit den DRG-Projekten in Zürich" (Frustration with DRG projects in Zürich). In *PCS-DRG: Tools for what?* Proceedings of a conference in Lausanne. Lausanne, Switzerland: Institut Suisse de la Santé publique et des Hopitaux, 1992.

Rey, J. "Stand kantonaler und internationaler Projekte" (The state of cantonal and international projects). *DRG News*, 1991, *3*, 6–8.

Ro, K. "Patient Characteristics, Hospital Characteristics and Hospital Use." *Medical Care*, 1969, 7, 295–312.

Sagmeister, M. "Einflüsse der fallbezogenen Krankenhausfinanzierung auf das Spitalsmanagement unter Berücksichtigung der Demographie" (Influences of case-related hospital financing on hospital management in relation to demography). *Gesundheits-Oeconomica*, 1991, *1–2*, 55–68.

Sanderson, H. F., and Andrews, V. "Monitoring Hospital Services: An Application of Diagnosis Related Groups to Hospital Discharge Data in England and Wales." Occasional paper, London School of Hygiene and Tropical Medicine, London, 1984.

Schenker, L., and Paccaud, F. "Anwendungsbeispiele der DRG-Einführung" (Examples of introducing DRGs). In F. Paccaud and L. Schenker (eds.), *Diagnosis Related Groups: Gültigkeit, Brauchbarkeit, Anwendungsmöglichkeiten*. Bern: Huber, 1990, 153–154.

Sommer, J. *Kostenkontrolle in Gesundheitswesen* (Cost control in the health services). Diessenhofen, Switzerland: Rüegger, 1983.

Souteyrand, Y. "Caractéristiques de la clientèle: gestions méthodologiques" (Characteristics of the customers: Methodological problems). In C. Tilquin (ed.), *Systems Science in Health Care* (pp. 1346–1356). Toronto: Pergamon Press, 1981.

Staatskanzlei St. Gallen (ed.). *Spitalplanung 1985* (Hospital planning, 1985). St. Gallen, Switzerland: Staatskanzlei St. Gallen, 1986.

Ulrich, W. *Neue Möglichkeiten der Standardisierung von Spitalkennzahlen* (New possibilities for the standardization of hospital codes). Bern: Gesundheitsdirektion des Kantons Bern, 1987.

Vereinigung Schweizerischer Krankenhäuser (ed.). *Kontenrahmen und Statistik der schweizerischen Krankenhäuser* (Accounting system and statistics of Swiss hospitals). Aarau, Switzerland: Vereinigung Schweizerischer Krankenhäuser, 1985a.

Vereinigung Schweizerischer Krankenhäuser (ed.). *Kostenrechnung der schweizerischen Krankenhäuser* (Cost accounting in Swiss hospitals). Aarau, Switzerland: Vereinigung Schweizerischer Krankenhäuser, 1985b.

Vereinigung Schweizerischer Krankenhäuser, Kommission für Medizinische Statistik und Dokumentation (ed.). *Code des opér-*

ations 1986 (Code of operations, 1986). Aarau, Switzerland: Vereinigung Schweizerischer Krankenhäuser, 1986.

Vereinigung Schweizerischer Krankenhäuser, Kommission für Medizinische Statistik und Dokumentation (ed.). *Code des diagnostics 1979 basé sur la Classification Internationale des Maladies de l'OMS (CIM)* (Code of diagnoses, 1979, based on the international classification of the OMS [CIM] illnesses). (9e revision) Aaru, Switzerland: Vereinigung Schweizerischer Krankenhäuser, 1987.

Vereinigung Schweizerischer Krankenhäuser. "Das schweizerische Krankenhaus im Spiegel der Statistik 1989" (The Swiss hospital as reflected by 1989 statistics). *Das Schweizer Spital*, Nov. 1990.

Zweifel, P., and Pedroni, G. *Die Spitalfinanzierung in der Schweiz* (Hospital financing in Switzerland). Basel: Pharma Information, 1987.

Seven

Portugal: National Commitment and the Implementation of DRGs

João Urbano
Margarida Bentes
James C. Vertrees

At the beginning of 1990, Portugal implemented the use of DRGs for allocating its national budget for inpatient health care. This represents the first time that a true case mix–based system has been used for resource allocation in Europe. The purpose of this chapter is to describe the Portuguese system and its genesis. In the first section we describe what we judge to be the main features of the Portuguese health care delivery system. In the second section we describe the practical history of the introduction of diagnosis-related groups (DRGs) in Portugal up to their use as a basis for resource allocation to hospitals. Next, we consider the information resources that were available to establish the budgets and the way that this information was used. In the final section we describe the expected future directions of this system.

The Structure of Health Care

Portugal has provided universal access to medical care for all its citizens since 1979. The right of every citizen to affordable

Note: The authors wish to thank Maria Luisa Sequeira, Maria Suzete Tranquada, and Jorge Vasco Varanda for reviewing this chapter.

health care has been embodied in several significant legislative reforms, beginning with the Reform Bill of 1971. This led to the rapid development of public health services, the creation of public hospitals, and better provision of low-cost care for the disadvantaged. The 1974 democratic revolution brought additional changes to the health care system, including the creation of new management structures for hospitals. Finally, the constitution approved in 1976 and revised in 1982 guaranteed universal health care coverage to all citizens, proclaiming nothing less than the socialization of medicine.

Health care is financed and administered through the National Health Service (NHS), which is funded entirely through taxes. In 1987, NHS expenditures (operation and capital) represented 58.3 percent of total health care expenditures (Departamento de Estudos..., 1990a). Hospital budgets centrally financed from NHS revenues represent the largest portion of public expenditures for health care. At present, the typical public hospital receives about 10–15 percent of operating expenses from local revenue. The proportion is even lower for health centers. Copayments for such services as ambulatory tests, high-technology tests, and inpatient hospital care represent less than 5 percent of total revenue (Campos, 1990a).

Despite an intention to move toward universal coverage for all medical care, the NHS has been unable to absorb all existing workplace insurance plans. Only 76 percent of the population has the NHS as the sole health insurer; the remaining 24 percent uses cumulative coverage. Private health insurance as the sole source of coverage is used by 1.5 percent of the population (Campos, 1990c).

The overlapping of health insurance plans for an individual or for his or her family makes separation of the public and private sectors difficult. Patients will try to get the best of both systems, and the lack of overall administrative control prevents optimal use of the different health services (Campos, 1990a). The NHS does not directly provide all types of care. Private services are used by beneficiaries primarily for ambulatory care (physician consultations and ancillary services). In 1987, 36 percent of the total NHS budget was expended through

payments to the private sector (Departamento de Gestão...,
1989). On the other hand, care in the more complex clinical
specialties, where the private sector does not have adequate
resources, is provided to beneficiaries by the NHS. This division
of care has led to a case selection policy in which the subsystems
choose the most attractive and least costly cases, which leaves the
NHS with the most complex and costly cases.

The current health care delivery system is a mix of public
and private markets, each of which provides a variety of different services. In 1987, 68 percent of services was provided by the
public sector and 32 percent by the private sector (Departamento de Gestão..., 1989). The total health care budget then
accounted for 6.4 percent of the gross domestic product, 61
percent of which was public sector spending (Departamento de
Estudos..., 1990a).

Most hospital care is provided by the public sector. At
present, 78 percent of hospital beds are in government hospitals,
4 percent are in investor-owned hospitals, and 18 percent are in
private not-for-profit hospitals (Departamento de Estudos...,
1990b). There are also a large number of psychiatric private
beds run by philanthropic institutions. In general, private sector hospitals mainly provide low intensive care such as elective
surgery and deliveries. Conversely, more than one-quarter of
ambulatory visits — including 18 percent of general practitioner
consultations, 44 percent of specialty visits, and 77 percent of
dental care — are provided by the private sector, as well as 66
percent of diagnostic tests (Campos, 1990c). Most ambulatory
specialized care, such as renal dialysis, physical therapy, and
imaging procedures (for example, computerized tomographic
scanning, ecography and MRI), and most common lab tests are
provided by small private companies run by physicians who
simultaneously work in government hospitals.

High-technology equipment is generally underused in
public hospitals and probably overused in the private sector,
often by the same professionals, whose conflicts of interest tend
to be solved at the cost of public efficiency. In fact, medical
practice in Portugal has a long tradition of mixing public employment and private practice outside public institutions. This

is particularly true for physicians, who until recently were granted the right to work in both sectors. Public hospitals and health centers, despite their poor facilities (and equipment), tend to have a better scientific reputation than corresponding institutions in the private sector (Campos, 1990b). However, money earned in private hospitals supplements public salaries, which are usually rather low.

More recently, there have been significant increases in salaries of physicians who choose to work exclusively for the public sector. About 15 percent of hospital physicians and 60 percent of general practitioners have accepted this status (Campos, 1990c). Of the few physicians who work on a full-time basis in the private sector, most are engaged in profitable activities such as the drug industry, laboratories, renal dialysis, and imaging. Only a negligible number of physicians work in private solo practice. Table 7.1 summarizes these figures of Portuguese health care.

The Public Health Sector

NHS services are administered at two main levels: the central level (the Ministry of Health) and the regional level (the regional health administrations). While much authority is decentralized, the Ministry of Health in practice still retains most of the power. This is particularly true in regard to hospitals, where the ministry controls policy development, strategic management, financing, and inspection and evaluation.

At present, the NHS comprises twenty-four central acute care hospitals, nine of which are specialized. There are, in addition, four nonacute specialized hospitals and sixty-three district hospitals (all acute care). Of these, twenty-four were previously country hospitals that have attained the status of district in recent years. Thus a total of ninety-one hospitals are directly under the financial control of the Ministry of Health. A small number of other government hospitals (eleven) is controlled by different ministries.

Virtually all general hospitals provide inpatient, out patient, and emergency care services (comprising both trauma

Table 7.1. Key Figures in Portuguese Health Care.

Country area (square km.)	88,944
Population (thousands)	9,808.9
Density of population (inhabitants per square km.)	110
Percent of population over 75	5.27%
Life expectancy (1988)	
Male	70.7 years
Female	77.6 years
Infant mortality rate	12.0%
Income per capita ($US)	6,737
Expenditure on health per capita ($US) (1987)	386
Percent of GNP devoted to health (NHS) (1980)	3.65%
Percent of GNP devoted to health (NHS) (1989)	3.98%
Number of acute-care hospitals	173
Public	98
Ministry of Health (MOH)	87
Others	11
Private	75
Number of acute-care beds	27,959
Public	23,860
Ministry of Health (MOH)	22,173
Others	1,687
Private	4,099
Number of acute-care beds per 1,000 population	2.85
Number of discharges in acute-care beds (MOH)	659,750
Average length of stay (MOH) (days)	8.96
Number of physicians	26,982
Ratio of population to physicians	364
Number of nurses (MOH)	24,730
Ratio of population to nurses	397

Sources: Departamento de Estudos e Planeamento da Saúde (DEPS), 1990b, 1991; Departamento de Gestão Financeira dos Serviços de Saúde, 1990; Organization for Economic Cooperation and Development, 1989.

and primary care). Hospitals' modes of service differ primarily in terms of the numbers of clinical specialty services provided.

In central hospitals, more than thirty specialty services are typically available, all of which may be represented in outpatient clinics and in the emergency rooms, as well as in the inpatient areas. Exceptions obviously apply to specialized central hospitals, which have a very limited variety of specialties. The typical district hospital, however, is unlikely to provide more than fifteen specialty services and, in some cases, will have only the basic medical, surgical, pediatric, and obstetric specialties.

It is fair to conclude that planning of the roles and functions of each hospital within an integrated health care delivery system has been relatively successful in Portugal. However, some factors have not been adequately controlled. For example, some services that should exist at the district level cannot be maintained because of the difficulty of recruiting staff (who prefer to live in larger metropolitan areas). In addition, hospitals continue to provide primary care services that might be more cost effective if delivered by health centers.

The health centers program formally commenced in 1971 but was relatively slow to develop until the 1982 reorganization. Responsibility for the operation of health centers rests with the regional health administrations, one for each of Portugal's health regions.

At present, there are 353 health centers (Departamento de Estudos. . . , 1991), providing reasonable access in all parts of the country. The typical facility provides health education, sanitary engineering, health inspection, antenatal services, and well-baby clinic and immunization, in addition to diagnostic and ancillary services with referrals to hospitals as appropriate. In many areas (particularly outside the main urban areas), health centers provide some inpatient care in addition to ambulatory clinics. Many health centers were not specifically constructed as such but rather were adapted from existing facilities. Thus, they may have significant limitations in terms of quality and range of services.

Portugal has thirty-seven mental health facilities, comprising six psychiatric hospitals, twenty-three health centers, and eight rehabilitation centers (Departamento de Estudos. . . , 1991).

Hospital services continue to consume most of the community's health care resources. Public hospitals account for about 43 percent of the public sector health budget, public primary care services account for 33 percent, and medications account for about 21 percent (Campos, 1990c). For this reason, the government's focus has been on hospital services, and the predominant view has been that improvements in hospital care are of highest priority. There is, however, a growing realization that hospitals cannot by themselves influence the health status of the community; therefore, there is a need for closer coordination between hospital and nonhospital services. Because the boundaries of each type of health care service have yet to be defined clearly, it is not yet possible to measure demand for each service and hence determine the desired resource mix.

Hospital services are centrally controlled, whereas administrative control over nonhospital services is significantly decentralized. This organizational structure has some inherent weaknesses. For example, where local problems concerning links between a hospital and a health center exist, the hospital might refer problems to the Ministry of Health at the central level, whereas the health center is more likely to seek approval from the regional health authority.

It is important to note in evaluating these problems that the current structure was not designed with the primary intention of facilitating the delivery of integrated health care services. A law was recently passed in Parliament that integrates hospital and primary care services at the regional level; however, it has not yet been implemented.

Financing of Health Care

Until 1980, under Portugal's hospital financing system, NHS hospitals were reimbursed on the basis of actual costs. The disadvantages of cost reimbursement are well known and include the lack of incentives to control resource consumption and avoid unnecessarily high production costs.

These problems were reduced in 1981 when the financing system was partially linked to outputs—both final products (such as numbers of patients treated by medical specialty) and intermediate products (such as diagnostic procedures). In effect, a crude output-based funding approach was adopted. Inpatient services were funded at different rates for each clinical specialty and varied with length of stay and occupancy rate. Outpatient services were funded based on the number of visits, with no discrimination for patient type. Ancillary services were paid at average unit prices, based on numbers of nonweighted units of service provided. Overhead costs were reimbursed separately, and capital funding was determined by a negotiation process, with some attempts at prioritization of project proposals.

Although this payment system represented a major step forward, it was considered far from ideal because the case mix classifications were extremely crude. Moreover, since ancillary services with different production costs were paid at the same rate, incentives existed to substitute low-cost diagnostic procedures for high-cost procedures, which risked jeopardizing quality of care (Bentes, Urbano, and Hindle, 1989).

In 1987, a more sophisticated type of output-based funding, drawing mainly on U.S. experiences with prospective payment was initiated. In the long term, the intention is to move to output-based funding for all types of hospital products, including acute inpatient care, nonacute inpatient care, and ambulatory care. The first and most critical issue, however, was the development of the inpatient component, using DRGs as the case mix measure upon which to base inpatient funds. As a result of these efforts, implementation of an inpatient resource allocation model was started in 1990. In this model, hospital budgets were set in part on the basis of the hospital's DRG production.

Nonhospital services are funded essentially on the basis of historical expenditures corrected for inflation and adjusted according to the current year's performance. Although attempts have been made to introduce more rational modes of funding that ultimately take into account health care needs by geographical area, no step has yet been taken or is envisioned in the short run to change the current system.

Weaknesses of the Health Care System

Many problems are evident in the Portuguese health care system. One of the most important is the underfinancing of NHS hospitals. This results in chronic deficits, limited management power, delays in meeting expenditures, and an overall lack of confidence in the system on the part of both users and suppliers of health care. Other pitfalls include the following:

1. Lack of integrated planning between hospital and non-hospital services, including undefined boundaries between primary care and emergency treatment in hospital emergency departments and unavailability of intermediate and domiciliary care services to which patients no longer needing acute care can be discharged.
2. Lack of comprehensiveness of the NHS services; for example, insufficient provision of dental care, physical therapy, and care to the elderly and the handicapped.
3. Weaknesses in identification of the costs of hospital and nonhospital care and hence inability to determine the relative cost-effectiveness of hospital and nonhospital options.
4. Nonoptimal use of human resources due to geographical distribution and cumulative employment with the private sector, especially for physicians.
5. Communication problems between different types of health care personnel.
6. Absence of fair competition between different agencies with respect to the financing and provision of health care, and hence the absence of appropriate mechanisms to determine the balances in the community's best interests.
7. Lack of understanding of costs of optional kinds of treatments in hospitals and unwillingness of individual physicians to consider the need for rationing of limited resources.
8. Low level of use of scientific methods to identify and then resolve problems of efficiency, such as those relating to supply acquisition and storage, the allocation of home visiting and nursing staff to patients and areas, and operating room allocation in hospitals.

The Privatization Issue

Although the level of private sector activity has declined significantly since 1979, there has been recent interest in encouraging investor-owned developments in hospital ownership.

A revision to the Portuguese Constitution in 1989 determined that access to health care is no longer totally free of charge but "tendentially free," reflecting a switch in the aim of NHS from socialization of medicine to socialization of health care costs.

In 1990, a law was passed in Parliament that allows copayment by individual patients. Copayments will not, however, be easy to impose because of a constitutional argument for universality of access to all citizens. The impact of copayments on equity of access is unknown.

The same law allows payment of real costs, as opposed to political prices, for private or public schemes other than the NHS when using public services. This provides an opportunity to bolster the NHS budget, which is now supporting a considerable portion of the subsystems' responsibility (Campos, 1990c).

The government is committed to stimulating and supporting private initiatives that to date have been merely tolerated. It is believed that this response will help to reduce long waiting lists for some specialties in public hospitals and improve the quality of care through increased competition between the two sectors. An example is the recent consideration given to private management of public hospitals and health centers. The property of these institutions would still be public, but management would operate within the rules of the private sector. In this context, private investors consider the health sector as a promising business area, and several projects are under development to create private hospital facilities.

The NHS will continue to play a major role in Portugal, at least in the foreseeable future. It is, in fact, the most economic way of providing care of reasonable quality at a low price to the majority of the population. However, new tools will arise within the current context of increasing privatization of the public sector, and new insurance companies, as well as new insurance policies and associations of physicians in cooperatives or in private for-profit companies are expected to be major actors in promoting health sector reform (Campos, 1990a).

Portugal provides good conditions for research and experiments in the public-private mix of the health sector. Such efforts will test the hypothesis that increments of private care, along with a clarification of the boundaries of the public and the private sectors, can make the health system and NHS much more effective and efficient.

Evolution of DRGs in Portugal

DRGs were formally introduced in Portugal through a contract between the Portuguese Ministry of Health and the U.S. Agency for International Development (AID) for the development of a hospital cost control project to be financially supported by AID. The general goal of the project was to reduce hospital costs and increase productivity. This would be accomplished through the implementation of a fully integrated information system for the management and financing of hospitals. The system would allow the Ministry of Health to fund hospitals in a rational manner that would create incentives to increase productivity and reduce costs and to develop within hospitals the appropriate types of modern management systems that would give them the capability to respond to those incentives.

More specifically, the first objective of the project was to create an integrated information system for hospital management based on a set of necessary and uniform data, which would allow all levels of management to measure and control their productivity, support their decision making, make plans and budgets, and establish equitable financing criteria. The second objective was to develop an information system that could efficiently collect, treat, analyze, and transmit information within hospitals, between hospitals and central departments, and among central departments.

The planned system was based on hospital management and cost control models that had been developed and tested in the United States. One of the key elements of its structure was the fully operationalized concept of DRGs developed by Yale University. The decision to choose DRGs followed a conference at Brandeis University in September 1984 on the ideas presented by the developers of the major patient classification systems.

Subsequently, the U.S. experience with DRGs was carefully watched, as were evaluations from the various debates between the proponents of alternative systems. Because Portugal had very few means for research and the DRG system appeared to be the most operative and tested of all systems, the idea of using DRGs as a case mix tool for management and financing was reinforced. Further, contacts with our European peers, the great majority of whom were in favor of DRGs, were important in influencing the Ministry of Health to study the feasibility of implementing DRGs in Portugal.

At the end of 1984 Yale University presented a proposal to provide technical assistance in developing a DRG-based funding system for hospitals in Portugal. A detailed work plan was set up between the Health Systems Management Group under the direction of Yale University professor Robert Fetter and the Ministry of Health working group Sistema de Informação para a Gestão de Serviços de Saúde (SIGSS) under the direction of João Urbano. The Fetter group and the SIGSS team were each assigned primary responsibility for specific tasks, although the resulting work was a joint effort.

An important phase of the analyses took place in Portugal, where Fetter, Jean Freeman, Robert Mullin, and members of the SIGSS staff conducted a series of seminars and working sessions to discuss DRG concepts and the methodology of the project with hospital managers at various levels of responsibility.

The aim of the first two phases of the work was to examine the extent to which DRGs as currently defined could be used in Portuguese hospitals and to classify hospital discharges into DRGs in order to examine patterns of resource use. Specifically, the objectives were (1) to assess the technical feasibility of assigning DRG numbers to Portuguese discharge abstracts, (2) to evaluate the adequacy of the utilization model defined by the DRGs for the Portuguese data, and (3) to compare the case mix and case-specific average lengths of stay in Portuguese hospitals to those for U.S. acute-care hospitals. These initial phases would also include the adaptation of the Yale cost accounting model to Portuguese hospitals so that costs by DRG could be determined for a group of study hospitals. Support would also be given for the development of a standard discharge abstract to include sufficient data to implement the cost model.

In the third phase of the project, the cost accounting model would be generalized from the study hospitals to all Portuguese hospitals and a transfer module developed for application in Portugal. The budget model would be adapted to produce budgets for Portuguese hospitals and to allow examination of the effect of alternative payment approaches, including case payment. In this work, DRG-based cost analyses would be tied to manpower productivity reports currently in use in Portugal. This was expected to result in a basic management information system based on DRGs, along with utilization review and quality assurance modules.

Finally, in the fourth and last phase, the system would be expanded so as to be appropriate for the implementation of a product-line management system in selected hospitals.

As a first development of the proposed work, a data base of Portuguese hospital discharge abstracts containing about 100,000 discharges from sixteen hospitals covering the period from January 1983 to March 1984 was sent to Yale to be processed. The data were converted into a form compatible with the DRG assignment software, DRG codes were assigned to Portuguese discharges, and some utilization statistics were generated and compared to those from a data base of U.S. hospital discharges (descriptive summaries of case mix, case-specific lengths of stay, and coefficients of variation).

The Portuguese diagnostic data were translated from ICD9 to ICD9-CM codes using a conversion table developed by Robert Mullin. Procedure data were coded using an internal coding scheme and recoded to ICD9-CM by Mullin and a team of Portuguese physicians. After these conversions, some ambiguity in DRG assignment remained for about 10 percent of the data base, and for approximately 8 percent of the data base a valid DRG number could not be assigned due to coding or other data problems.

The general structure of the DRG model, originally developed using U.S. data, was, for the most part, consistent with Portuguese data. However, descriptive analyses suggested that the relationships among the variables used to define the DRGs were stronger in the United States than in Portugal. Overall, DRGs in Portugal appeared to be slightly less homogeneous than in U.S. hospitals (a fact that was expressed by higher coefficients of variation), but the relative variability among DRGs appeared to be similar in the two countries, which means that the DRGs with high variation in Portugal tended to be those with high variation in the United States.

The hierarchy of surgical procedures observed in the United States also existed in Portugal, and patients over seventy years old and/or with a significant co-morbidity or complication tended to stay longer than patients who were less than seventy years old without a significant co-morbidity or complication, and patients with a malignancy diagnosis stayed longer on average than patients without a malignancy diagnosis (Freeman, Fetter, Newbold, and Mullin, 1985).

Finally, lengths of stay in Portuguese hospitals were consistently longer than lengths of stay in the U.S. hospitals. However, since the data from the two countries were collected under different information systems and using different procedure and diagnosis coding conventions, the observed differences could be attributed to the methods of collecting, abstracting, and coding the discharge information.

In 1985, after the problems with the first data base had been identified and partially corrected, a new data base containing about 115,000 discharges from seventeen hospitals was sent to Yale to repeat the evaluation of the DRG model. Since the results of this analysis were quite encouraging, the Ministry of Health decided that the DRG system should be extended to all public acute-care hospitals and that its use as a resource allocation tool should be planned.

As part of this preliminary work, three hospitals carried out a pilot study in 1985 to attempt to measure costs per case. The objective was to determine the needs and constraints in cost data production at the patient level in order to implement a case-based cost accounting model that could be generalized from the study hospitals to all hospitals. This model was intended to be the basis for producing budgets for Portuguese hospitals. The model would also allow an examination of the effect of alternative budgeting approaches.

Hospital data collection was designed by the SIGSS and the Fetter teams, and data processing was done at Yale to determine costs per case for the three Portuguese hospitals. Some critical problems were identified.

First of all, information regarding the total resource use for an individual patient was not routinely collected. Portuguese hospitals have reasonable accounting systems, but these systems are more oriented toward providing data regarding input costs. They do not link these inputs to the products (the care provided to individual patients). In fact, most Portuguese hospitals use a cost center structure under which expenditures are allocated to cost centers from the general ledger. The end of the allocation chain, however, is the various clinical services and not the individual patients. Therefore, there was no data available on the actual use of resources (procedures, drugs, nursing, and so on) by patients, but only standard costs per patient per clinical service.

In addition, there were differences in cost center definitions, and different allocation statistics were used across hospitals. It was not possible to accurately compare hospitals at the cost center level because there are many accounting variations between hospitals. Even when the name of the cost center is the same, there is no guarantee that it contains the same types of expenditures and functions.

Finally there was a lack of detail in the chart of accounts such that expenditure items that should be treated differently in cost analyses were not able to be disaggregated.

These difficulties pinpointed the need to redefine the Yale cost-identifying model to fit Portuguese hospital accounting methods and to design a data collection strategy at the hospital level to obtain crucial information at the patient level.

Until 1987 progress was slow in implementing a DRG-based resource allocation model that included the development of a case mix–based cost accounting system. The political environment was unstable, and, although there has always been formal support from the Ministry of Health for the DRG project, there was not, in practice, much support in terms of providing the means to introduce real change. For example, hospital information systems were very weak, and the vast majority of hospitals did not have computers. Most computing activities were handled at regional centers, which are functionally limited. In addition, intermediate staff categories were unskilled and needed extensive training.

After 1987, efforts to overcome these weaknesses accelerated. Important investments were made to implement a hospital output-based funding system using DRGs as the case mix measure; that is, as the basis for allocating resources for hospital inpatient care. As a key part of this effort, Don Hindle from Wisconsin University was contracted as a full-time consultant, first as a member of the Yale team and subsequently as the sole consultant for the whole DRG project.

The changeover to a funding system based on DRGs represented new challenges for the hospitals, which needed to be able to respond constructively to the incentives provided by the system. This meant that hospitals had to be given both the tools and an understanding of their use. Several actions were taken in this regard.

Diagnosis and procedure coding was changed to ICD9-CM, and training courses in coding for physicians were implemented. Although most of the hospitals in Portugal had centralized medical record departments, there were few specialized professionals in this area. As the training of medical recorders was not feasible in the short run, the Ministry of Health decided that physicians should be assigned responsibilities for coding activities. From November 1988 to May 1989, 377 physicians attended fifteen training programs of eight days duration, equivalent to forty-one working hours per physician. The objectives of these training sessions were to give specific training in ICD9-CM coding of diagnoses and procedures, to explain the purpose and structure of the DRG classification system and the relationship between ICD9-CM coding and DRG assignment, and to design a quality control program for monitoring ICD9-CM coding and DRG assignment.

A standard microcomputer-based discharge-abstracting

and DRG grouper package was implemented at the hospital level, including a wide range of management reports. Clerical staff of all hospitals have been trained in its use, and grouping started to be done on an ongoing basis at each hospital in January 1989. In addition to the above package, a much more comprehensive microcomputer package was developed and is still under test at selected sites. This provides a wide range of patient-related master index and admission-transfer-discharge functions, in addition to discharge abstracting and grouping. It is also linked to modules for emergency department and outpatient clinic visits and has the capability to incorporate an ambulatory grouper in due course.

The Yale cost model was also adapted for use with microcomputer software at the hospital level, in order to enable Portuguese hospital managers to identify weaknesses in their cost structures. The basic process involves capturing data on hospital inputs as recorded in the general ledger and tracing those inputs through several stages: from initial cost centers to final cost centers, and from final cost centers to products. These products are not the individual patients but rather DRGs (Urbano and Hindle, 1987). Given the fact that in the Portuguese health care delivery system there is no need to bill patients, the development of patient-level costing capabilities would be very expensive and difficult to implement. Therefore the cost model was designed to derive standard DRG costs by apportionment of cost center costs to DRGs. Although this package has been tested and documented, the main work still needs to be done. This involves the development and implementation of methods to capture the required data together with allocation statistics whereby costs recorded in the general ledger can be ultimately related to the DRGs.

Finally, a national standard cost center structure was defined through which component cost data will be comparable at higher levels of aggregation. Work is already advanced in terms of developing a standardized set of cost centers arranged in hierarchical form to facilitate comparison between hospitals of different size. A common set of allocation statistics was also defined. A team including representatives from hospitals and central departments has completed the design work. The remaining tasks include negotiations with the individual hospitals to achieve widespread acceptance.

It would be a mistake to consider that all these activities began in 1987. The trends, which accelerated after 1987, were for the most part already evident before that date. For example, in 1985 and 1986 a standardized discharge abstract was developed and DRG grouper software was adapted to Portuguese computer systems. Preliminary discussions with hospital managers and physicians had already taken place regarding standardizing cost centers, units of service, and allocation statistics. Above all, extensive seminars and training sessions had been held since 1984. These seminars were mainly directed at physicians and hospital managers in order to promote the DRG classification system and its use as a hospital management tool.

DRGs were from the beginning well accepted by most people, including hospital physicians and the medical association. There was no severe criticism or formal opposition, and most of the discomfort some people experienced when confronting the new concept has been overcome. Special reference should be made to the role played by hospital managers in this acceptance process. Their demand for change in respect to information systems and management tools made them strong supporters of the introduction of innovative concepts, thus facilitating the diffusion of DRGs in their hospitals. One of the appealing features of DRGs is that they fulfill the role of a common language between physicians and managers, which is essential for the involvement of the former in the management of hospital resources. The concepts of product-line management and matrix management have been extensively presented to physicians to show their expected involvement in the hospital's managerial process and their accountability for resource use. However, effective implementation of these organizational models is still very limited due to the fact that hospital-level information systems based on case mix are not yet fully installed in Portugal.

The Ministry of Health's strategic plan outlined after 1987 ultimately envisions allocating resources using a combination of needs-based budgeting and output-based payments. Under that approach, resources would be allocated to each region based on measures of the health status of its population, and the regional health authorities would then distribute funds to health care providers within the region based upon measures of their production as adjusted for case mix. Currently, however, systems development is focused on allocating resources to hospitals for acute inpatient care without changing responsibilities for payment administration.

In July 1989, after Hindle's withdrawal from the project, the Ministry of Health entered into a contract with SOLON Consulting Group for the provision of technical assistance for the development and operationalization of a DRG resource allocation model for the hospital inpatient sector. During the first phase of the project, the staff of SOLON, under the direction of its president, James Vertrees, and in collaboration with the SIGSS team, identified the data needs for resource allocation and began to design the information and funding systems, including a set of preliminary regulations. Following the success of the initial project, a supplemental agreement was made to continue efforts to improve the information systems and simulation models developed during the first phase of the project, to identify, investigate, and recommend specific policy options, and to update the resource allocation regulations based on the evaluated policy issues. Hospital budgets were first allocated using DRGs in 1990.

The current DRG resource allocation system is described in the following section of this chapter, including its objectives and key aspects of the implementation process.

DRG-Based Resource Allocation

The objectives of the DRG resource allocation model are (1) to provide a more rational allocation methodology by basing funding on the clinical complexity of the cases treated at a particular hospital rather than on volume alone, (2) to provide for equity in resource allocation by defining hospital products and paying the same rate for similar products, (3) to promote efficiency and effectiveness in managing care through incentives to eliminate unnecessary services and hospital days, and (4) to control costs while maintaining quality of care (Sistema de Informação para a Gestão de Serviços de Saúde, 1990).

It was necessary to design a system that could achieve these objectives and also be feasible to implement in 1990. As a practical matter, the initial system design included several specific factors used by the U.S. Medicare program, as this has been a principal source of experience in the use of DRGs. For example, the definition and credit rules for long-stay outliers in Portugal are generally similar to those used by Medicare, except that, as extended-care facilities are very few in Portugal, an additional class of very-long-stay outlier cases had to be created. In a similar vein, short-stay outlier definitions initially followed Medicare. However, experience in 1990 showed that the number of short-stay outliers was higher than expected as it appears that people who would be classified as outpatients in the United States may be treated as one-day admissions in Portugal. For this reason, the short-stay outlier definition may be modified in the future to include somewhat longer stays.

There are several other important differences between U.S. and Portuguese health care financing that influenced the initial design of the Portuguese system. For example, in the United States the Medicare DRG system is responsible for about 40 percent of hospital revenues, hospitals are independently owned, physicians are independent of hospitals, and physicians and hospitals are paid separately by Medicare. Medicare is not responsible for maintaining the financial solvency of particular U.S. hospitals. Conversely, the Portuguese NHS is responsible for the vast majority of hospital revenues (87 percent on average), most hospitals are publicly owned, and hospitals employ physicians. Thus, the government in Portugal is simultaneously the dominant payer and provider of care and is responsible for the financial solvency of its hospitals (Bentes, Urbano, Carvalho, and Tranquada, 1991).

Since hospital employees (including physicians) are government employees, and since the hospitals are governed in some detail by regulations, a large proportion of operating costs in Portugal represents fixed costs. The budget available for inpatient hospital care is also fixed by a political and social process that is largely external to the health care sector (Bentes, Urbano, Carvalho and Tranquada, 1991). Finally, the rules of public accounting determine that payments must be based on budgets and delivered in monthly allocations.

Ideally, a DRG-based resource allocation system would be based entirely on the costs known to be necessary to provide quality care within each DRG, and we could assume that these costs would be the same for each hospital. Under this ideal approach, the relative weights, and thus the allocation rates for each DRG, would be determined by adding the average cost per patient (however defined) within the DRG and then adding these sums across DRGs for each hospital. This is the general method used by the Medicare program and many other DRG-based prospective payment systems in the United States. However, this approach was not feasible for Portugal because of certain data limitations. In the first place, hospitals do not currently report costs at the patient level; instead, costs are available only at the hospital and service levels. In the second place, there is a lack of cost information for some hospitals and a lack of DRG information for others. In the third place, there are imperfections in the diagnostic and procedure information used to classify cases into DRGs due to the fact that hospitals have only been asked to provide this information since the beginning of 1989.

These obstacles to the successful implementation of the allocation methodology were overcome by (1) using information from an external source with cost information from national hospitals to produce DRG cost weights suitable for use in Portugal, (2) estimating costs and DRG case mix for hospitals where this information was missing, and (3) creating an allowance in the budgeting formula to compensate for improvements in the accuracy of coding for individual cases.

Thus, though the SIGSS group did not use nationwide averages for the costs, the basic structure of adding averages within and then across DRGs for each hospital became the basis of our financial model for the hospital. This is a simple way to characterize a hospital's financial structure. We anticipate that

this model will need to become more realistic and more complex over time as, for example, fixed, variable, marginal, and
direct and indirect costs are recognized in the model.

Data Sources

Three data sources are used to determine hospital allocation
levels: hospital DRG claims data, annual hospital cost report
information, and service weights developed and used by
Maryland's Medicaid program. These data sources cover all
eighty-seven NHS acute-care hospitals, of which eighty actually
submitted usable data. Each of these data sources is described
below.

The DRG claims data are collected at each hospital using
Portugal's LDRG computer data base, currently with version 6.0
of the grouper program. Collection of these data is mandatory
from a uniform discharge abstract. This system collects patient
demographic information (for example, birth date and sex),
diagnoses, services provided, surgical procedures, transfer information, length of stay, and disposition status for each discharge. Each hospital forwards its LDRG data on floppy disks on
a monthly basis to the national health care office, which integrates the data into a national data base to be used for budgeting. The base year for which data were drawn to set allocation
levels was 1989.

Hospital cost report information is submitted to the Ministry of Health's Department of Finance on an annual basis for
budgeting. (This source is now also used to develop allocation
schedules.) These data include costs, revenues, and expenditures for each hospital and for each specialty within the hospital. A stepdown method similar to that used by Medicare is used
to allocate indirect costs. Again, 1989 is the base year for this
data source.

The Maryland cost review program prospectively controls hospital revenue based on the relative resources required
by each service (for example, physicians, nursing, room, board,
laundry, and so on) provided during an average hospital stay
within a DRG. The service weights reflect the cost of a service

relative to other services. Weights for ancillary services (services that were determined to vary only by number of discharges) were used from this source along with total costs in Portugal for the ancillary service in question as part of the calculation of Portuguese-specific DRG relative weights. Costs that vary with length of stay (for example, physician salaries) are allocated to cases using the actual length of stay of the case. To compute the DRG relative values, these costs are summed within the DRGs and the result for each DRG is divided by the national average cost per case.

Resource Allocation Methods

Under the DRG-based system, Portuguese hospitals are allocated resources for inpatient care on a per-discharge basis. Patient diagnoses are grouped into one of the 477 DRG classifications. Cases are assigned to DRGs based on diagnoses, whether surgery was performed, patient age, secondary conditions, and discharge status.

The basic method for setting appropriation levels for hospitals is determined by multiplying each hospital's case mix index (CMI) by its expected number of cases (N) and the budget rate (R), which is the national average cost per case (SIGSS, 1990). Thus, under this framework, the allocation level (A) for each hospital (h) can be represented by the following equation:

$$Ah = CMIh \times Nh \times Rh$$

The case mix index is determined using the DRG weights, or relative values. Each DRG group is assigned a relative resource weight, which expresses the relationship of one DRG to another in terms of their resource requirements. The relative values do not vary by hospital—a single value for each DRG is calculated and used for all hospitals. The general method for calculating the DRG weights (the method used by the Medicare program and most other DRG-based prospective payment systems) involves assigning a specific cost to each case within a DRG using hospital claims or cost data. The geometric mean cost for all cases, as well as for each classification group, is then determined. The ratio of the mean cost for a group, weighted by the number of cases within the group, to the overall mean cost is the relative weight for that group. A DRG with average costs will have a relative weight of 1.0, while a DRG that is twice as expensive as the average will have a relative value of 2.0. The geometric mean is used instead of the average to calculate DRG weights because the distribution of average hospital costs is lognormally distributed; thus, the geometric mean is a more stable measure of central tendency. This means that the relative values will not change considerably over time as allocation rates are recomputed.

The first step in this method, assigning specific costs to each case, requires that data on hospital costs be available at the patient level. As noted above, this is not the case in Portugal. Rather, cost information is available only at the hospital and service level. To circumvent this problem, a method has been devised that converts global facility costs to DRG-specific costs. A proxy (the service weights developed and used by Maryland's Medicaid program to reimburse hospitals) is used to assign costs in escudos at the DRG level for ancillary services. Maryland's system assigns each service provided during a hospital stay (for example, diagnostic radiation, laboratory, and so on) a weight that reflects that service's costs relative to other services in each DRG. By assuming that Portuguese hospitals exhibit the same pattern of service use as hospitals in Maryland but at different levels, we can determine the relative costs of each of the services that comprise total hospital costs by DRG in Portugal.

Specifically, patient-level costs by DRG are calculated using hospital cost report data, information on total discharges and hospital days, and the Maryland service weights. Analysis of annual hospital costs from the hospitals' cost reports showed that costs for some services (for example, physicians, nurses, laundry) vary by length of stay, while other services (for example, ancillaries) are associated only with number of discharges. Thus, total hospital costs by type of service were broken down to either a cost per day or a cost per discharge, depending upon the service. Next, these costs were, with the exception of physician costs, associated with the Maryland service weights so that the relative costs for each could be determined by DRG. This method led to cost-based DRG relative values that could be used to calculate hospital case mix indices.

Each hospital must prepare a budget request for the upcoming year. The number of discharges for each hospital is estimated by the hospital using its data for previous years. In general, for hospitals with a complete year's data, the number of discharges is estimated from the experience during the prior year and a trend factor. As new information is likely to be both more relevant and more accurate than older information, newer information is weighted more heavily in computing the trend. If a hospital does not have twelve months of data, the number of discharges is estimated using a rolling weight. This estimate is then compared to estimates prepared by the Department of Finance, which has historically tracked hospital discharges. Large discrepancies require an explanation.

As the actual number of discharges may differ from that forecast by the hospital, at the end of each year the budget must be reconciled with actual experience. Hospitals experiencing an increase in the number of discharges will have this increase funded through settlement payment. Hospitals with decreases will have their settlement netted out of the next year's budget for inpatient operating costs. This reconciliation was not done for 1990 as the counts of patients used to set the 1990 budgets were not sufficiently reliable. However, in future years, the settlement will be based on the marginal cost of care within a DRG.

Once determined, the DRG weights and discharge estimations are used to calculate each hospital's case mix index. The index reflects the composition of a hospital's patients relative to other hospitals and is determined by weighting each discharge by the relative weight of the DRG to which the discharge has been assigned. The sum of the weighted discharges, divided by the total number of discharges, is the case mix index.

Modifications to the general allocation model illustrated by the above equation are made to account for special cases that are outliers or transfers. DRGs were designed to group cases that should require similar amounts and kinds of resources; however, the groupings are not perfect in this regard. Two cases with the same diagnoses may be quite different in terms of severity of illness and response to treatment. Therefore, some cases in a particular DRG will be outliers in that they will require significantly more or fewer resources for treatment than a more typical case in that DRG.

Cases with short or long lengths of stay relative to average cases within a particular DRG are termed short- or long-stay outliers. Three types of outliers are considered in the determination of appropriations to Portuguese hospitals: short-stay, long-stay, and very-long-stay. Each type is defined below.

A short-stay outlier is defined as a discharge with a length of stay greater than 1.96 standard deviations (in logarithms) below the geometric mean, or 1.0 day, whichever is greater. Short-stay outlier cases are credited to the hospital at 100 percent of the DRG per diem national rate. Thus, a short-stay outlier of one day in a DRG with an average length of stay of five days will receive one-fifth of the normal DRG credit. These outliers are included in the count of cases for the hospital (Nh) in the allocation equation at a weight equal to the number of short-stay days divided by the average length of stay of the DRG (one-fifth in the above example).

This expresses the short-stay credit in terms equivalent to inpatient discharges. As utilization review in Portugal is limited, some patients who could be treated as outpatients may be one-day admissions in Portugal. This implies that a wider definition of short-stay outliers may be desirable. However, this concern must be seen in context: Portugal is preparing a case mix–based system to fund outpatient care. As short-stay outlier policies will need to be integrated with ambulatory care reform, these reforms might be best accomplished simultaneously.

A long-stay outlier is defined as a discharge with a length of stay greater than 1.96 standard deviations (in logarithms) above the geometric mean, or seventeen days above the length of stay for the DRG, whichever is less. Allocation for long-stay outliers is based on the length of stay beyond this trim point. Cases with a length of stay of 3 standard deviations or less (but meeting the outlier definition) will be allotted an additional amount of 60 percent of the DRG per diem rate for each day over the upper limit. These credits begin when the cases cross the outlier threshold and continue until the patient is discharged or until the stay reaches the 3 standard deviation maximum. Thus, a long-stay outlier of fifteen days in a DRG with a trim point of ten days will receive five times 60 percent of the normal DRG credit. As with short-stay outliers, these outliers are included in the count of cases for the hospital (Nh) at the weight equal to the number of long-stay days times 60 percent.

Facilities that specialize in providing nonacute care are almost nonexistent in Portugal; their role is filled, to a large degree, by the extended family. However, some cases require extended hospital stays. This implies that an additional category is needed for cases with very long stays. Cases with a length of stay of more than 3 standard deviations above the geometric mean are termed very-long-stay outliers and will receive an additional amount, equivalent to room and board costs per day as defined by the Department of Finance, until the patient is discharged or until continued stay review denies additional credit. The DRG-based budget allocation system is expected to greatly reduce the number of these cases. However, there is legislation under which hospitals provide room and board for people (for example, a mother) who reasonably need to stay with a patient during the patient's hospital stay. These individuals are not captured by the DRG data systems at present, but some accommodation for this humanitarian practice will need to be built into the information and budgeting systems. This accommodation will probably resemble the policy for very-long-stay outliers.

Under the DRG-based allocation system, transfer cases are handled in two ways. Most transfers are treated in the same manner as short-stay outliers in that the transferring hospital will be credited at the DRG per-diem rate up to the full DRG rate. Alternatively, for two kinds of transfers (burn and neonatal cases), the transferring hospital is given a transfer DRG and will be credited at the appropriate DRG rate. Thus, the number of cases (Nh) in our allocation formula is increased to account for those transfer cases that are not credited through the DRG system by the actual length of stay of the transferred cases divided by the average length of stay of the DRG. This value is constrained to be less than or equal to 1.0.

Portugal has a fair number of cases that are admitted to a small hospital, transferred to a larger hospital for treatment, and then returned to the small hospital for recovery. It seems reasonable to limit the credit for the recovery to the DRG amount, but tracking patients requires that an identifying number always be present in the record systems. Though such a number exists in Portugal, hospitals are not required to obtain this number from patients nor to include it in the encounter records, though many do. This is because most people are covered by the national health service and no one wishes to delay an admission or treatment simply because someone forgot his or her number. This is an issue that will require further exploration.

Including the discharge equivalents for short- and long-stay outliers and for transfer cases in the allocation equation given above modifies the variable for the number of cases (Nh). In addition, the hospital case mix index ($CMIh$) is modified by computing this variable as the weighted average of all discharges, including the discharge equivalents for short- and long-stay outliers and for transfer cases.

One objective of the new approach to providing resources to hospitals based on DRGs was to increase the rationality of the resource allocation process by basing allocation levels on hospital output and by rewarding hospitals that achieved increased efficiency in treating their patients. Implementation of the new system has been carefully considered to minimize the impact on hospitals of unexpected resource shifts and to provide all levels of management with the maximum opportunity to learn and benefit from the system. These objectives have been met by blending hospital-specific and national average costs in setting the DRG payment rates and by providing hospital administrators with positive incentives to, for example, increase the efficiency of patient care. Finally, the allocation formula includes a measure to ensure budget neutrality.

If hospital payments from the NHS were based entirely on

DRG rates computed at the national average, some facilities would face large and sudden reductions in funding while others would enjoy large increases. Changes of these magnitudes could threaten the stability of the health care delivery system, with serious consequences for the citizens of Portugal. Thus, during the early years of the system, DRG rates used to compute hospital budgets will be based in large part on the prior budgets of the hospital itself. Only a small part of the DRG rate will be based on national average costs, but this part is to increase over time. A virtue of this approach is that it is simple to administer and to understand. In addition, it is easy to establish a schedule for the increase in the national component of the hospital's rates over time. The proposed schedule called for 10 percent of the DRG rate to be based on national average costs in 1990, rising to 30 percent by 1994 and stabilizing at 50 percent in 1995.

To understand how using a blend of hospital-specific and national average costs to set the budget rate changes the allocation formula, we must first define several financial terms. ACh is the average inpatient operating cost per patient for hospital h, inflated to the subject year (1990 in this instance). Note that the hospital's costs (Ch) include the financial effects of the mix of cases it is expected to treat. These case mix effects can be removed by dividing these costs by the hospital's case mix index, that is:

$$ACh = Ch \div CMIh$$

ACp is the Portuguese average cost per case; that is, the sum of ACh divided by the number of hospitals, computed as if all hospitals treated an average (CMI = 1.0) case mix. This calculation is based on the hospital's costs projected to 1990. A blended rate for hospital h will combine the Portuguese national average cost with the hospital's own cost in the proportion for a given year, which we will call α. Thus the blended rate (BRh) can be written as:

$$BRh = \alpha ACh + (1 - \alpha)ACp$$

If the hospital were paid using this blend of hospital-specific and national costs, then its allocation (Ah) under this system would be:

$$Ah = CMIh \times Nh \times BRh$$

The national expenditure (E) under the DRG-based system described by the above equation would be the sum of the allocation levels for all hospitals, or:

$$E = \Sigma Ah$$

However, the National Budget (NB) for inpatient hospital care for a given year may well be more or less than this amount. In addition, extra payments for very-long-stay outlier cases must be added to the hospitals' allocations. Finally, it is necessary to adjust for the apparent increase in case complexity at hospitals due to more complete coding ("code creep") and to set aside monies for unanticipated contingencies. Based on experience elsewhere, code creep is expected to result in increased spending over that anticipated by the model by 3 percent of the total budget. For 1991, for example, it may be decided that 1 percent of the total budget should be reserved out of prudence as a contingency fund. (These funds, if not needed in the given year, would be returned to the system the following year.) Therefore, the funds available for distribution through normal DRG rates (including credits for outlier and transfer cases) would be 96 percent of NB for 1991.

To ensure that the amount expended under the DRG-based system is budget neutral (in other words, that it does not exceed the national budget for inpatient care), it may be necessary to adjust the hospital allocation rates. At this point, we have determined a hospital's allocation under the DRG-based system to be:

$$Ah = Nh \times CMIh \times BRh$$

where Nh is the number of cases or discharges, including an adjustment for short- and long-stay outlier credit and for transfer cases (except for burn and neonatal transfers that are credited through the DRG system). Thus, we have an estimate of total spending (E) if all hospitals were credited using blended rates at the level of their costs. In addition, we have an adjusted national budget amount $(0.96\,NB)$ that takes into account code creep and unanticipated contingencies.

Through a recursive process, rates that exactly spend the budget can now be determined. For example, assume that the adjusted national budget amount $(0.96\,NB)$ is 99 percent of total expenditures, the sum of hospital allocations. Each hospital's blended rate $(\alpha ACh + [1 - \alpha]ACp)$ would then be decreased by multiplying by 0.99 and E would be recalculated. Next, E and $0.96\,NB$ would be compared again, another (smaller) correction factor calculated, and the comparison repeated. This process continues until the two amounts are identical.

Although the blended rates were a policy option to compute the hospitals' NHS budgets, it should be noted that the non-NHS component of the hospitals' inpatient revenue (payments from occupational insurance subsystems and private insurers) results from per-case payments at the national DRG rates.

The credit rules for non-NHS short-stay, long-stay, and transfer cases are the same as for the NHS patients, but payments are delivered on a per-case basis.

Looking Ahead

A brief overview of possible future directions for Portugal must be limited to an outline of broad policy guidelines as the details of any one of these directions would require a separate document. For convenience, these broad directions have been divided into four groupings representing needs-based capitation from the center to the regions, outpatient care, nonacute care, and acute inpatient care. We must emphasize that the following descriptions are intended only to indicate directions that we plan to explore further over the coming years. We have neither the authority nor the desire to commit the government of Portugal to any particular direction; nor can we precisely forecast changes in both the health care and the political arenas that past experience warns us to expect.

Needs-Based Capitation

The needs-based capitation system will measure the health status of the population of a region at a point in time and allocate resources in proportion to the derived demand. This provides regions with powerful incentives to provide care efficiently but also to underprovide care. To offset this negative incentive to underprovide services, provisions will be built into the capitation system to reward regions for improvements in quality of care and efficiency, where high-quality care provided efficiently is defined as care that maximizes the active life expectancy of the population within the resource constraint implied by the region's budget allocation (Woodbury and Manton, 1977).

Rewarding providers for maintaining or improving quality of care is difficult using conventional approaches to capitation payment. In large part this inability to represent the care maintenance function occurs because of the difficulty in measuring it. One of the most difficult problems in developing a capitation system that has internal incentives for quality of care is the creation of a measure for quality of care that can be balanced in an optimization procedure against cost constraints. In this project we plan to use a concept based on an advanced concept in measurement called fuzzy set logic (Zadeh, 1965). DRGs are an example of fixed set logic; fuzzy sets define an individual as more like one type and less like another. This concept is much more powerful than fixed set logic, and it allows one to define "active life expectancy" and use this definition to measure quality of care as an outcome that improves active life expectancy. That is, the effects of the services provided to a regional population will be measured both in terms of their cost and their effect on the active life expectancy of the region's population (Woodbury and Clive, 1974; Manton, Vertrees, and Woodbury, 1990).

In its representation of the quality of care outcome, the

concept of active life expectancy weighs both the duration effect (that is, the extension of time in a given health state) and qualitative features of that outcome defined in terms of the ability of the individual to maintain several dimensions of physical and cognitive functioning and social autonomy. Thus, this quality of care measure represents a very general and flexible indicator of the social and human capital preserved by the care delivered.

This approach is potentially far superior to systems where quality of care is maintained by an independent regulation and review process in which the goal of care efficiency at the level of the individual patient may not be consistent with that of the regional resource allocation system. To illustrate the differences in concept, a person who suffers from a stroke may require rehabilitative care in order to return to a more nearly normal (active) life. Efficient care in this context is the mix of kinds of care (whether extended care or technologically innovative medical care) that achieves this objective for the largest number of people in a region, given the total resources available. Note that this is quite different from providing for all of the needs of a single individual at the minimum cost.

Having received budgets based on need, the regions will allocate resources to providers based on their production. As it is more efficient for the production-based systems to be designed and developed centrally and distributed to the regions, the three following sections describe plans for a complete and comprehensive production-based allocation system. It is, however, useful at this point to note that the total of these parts provides the government with a great deal of flexibility. For example, one could centrally allocate resources to providers based on production and use the capitation model for capital planning and quality assurance.

Outpatient Care

The model for outpatient care is related to the inpatient DRG system. As for inpatient care, a set of categories and their related weights are the basic components. Ambulatory patient groups

(APGs) is the term for an outpatient classification system that is analogous to DRGs (Averill and others, 1990). Use of APGs is planned in Portugal. APGs are used to classify ambulatory visits in much the same way that DRGs classify inpatient hospital discharges. APGs are a refinement of ambulatory visit groups (AVGs), which were developed by Robert Fetter while he was at Yale. There are fewer APGs than AVGs, and the new system will handle outpatient testing and all other outpatient services.

APGs will need to have weights appropriate for Portugal estimated and linked. The actual allocation level will need to be related to the allocation level for DRGs so that hospitals have an incentive (or at least no disincentive) to treat cases on an outpatient basis whenever possible. Finally, the system will require the necessary rules for its implementation.

Nonacute Care

Extended or nonacute inpatient care is needed by patients who cannot be sent home after an acute hospital episode, even though they no longer require acute care. These patients may, for example, be too frail to care for themselves, and there may be no relatives or friends who are able to fill this role. Alternatively, in certain cases (such as hip fractures) inpatient treatment can be completed fairly quickly, but the time needed for recovery is much longer.

Under Portugal's current DRG-based system, hospitals are allocated a per diem to cover the room and board of extended-care patients. At a minimum, the nonacute-care system will recognize the case mix of extended-care patients in much the same way as DRGs measure inpatient case mix (Manton, Vertrees, and Woodbury, 1990). However, there are numerous uncertainties involved in a project of this nature. Some of these uncertainties stem from the fact that an allocation system for this area of care has not been set up before. Thus, even issues as basic as whether time (length of stay) can be included in the system must be resolved.

Acute Inpatient Care

While the initial resource allocation system operationalized the payment rules and regulations, it did not fully reflect the true economics of the budgeting process in Portugal. In reality, budgets are developed by combining fixed costs and average variable costs, whereas the initial system simply projected an average cost by DRG. We are currently planning to incorporate fixed and variable costs in the budget formula. However, neither fixed nor variable costs are appropriate for use in reconciling budgets at the end of the year for the difference between planned and projected discharges by DRG. For this purpose one must recognize the change in total costs that results from an increase or decrease of one unit of output.

Marginal cost is defined as the change in cost associated with a change in the number of cases treated from the number projected. Thus, we plan to explore an interim method for recognizing marginal costs that will assume marginal costs for each DRG to be a percent of average variable costs. The revised budget estimation process may also take into account the differences between hospitals that can affect costs (for example, geographic location, number of beds, teaching status) through the use of peer groups or a formula. In either case, indirect measures such as number of beds are used to define hospitals' roles.

While the interim approaches described above represent improvements to the current resource allocation system, they are to be replaced by more advanced methods. Specifically, a more sophisticated marginal cost pricing model has been developed (Woodbury, Manton, and Vertrees, 1993). This model calculates true marginal costs by DRG. In addition, the model provides nonstochastic estimates of the number of discharges for each hospital for each DRG, and it defines each hospital's role in delivering health care along with an appropriate budget adjustment factor that reflects the cost implications of this role. SOLON and Duke University have constructed a prototype of this multipurpose model, and it will need to be calibrated for use in Portugal.

Two additional tasks are planned that will complete the acute inpatient resource allocation system. These are the development of quality assurance and utilization review mechanisms and the implementation of revised DRGs.

Clearly these are ambitious plans. However, the ambition stems from the scope and complexity of the problems that we must attempt to handle in the most rational possible way. If our ambition were more constrained, our achievements could not match the challenges of the coming decade.

Epilogue

Since this chapter was written, preliminary information regarding the performance of the system has become available, and two significant changes have been implemented.

DRGs give hospitals a positive incentive to reduce average length of stay. In this regard, the preliminary findings are positive. Though length of stay was slowly declining in Portugal prior to the introduction of the DRG system, this trend appears to have continued at a slightly faster rate. In addition, the system has been well received and is supported by most hospital administrators and physicians, although they would like more assistance in using the DRGs for management and quality control than we are able, at present, to provide.

While the above results are positive, DRGs have also been used to identify problem areas within the system. First, the number of short-stay outlier cases was increasing beyond our expectation. Apparently some hospitals are keeping day patients overnight to qualify these cases for the full DRG payment. Since ambulatory services are funded based on the previous year's budget and since there is a chronic underfinancing, hospitals are not encouraged to enhance outpatient care as an alternative to inpatient admissions when clinically appropriate. In addition, excessive numbers of short-stay outliers harm the hospitals in that these cases inappropriately reduce the inlier DRG rates.

While an eventual solution to this problem will involve more adequate payments for outpatient care based on the new

APGs, this solution was not relevant for the near term. Therefore, as an interim approach, it was decided to change the short-
stay outlier criteria to make it more difficult for a case to qualify
for the full DRG credit. While not a true response to this
problem, it will serve until more appropriate steps can be taken.

Second, the financial impact of increasing the national
percentage of the hospitals' blended rate has been systematic by
type of hospital. Large central and high-technology hospitals
have tended to lose revenue, while smaller district and maternity
hospitals have gained revenue. This meant that the national
percentage of the hospitals' blended rates could not be increased to the level that was initially planned unless actions were
taken to even out this effect.

This issue was addressed by recognizing that hospitals
play different roles in delivering health care services and that
these roles have financial implications that are not accounted
for by simply adjusting for case mix. If additional adjustments
were not built into the system, some hospitals would be penal-
ized for the role that they fill.

We explored alternative approaches to this problem and
decided on a peer grouping methodology based on a modification of the current administrative hospital groups, which were
being used in Portugal for a different purpose. The result is that
hospital budgets are now based 20 percent on their peer group
rate and 80 percent on the hospital's own cost. While these
groups are useful, they are somewhat ad hoc. Therefore, we plan
to continue to explore alternative approaches to defining and
using peer groups for hospital funding.

In summary, the Portuguese DRG resource allocation
system appears to be reasonably successful. Physicians and hospital administrators are, in general, pleased with the system,
despite the initial problems that almost invariably accompany
change. Hospitals appear to be responding to the incentive to
treat patients more efficiently by reducing the average length of
stay. The system is also useful in that it enables us to identify
problem areas. Two problem areas—admitting day cases and
the biased impact of the national rates—have already been
identified, and initial responses have been formulated.

References

Averill, R., and others. "Design and Evaluation of a Prospective Payment System for Ambulatory Care." Final report. New Haven, Conn.: 3M Health Information Systems, 1990.

Bentes, M., Urbano, J., Carvalho, M., and Tranquada, S. "Using DRGs to Fund Hospitals in Portugal: An Evaluation of the Experience." Paper presented to the 2nd EuroDRG Workshop on DRGs Linking Patient Information and Costs, Dublin, Apr. 1991.

Bentes, M., Urbano, J., and Hindle, D. "Output-Based Funding in Portugal: Taking the First Steps." Paper presented to the 3rd International Conference on the Management and Financing of Hospital Services, Washington, D.C., May 1989.

Campos, A. "A Hora da Reforma: Linhas Gerais para a Revisão do Serviço Nacional de Saúde em Portugal" (Time to Change: Guidelines for Revision of the National Health Service in Portugal). *Farmácia Portuguesa*, 1990a, *63*, 45–49.

Campos, A. "Estado-Providência. Perspectivas e Financiamento. O Caso da Saúde" (The Providence State. Perspectives and Financing. The Case of the Health Sector). Paper presented to the 1st Luso-Afro-Brasilian Congress on Social Sciences, Coimbra, Portugal, July 1990b.

Campos, A. "Public Needs, Private Sector. The NHS and the Public-Private Mix in Portugal." Paper presented to the World Bank Conference on Private Provision of Social Services, Bellagio, Italy, October 1990c.

Departamento de Estudos e Planeamento da Saúde. "Elementos Estatísticos: Saúde/88" (Statistics on Health: 1988). Lisbon: Portuguese Ministry of Health, 1990a.

Departamento de Estudos e Planeamento da Saúde. "Estabalecimentos Hospitalares" (Statistics on Hospital Facilities: 1989). Lisbon: Portuguese Ministry of Health, 1990b.

Departamento de Estudos e Planeamento da Saúde. "Portugal Saúde 1989" (Statistics on Health: 1989). Lisbon: Portuguese Ministry of Health, 1991.

Departamento de Gestão Financeira dos Serviços de Saúde. "Relatório e Contas" (Annual Report). Lisbon: Portuguese Ministry of Health, 1989.

Departamento de Gestão Financeira dos Serviços de Saúde "Elementos Estatísticos" (Statistics). Lisbon: Portuguese Ministry of Health, 1990.

Freeman, J., Fetter, R., Newbold, R., and Mullin, R. "Development of a DRG Based Payment System for Hospitals in Portugal." Final report. New Haven, Conn.: Health Systems Management Group, School of Organization and Management, Yale University, 1985.

Hindle, D. and Urbano, J. "Grupos de Diagnósticos Homogéneos—DRGs in Portugal." Paper presented to the 2nd International Conference on the Management and Financing of Hospital Services, Sydney, Australia, February 1988.

Manton, K., Vertrees, J., and Woodbury, M.: "Functionally and Medically Defined Subgroups of Nursing Home Populations." *Health Care Financing Review*, 1990, *12*, 47–62.

Organization for Economic Cooperation and Development. "Fichiers de Données sur la Santé" (Data Files on Health), Paris: OECD, 1989.

Sistema de Informação para a Gestão de Serviços de Saúde. "O Novo Sistema de Financiamento dos Hospitais" (The New Funding System for Hospitals). Final report. Lisbon: Portuguese Ministry of Health, 1990.

Urbano, J, and Hindle, D. "Cost Modelling in the Portuguese Government Hospital Sector." Paper presented to the 2nd Patient Classification Systems–Europe Working Conference, Lisbon, June 1987.

Woodbury, M., and Clive, J. "Clinical Pure Types as a Fuzzy Partition." *Journal of Cybernetics*, 1974, *4*, 111–121.

Woodbury, M., and Manton, K. "A Random Walk Model of Human Mortality and Aging." *Theoretical Population Biology*, 1977, *11*, 37–48.

Woodbury, M., Manton K., and Vertrees, J. "A Model for Allocating Budgets in a Closed System Which Simultaneously Computes DRG Allocation Weights." *Journal of Operations Research*, 1993.

Zadeh, L. "Fuzzy Sets." *Information Control*, 1965, *8*, 338–353.

Eight

Norway: Innovation and the Political Agenda

Torbjørg Hogsnes

Norway is a country of 320,000 square kilometers with a population of slightly over 4 million (Table 8.1). It is governed by a three-tier parliamentary system; each tier is governed by a popularly elected body, the Parliament, the county council, and the municipality council. The country is divided into nineteen counties and 448 municipalities.

The Parliament sets laws and general policy; the county council and the municipality council are responsible for formulating and implementing policy within the general framework of responsibilities delegated to them by Parliament.

All public services, including health care, are organized on a county and municipality level (Table 8.2).

The Norwegian government became decentralized in the 1980s. The financing system for the counties and municipalities has changed as a consequence. County and municipality budgets are now derived from the state and from local taxes. The combined county and municipality taxation level (21 percent in 1991) is set by the state. Since 1986 the country's global budget has covered all public services noted in Table 8.2 and is calcu-

Note: The author wishes to thank Ola Kindseth and Harald E. Hauge for reviewing and commenting on this chapter.

Table 8.1. Key Health Care Figures for Norway.

Country area	320,000 sq. km.
Population, 1989	4.2 million
% of population over 75	6.9%
Average income per household, 1988	NKr 157,400 ($24,215)
Per-capita spending on health care, 1988	NKr 10,600 ($1,630)
% of GDP spent on health care	
1980	6.6%
1988	7.6%
Number of acute-care hospitals, 1989	85
Ratio of acute-care hospital beds to inhabitants, 1989	3.57 per 1,000
Number of acute-care hospital discharges	
1988	631,901
1989	607,054
Average length of stay in acute-care hospitals	
1988	8 days
1989	7.6 days
Hospital outpatient episodes	
1988	2.62 million
1989	2.56 million
Number of physicians (approx.)	10,000
Number of physicians in hospitals (approx.)	5,000
Ratio of physicians to inhabitants	1 per 420

lated according to certain allocation statistics for each type of service. A general contribution equalizes any difference in tax income. This ensures that the counties and municipalities can provide equitable services to their inhabitants because their sector support will equalize any difference in costs, and the general contribution will equalize any difference in tax income.

Table 8.2. County and Municipal Services.

County	Municipal
High schools	Primary and secondary schools
Hospitals, health care specialists, and dental services	Primary health and social services
Ambulatory service	Nursing homes and care for the mentally retarded
Institutions for alcohol, drugs, and child care	Culture
Communication	

Table 8.3. Method of Allocating Health Expenditures to Counties.

Criteria		Weight
Inhabitants	0–15 years	0.11
Inhabitants	16–66 years	0.50
Inhabitants	67–79 years	0.16
Inhabitants	>80 years	0.10
One-person household	>67 years	0.05
Land area		0.02
Inhabitants in sparsely populated areas:		0.06
In addition to Oslo	10%	
In addition to Troms	2.5%	
In addition to Finnmark	15%	
Total		1.0

The state finances approximately 30 percent of county and municipality budgets.

Approximately 35 percent of county and 65 percent of municipality expenditures for health and social services are financed by the state. State support is based on certain allocation weights or statistics, and the counties and municipalities receive the money as part of the global budget for all their services. The allocation method for health services is as shown in Tables 8.3 and 8.4.

The allocation system helps control total spending on health care and gives the government the ability to implement national goals according to the general health policy set by Parliament. One goal has been that the growth in spending for hospital care should be lower than for primary health care. Annual expenditures grew 2.2 percent between 1984 and 1987 for acute hospital care compared with 4.8 percent in the same period for primary health care.

Hospitals in Norway are public and are owned by the counties. A few are owned by voluntary organizations, but these are on the county health plan and receive public support as the others do. Only two hospitals with a total of fifteen beds are run for profit. Service in these hospitals is privately paid for, unlike public hospitals, where inpatient care is free. During the last

Table 8.4. Method of Allocating Health Expenditures to Municipalities.

Criteria		Weight
Inhabitants	0–15 years	0.08
Inhabitants	16–66 years	0.14
Inhabitants	67–79 years	0.18
Inhabitants	>80 years	0.40
Inhabitants in sparsely populated areas		0.06
One-person household	>67 years	0.05
Social clients		0.02
Basic allocation: (each of 448 municipalities receive equal share of $\frac{1}{448}$)		0.07
Extra to:		
Oslo	10%	
Bergen	7.5%	
Trondheim	5%	
Stavanger	5%	
Troms	2%	
Finnmark	15%	
Total		1

Source: Ministry of Health and Social Affairs, 1990–1991.

years there has been considerable debate over whether to allow the existence of private hospitals. A legal case is currently under way to determine whether politicians can prohibit private hospitals from existing if public hospitals cannot adequately serve the citizens. The question arose because there are long waiting lists for certain treatments (in orthopedics specialties; general surgery; ear, nose, and throat; gynecology; hip replacement; and cataract removal). At the end of 1989, 105,000 patients were on waiting lists for hospital treatment.

Hospitals are organized in a hierarchical structure across regions, counties, and districts. This structure was set out in the Hospital Act of 1970 and a parliamentary report of 1974–1975. Norway is divided into five health regions, each with its regional hospital. Four of the hospitals are owned by the county in which they are located. The fifth hospital, which serves as a national hospital for highly specialized services, is owned by the state.

Each of the nineteen counties has one county and several district hospitals. There are a total of sixty-six district hospitals. The organizational structure for the entire hospital sector is based on the principle of treatment for all patients at the lowest efficient level of care. The first level is primary health care, which includes basic health services and is the foundation from which all other services and care proceed. This is stated in the Act on Municipality Health Services that came into force in 1984. If a person needs more specialized services, the primary care physician chooses which hospital the patient should enter, normally one within the county of residence. Only if acute care is necessary is the patient allowed to enter a hospital on his or her own.

Hospital budgets are set by county councils as a global budget at the beginning of each year. For outpatient treatment, hospitals are paid fixed prices directly by the National Insurance System. This is an outgrowth of an older system under which physicians were allowed to treat outpatients in hospitals on a private basis. In the past, prices were the same for treatment in private practice and in hospitals, but since 1988 the price lists have been separate. The state now sets the prices for outpatient care in hospitals. Private practice prices are set after negotiations with the Association of Physicians.

Hospitals are paid separately by the state for research and teaching services. The state also sets prices for specialized services bought outside the county. As of 1991, three different prices had been set for services bought from regional hospitals. The prices are fixed and are not calculated according to the hospitals' real cost. The county is not allowed to reduce the prices or give discounts.

The global budget system has been effective in achieving cost containment, but it gives hospitals no incentive to produce more services. In the case of rationalization, the county council may sometimes withdraw the surplus and use it for other health care services. The county council will also give extra money to hospitals if there is a deficit at the end of the year. This has caused hospitals to have weak budget discipline and no incentive for efficiency. As an incentive to use resources more wisely, hospitals are now given more freedom over their budgets to the

extent that they are allowed to keep any surplus at year's end. At
the same time, they may also bear the risk of any deficit.

This method of financing hospitals, combined with the
shift to a more decentralized system in the last decade, means
that hospitals are no longer subject to tight control and detailed
scrutiny from the national level. Some specific rules remain,
however, such as the state-controlled guidelines on employing
physicians in hospitals. Because Norway is a large but sparsely
populated country, it is difficult to attract people with higher
education to the northern and western regions. The market for
specialists in hospitals is, therefore, regulated. Hospitals are not
allowed, for example, to hire a heart surgeon if the committee
(*Legefordelingsutvalget*) has not given its approval.

The role of the state is also to influence and develop new
technology or health care methods. For developing such work,
hospitals and counties are supported with extra money from the
state because the global budget only covers running costs. The
Ministry of Health and Social Affairs decides what work should
be supported. Normally, projects given high political priority
are those that seek to reduce waiting lists, educate nurses, or
stimulate people to work in the northern part of Norway. There
has been no national strategy for developing information systems because this has been viewed as the responsibility of the
counties and municipalities. The consequence of this policy is
that the use of information technology in the health care sector
lags behind other sectors and varies greatly across hospitals. On
the national level, several institutions are collecting information
about health, activity, and resources in the health care sector.
Different reports are produced by the Directorate of Health, the
Central Bureau of Statistics, and the National Insurance System.
Efforts have been made to establish a national health information system, but so far this has not been approved because of
political opposition to plans to attach the information to the
personal identification numbers of the individual patients.

The state plays an important but not absolute role in
setting health care policy. Nevertheless, it is still usual for the
counties and municipalities to blame the government—and at

the same time ask it for help when things go wrong in the health care sector.

The Health Care Debate

In 1983 the health care debate became rather intense in Norway. The waiting time for certain elective surgery procedures was very long. The country's oil income had declined, and the growth of health care expenditures had become a political problem. Within the last decade, hospital expenditures had increased by 50 percent, so that by 1983 annual spending exceeded NKr 25 billion ($3.85 billion). The political focus was on the increasing numbers of elderly people, long waiting lists, and increasing costs in the health care sector. The debate centered on whether to allow private hospitals or not. Newspapers published daily accounts of mistakes and inefficiencies in public hospitals. Forced to do something, politicians decided to give priority to increased efficiency.

The Ministry of Health and Social Affairs became responsible for determining appropriate directions. A steering committee was established under the leadership of the deputy minister. Two working groups, one for hospital and one for primary health care, were also created to give advice and follow up on different kinds of projects. Roughly NKr 5 million ($770,000) was earmarked for the work, and a secretary was appointed in the ministry.

This was not the first time the Ministry of Health and Social Affairs had decided to increase efficiency in hospitals. Since 1950 different reports and recommendations to the Ministry of Health and Social Affairs had pointed out the need for such reform. One 1950 report recommended that the director general of health have an advisory board concerning rationalization. In 1974 a public governmental investigation concluded that efforts to increase efficiency had been ad hoc and lacked any guidelines for application ("Effectiviseringsvirksomhet. . .," 1974). Efforts had mostly focused on solving serious problems, but resources to carry out the proposals were very limited. Although several recommendations were made, very little happened afterwards.

A new committee appointed by the director general of health in 1979 concluded that priority had been given to the expansion of all health care activities instead of to rationalization. The reasons given were the following:

- There had been growth in the gross domestic product and therefore no need for rationalization.
- There existed no simple, well-accepted criteria for effectiveness and efficiency.
- Efforts at rationalization had not been well organized, and the methods consequently failed.

As a result of the 1979 committee findings, the Ministry of Health and Social Affairs realized that better efforts to increase efficiency and effectiveness in the health care sector were necessary. Health care then was 11.5 percent of total public expenditures (NKr 20 billion of 174 billion), of which hospitals accounted for 75 percent. A new committee was appointed in 1981 and its recommendations came out in the same year. A major finding was that data on hospital production would be necessary if medical resources were to be effectively managed. Moreover, this information should be as detailed as possible and should include prices for hospital services. To rationalize at the departmental level, each department should know what it produced and what its costs were. These figures should be comparable to other departments ("Medisinsk rasjonalisering," 1981).

The information system hospitals used at the time was called Economic Medical Information. Developed at the national level, the system provided a minimum of information about production and costs. Not all hospitals used the system.

The counties' direct control over hospitals financing and management has been and is still under debate. The hospital's budget is approved by the county council. Hospital employees claim that county politicians get involved in internal hospital matters and that the staff are not given enough freedom to operate in an efficient way. Although a political board normally monitors hospital activities, the board lacks any responsibility for problems whenever the hospital registers a deficit. In recent years the hospital board has been given more power. A number of projects are under way to evaluate new ways of organizing the political decision-making process of hospitals.

Since 1981 efforts have been made to decentralize the responsibility for budgeting and cost accounting in hospitals. This is considered necessary if hospitals are to achieve efficiency. The Ministry of Local Government is changing the rules for hospital budgeting and cost accounting; the latest change came into force in January 1991.

Hospitals are run by a managing director who normally is not a physician. The director is assisted by a controller, a personnel manager, and a technical manager. A chief physician and chief nurse are also part of the management team.

At the departmental level, management is divided between a physician and a nurse. The experience from this organizational model is that the managing director has little influence on physicians' decisions at the departmental level. Divided leadership at this level has caused problems, especially when the department is responsible for its own budget and resource utilization.

In searching for new ways to organize relations between the county and the hospitals, changing the internal management system has been found to be rather cumbersome. In the regional hospital in Tromsø, the hospital board decided to try a new organizational model with only one leader at the departmental level who would be responsible for medical and administrative matters. The experiment caused such a conflict between the physicians and nurses that the Ministry of Health had to step in to calm things down.

In January 1990 the Ministry of Health and Social Affairs appointed the Andersland Committee under the leadership of the deputy minister to evaluate the management of hospitals and make suggestions for the future. The main purpose was to stress the importance of management in using hospital resources more efficiently. The group's main recommendation was to decentralize more power and responsibility from the county to the hospital general director. At the departmental level only one person should be given the responsibility for medical, economic, and administrative matters.

One of the problems pointed out both in the Tromsø hospital project and by the Andersland Committee was a lack of the necessary information to manage hospitals efficiently. Hospital departmental budgets are based on historical data, and the cost accounting systems vary from one hospital to another. No hospital is able to produce information about patient treatment and costs. The Andersland Committee concluded that it should be a goal to use diagnosis-related groups (DRGs) to produce management information in hospitals. (The report — Ministry of Health and Social Affairs, 1990b — will probably be acted on by some hospitals.) The regional hospital in Tromsø has already made the decision to have one top manager at the departmental level and is planning to test the DRG system as a managerial tool in one of the hospital's departments.

Diffusion of DRGs

As part of its long-term public policy goals for the period 1986–1989, Norway's Conservative government drew up strategies for health policy. Based on these strategies, the steering committee appointed by the Ministry of Health in 1984 under the leadership of the deputy ministry decided to support projects with the following goals:

- To reduce variations in medical practice
- To develop a national bank of ideas for improving and rationalizing work
- To investigate whether the DRG system could be used to measure hospital productivity
- To develop efficient management

The proposal to use DRGs was brought up by Jan Grund, an adviser to the Ministry of Health and Social Affairs who also was a member of the steering committee. He asked a consulting group to prepare a project proposal, which was passed to the ministry in April 1985.

Members of the working group for hospital rationalization had also recommended a similar project. A physician in the group, Trygve Høsteng, was then involved in a project on the economic analysis of hospitals in Hedmark. In trying to find a measure that could be used to develop a uniform plan and budget for all hospitals in the county, the researchers recommended the use of DRGS.

Physicians Bo Arnesjø, Jan Erikssen, and Trygve Høsteng also pointed out that DRGs could be useful in standardization and quality improvement. Any large variation in costs across hospitals for the same DRG should be investigated. They also suggested that treatment guidelines for patients under DRGs should be drawn up. Thus both hospital quality and efficiency would improve.

In the fall of 1984 the Norwegian Institute for Hospital Research (NIS) began a pilot study on the DRG system that was financed by the Ministry of Health and Social Affairs. The result, a literature review, was reported in September 1985 (Aas, 1985).

Two nurses from Aust-Agder central hospital, Tora Halvorsen and Anne Haugmoen Karlsen, also completed a report on DRGs in May 1985. They concluded that aspects of the DRG system could be used in Norwegian hospitals, and they referred to the growing interest in DRGs in England, the Netherlands, and Sweden at the time.

In October 1985 Bo Arnesjø invited people from NIS, Haukeland Hospital, and the Ministry of Health to Haukeland Hospital to discuss the DRG approach in Norway. The group developed a plan to launch a three-phase DRG project that would include the following:

1. An analysis of whether the American DRG system could be applied to Norwegian discharge abstracts in developing a Norwegian DRG
2. Development of a model for patient-related costing as a means of relating Norwegian cost weights to DRGs
3. Implementation of DRGs in some hospitals

One reason for developing specific cost weights was because otherwise the system would not have been accepted by Norwegian physicians. Another reason was that the American cost weights did not include the physician's fee; in Norway, hospital physicians are paid fixed salaries.

The project was approved by the Ministry of Health, and the research was conducted by NIS in conjunction with Haukeland Hospital. The project ran from 1986 to 1990. A steering committee was appointed whose members were county administrators Bjørn Walle and Per Roland, surgeons Bo Arnesjø and Hans Olav Myhre, researchers Sverre Harvey and Harald Buhaug, and I, representing the Ministry of Health and Social Affairs. The role of the steering committee was to monitor the project, but any final decisions about the project were made by the Ministry of Health and Social Affairs.

NIS sought the advice of Robert Fetter and his group of experts at Yale University in designing the Norwegian DRGs. Fetter's group had had considerable experience with DRGs, both in the United States and in other countries. In December 1985 Fetter visited both the Swedish Planning and Rationalization Institute of the Health and Social Services (Spri) in Stockholm and NIS in Trondheim in order to launch two projects on DRGs with Spri and NIS.

In January 1986 a research proposal from the Yale School of Organization and Management was offered to Norway. Fetter offered technical assistance for the development and implementation of a DRG-based cost accounting, budgeting, and management information system for Norway's hospitals. The project had four phases:

1. Assessing the technical feasibility of assigning DRG numbers to discharge abstracts in Norwegian hospitals
2. Evaluating whether the utilization model defined by the DRGs is adequate for Norway's hospitalization data
3. Adapting the U.S. DRG-based cost and budgeting model to make it applicable to Norway's financial data and hospital setting

4.   Reprogramming the cost model software for accounting
and budgeting analyses on in-house microcomputers

A contract between NIS and Yale was set up for phase one
in March 1987. The work in this phase involved translation of
diagnoses and procedure codes in Norwegian discharge abstracts to American standards (ICD9-CM). In early 1987 Norway
had converted from the ICD8 codes to the ICD9 codes. Norway
also has a national code list for procedures. Both coding systems
had to be converted to the American ICD9-CM.

The Yale group had previously mapped disease codes
from international ICD9 to ICD9-CM. This mapping had been
used in cooperation with several countries as a basis for national
disease-mapping tables. Quality control of this mapping table
had been performed by the different countries.

The present practice in Norway concerning use of disease
codes is to sometimes use classification on the three-digit level
even when a fourth digit is available. For this reason, all three-
digit codes in the Norwegian disease code book were included
in the mapping table when the information on the three-digit
level was sufficient for DRG grouping.

At this stage a preliminary DRG grouping was performed
for 87,245 hospital stays from thirty-seven Norwegian hospitals.
The material was analyzed and the mapping table improved. A
control of the DRG grouping was made for a total of 11,040
patients. The conclusion was that good control had been
achieved over possible errors introduced by mappings. The
frequency of erroneous DRG assignments after final corrections
to the mapping table was very low (less than 0.3 percent). Other
factors are more important for correct DRG assignment, such as
the quality of the input data.

A statistical test was conducted of DRGs homogeneous in
length of stay. The homogeneity of the Norwegian DRGs based
on Norwegian material showed results quite similar to the U.S.
results. A report summarizing the work in designing Norwegian
DRGs was submitted to the ministry in March 1989 (Aas, Freeman, Palmer, and Fetter, 1989).

Table 8.5. Cost Weight Components.

Cost	Share of Total (%)
Basic cost	56.3
Nursing	11.0
Intensive care	1.9
Surgery	14.5
Medical procedures	3.6
X-rays	4.9
Laboratories	4.9
Drugs	3.1

DRG Cost Weights

Work on DRG cost weights started in 1987. At the time, no hospitals had cost accounting systems that related hospital costs (for example, x-rays, lab test procedures) to the patient. It was therefore decided to combine different methods in collecting data and to use data from the different hospital cost accounting systems.

The method used to relate cost to DRGs was based on Fetter's cost model. The work was completed in 1990 (Slåttebrekk, 1990). In estimating the cost weights, three different kinds of data were used: average length of stay for 200,000 patients from twenty hospitals, allocation statistics for a number of services from Haukeland Hospital, and allocation statistics for laboratories and drugs from the cost weights of hospitals in Maryland.

The average length of stay was used to allocate 56 percent of the total costs. Together with nursing weights, the average length of stay is also used to allocate nursing costs, which amount to 11 percent of the total. This means that two-thirds of total costs are based on length of stay, though with a considerable variation among DRGs (see Table 8.5).

The cost of surgery was estimated on the basis of 23,000 operations, each measured by duration, personnel, and equipment used. Several studies were undertaken to establish allocation statistics for medical procedures, x-rays, and different therapies.

In this way it was possible to estimate 319 DRGs out of a total of 467. This covers 98 percent of the patients in Norwegian hospitals. For the remaining DRGs, we are using the American cost weights.

The basic cost is allocated only according to average length of stay, while the remaining cost components differ from one DRG to another. The cost of surgery will be dominant for some surgical DRGs, whereas basic costs and nursing will determine most of the costs within the medical DRGs. It was concluded that despite existing data, more cost information is necessary.

The cost weights in Table 8.5 should be viewed as a first set of cost weights. With better information systems in the hospitals and higher-quality medical data, the cost weights will need to be recalibrated.

When the Ministry of Health and Social Affairs received the cost report, the deputy minister gave an interview to *Aftenposten*, the largest newspaper in Norway, about the value of DRGs and the Norwegian cost weights. In the article ("Cost of Norwegian patients," 1990), he recommended the use of DRGs in hospitals. He pointed out that DRGs make it possible to compare hospital production and thus inspire higher quality and efficiency. At the same time he announced that the ministry would start a DRG-based prospective payment experiment in which four hospitals would be reimbursed 40 percent of their budget according to their DRG activity.

Shortly after the cost report, NIS worked out a price list for all DRGs that could be used by the Ministry of Health and Social Affairs in the DRG-based payment experiment. The prices were based on the average cost level in 1988 in twenty Norwegian hospitals with 200,000 discharges (Ministry of Health and Social Affairs, 1990a).

In the DRG research work, NIS collaborated with the other Nordic countries. This cooperation began in 1987 in Copenhagen. Since then researchers from Norway, Denmark, Sweden, Finland, and Iceland have met annually. The aim of the group is to discuss methods and results from their DRG re-search. Since March 1991 the group's name has been Resource Management Group to reflect the fact that its interests extend beyond DRGs.

Norway also participated in the European network on DRGs and thus got further reinforcement for its work on DRGs. Today Norway is a member of the Patient Classification System–Europe organization and is also participating in the Advanced Informatics in Medicine program in Europe.

DRGs in Hospitals

At the end of 1987 I took the initiative and invited NIS to begin implementing DRGs in one region that had ten hospitals. The idea was to establish whether the DRG system could be imple-mented in hospitals, what tools were required, and whether the system might be of any value in hospital planning and budgeting.

In keeping with the objectives and strategies of the minis-try's steering committee for rationalization, it was also of interest to find out whether the DRG system could be of value in compar-ing hospitals and in regional planning across county borders. Thus, a regional hospital and all other hospitals within that region were included because the local hospitals buy a lot of patient treatment from the regional hospital. It was also believed that using DRGs in hospitals would begin to improve the quality of the data.

Although the original plan was to begin implementing the system in 1990, the Ministry of Health and Social Affairs decided that NIS should begin implementation sooner. All the counties from one health region were invited to participate by the Ministry of Health and Social Affairs, and a meeting was arranged in each county with representatives from the county administration, the hospital administration, NIS, and the ministry.

At the meeting the kind of information the hospitals had to register in order to use DRGs and the tools they needed were discussed and defined. It was decided that NIS should develop the software necessary to group the patients in DRGs. NIS developed the necessary supplemental tools to use the 1985 Yale University grouper and the application software for analyses and statistics.

At this time the routine for collecting patient medical data varied greatly among the hospitals. Because hospitals did not even collect discharge data, it was not possible to implement the DRG system in all ten hospitals at the same time.

The project ran until June 1991. According to a preliminary report from NIS that was passed to the ministry at the end of 1990, the experience can be summarized as follows: A lot of work was necessary to develop the software for producing statistical reports on DRGs. People also had to be trained to use the system. Very few physicians were involved in the project. The contact between NIS and the hospitals was mainly through the general director and people in the computer information department. Some hospitals have produced statistics four times a year, others only once a year. When the project started, the Norwegian DRG cost weights were not attached to the DRGs. After implementing the DRG cost weights in 1990, political interest in DRGs rose, and the information was used to compare hospital efficiency and productivity.

No hospital has used DRGs for internal managerial purposes. The reason might be that the hospitals were not able to handle the DRG system. They did not really understand the logic and structure of DRGs to the extent necessary to use the system for managerial purposes.

The DRG-Based Payment Experiment

The most significant DRG project underway in Norway is the DRG-based Payment Experiment in Stykkprisforsoket. In its initial phase, from January 1991 through December 1992, four acute-care hospitals had their income based on a combination of standard reimbursement and variable DRG-based reimbursement. All patients were included in the project. For outpatient and day surgery, the hospitals were paid according to a fixed price list decided by the government. Of the four hospitals, one

Table 8.6. Characteristics of the DRG-Based Payment
Experiment Hospitals.

Hospital	Beds[a]	Discharges	Employees
Haukeland	1,140	45,158	4,000
Stord	111	4,504	350
Norland	373	15,331	1,450
Rana	80	3,856	350

[a] The average size of Norwegian hospitals is 200 beds.

is a regional and university hospital in Haukeland (one of Norway's largest hospitals), one is a county hospital, and two are district hospitals (see Table 8.6).

The recommendation to launch a DRG-based payment experiment was given by the Eilertsen committee, which had been appointed by the Ministry of Health in 1985 to evaluate the current system of organizing and financing hospitals and to propose options for more efficient resource utilization and management. The committee concluded that it was inopportune to undertake large political administrative reforms that would change the ownership structure and operating patterns of hospitals.

The committee did, however, recommend a new model for financing hospitals. According to this model, hospitals would receive the largest part of their funds as a fixed budget, but in addition they would receive payment for each patient treated. DRGs were recommended as a system for patient classification and reimbursement. This conclusion was based on a report about DRGs that the committee had commissioned from NIS about the possibility of using DRGs as a system for payment (Magnussen, 1986).

The reason for suggesting a new financing model for hospitals was, as stated earlier, that the global budget for hospitals did not encourage efficient resource utilization. When hospitals have a fixed budget at the beginning of the year, they benefit from treating fewer patients. To offset this tendency, a certain percentage of the budget should be tied to patient care,

272 The Migration of Managerial Innovation

and the rest of the budget should account for geographical and other differences that concern the organization of services.

The committee's proposal was to give hospitals 80 percent as a global budget and 20 percent as variable reimbursement ("Sykehustjenester i Norge," 1987). Variable DRG reimbursement is intended to create competition among hospitals, which in turn should stimulate the hospitals to higher productivity. The committee's conclusions were approved by Parliament in 1988, with nonpartisan agreement to the experiment.

The 1991–1992 DRG-Based Payment Experiment was run by the Ministry of Health and Social Affairs. The aim of the project was to increase efficiency in hospitals through economic incentives. A steering group monitored the project, but final decisions on its future will be made by the ministry (Hogsnes, 1990).

Using Norwegian DRG cost weights, the Ministry of Health and Social Affairs has published a price list for all DRGs. In the project, the hospitals are reimbursed 40 percent of the published price list according to their DRG activity. The remaining 60 percent is given as a block budget.

The DRG price does not cover costs for long-term patients, research, or medical teaching. The treatment of severe cases or long-term care is financially covered by the basic reimbursement, and for research and teaching purposes the regional hospital gets extra money from the state.

The model implies that the hospital budget is decided by the county and based on an activity plan that is set in terms of DRGs. The state uses the activity plan to determine how much estimated income from the prospective payment system to hold back from the budget. Each month a bill is calculated on the basis of the number of patients treated in each DRG and of the prices set by the state. This bill is sent to the National Insurance System, which in turn reimburses the hospital.

If the hospital fulfills its activity plan, the hospital will end up the same as under the old system. In the case of higher activity, the state will pay for the higher activity. In case of lower activity, the hospitals are worse off than under the old financing system, which means that they lose money.

The model gives the hospitals two incentives. First and most important is the incentive to treat patients with a minimum use of resources. Second is the incentive to utilize the capacity within the hospital to treat more patients. Paying for treatment above the committed activity plan will show which treatments will be given priority by the hospital. Will the priorities be according to demand or to economic surplus? This information will be of value in making decisions about the financing model.

Beyond Financial Incentives

To create motivation for cost consciousness and higher productivity in hospitals one has to combine financial incentives with other efforts. It is also necessary that the incentives reach those who decide and are responsible for resource utilization, that is, the physicians. Other efforts have therefore been included in the payment experiment. These include better planning and budgeting, incentives for physicians, improved cost accounting, staff education, and quality assurance systems.

The hospitals are obliged to use DRGs for planning and budgeting. The clinicians should be active in working out goals and activity plans for the whole hospital, which then have to be discussed with the county. Using DRGs will give politicians more information about hospital activities and hospital costs, which they can use in setting priorities for the hospital.

To create cost consciousness and make the hospital more efficient, incentives should be given to the physicians in the hospital. In the project each hospital has to set up rules about handling surpluses or deficits for the hospital. The rules should be approved by the county authorities. So far only one hospital, Haukeland Hospital, has established contracts with its clinics that are based on activity plans for each department and connected to the departments' budgets. Prospective payment rates per DRG are set for each department, reflecting the part of the treatment costs the department is responsible for. These payment rates are generally lower than the payment rates faced by the hospital. The other hospitals have decided to reward good clinicians with new technical equipment, education, and so on if the hospital turns out to be more efficient than before.

None of the hospitals in the project knows its own patient costs. Great efforts are being made to develop cost accounting systems in order to compare the patients' actual costs with the DRG price. In 1987 the Ministry of Health and Social Affairs supported a project in two hospitals, the Regional Hospital in Tromsø and Telemark Central Hospital, for developing cost accounting systems. From these projects we have learned that it is difficult to develop and introduce cost accounting systems in hospitals that are of value for the clinicians in planning treatment for patients.

Two characteristics seem to be important in hospital cost accounting systems: the information must be given in an understandable way, and the physicians must have incentives to operate more efficiently. In the DRG-Based Payment Experiment, the ministry now cooperates with these two hospitals. Though the DRG-Based Payment Experiment motivates the work, the work should be given higher priority by the county and hospital administrators.

To motivate its staff, each hospital has its own information and education plan. Special educational programs will be developed to use DRGs in management.

None of the hospitals involved in the project has any quality assurance system. Neither do other hospitals in Norway. Therefore it is hard to tell whether the payment system will reduce quality of treatment. We believe quality is good because we have well-educated staff in the hospitals; but in Norway, as in the United States and other countries, complaints about mistakes in hospitals are rising. To answer the question, Does DRG-based payment in hospitals reduce quality?, a research group from the Norwegian Institute of Public Health (*Folkehelsa*) will conduct a study of the impact of DRGs on quality. So far the hospital physicians have cooperated with the research group in this work. In addition to quality, hospital productivity and efficiency will be measured by NIS. The DRG-financed hospitals will be compared to other hospitals, and the DRG system will be used for comparison.

In March 1991 Robert Fetter visited Norway with representatives from the 3M Company at the request of the project
leader from the Ministry of Health and Social Affairs. Meetings
were arranged in Haukeland Hospital and the Central Hospital
in Nordland. The purpose of the meetings was to learn about
the development of DRGs in the United States and how far U.S.
researchers had come with a system of outpatient grouping. In
the payment experiment, Norway has been using the 1985 Yale
DRG grouper, but a current goal is to change to the latest version
of either Health Care Financing Administration (HCFA) or All
Patient grouper.

DRGs in Other Projects

Until 1986 national statistical reports for the health care sector
were mainly done by Norway's Central Bureau of Statistics. The
quality of the data was poor because of a lack of standardization.
Moreover, no one had ever been too concerned about the data
because they had never been used for comparing efficiency and
productivity in hospitals. No national discharge abstracts from
the hospitals had ever been collected.

In 1986, Ola Kindseth from NIS took the initiative to
collect discharge abstracts from all hospitals in a more standardized way. The proposal was passed to the Ministry of Health and
Social Affairs and the Association of Local Authorities (*Kom-
munenes Sentralforbund*), which both agreed to do this. One motivation behind the proposal was that it had to be done if DRGs
were to be used at a national level to compare hospitals.

In 1988 the first Samdata publication, a comparison of
data across counties and across hospitals, was released; the next
was published in 1989. In 1990 the ministry decided to use
DRGs for comparing hospitals at the national level.

All eighty-five acute-care hospitals collect information
that makes it possible to group patients treated in DRGs. Some
very small, specialized hospitals use their own procedure codes,
which makes it impossible to use the standard conversion table
to ICD9-CM. For other hospitals, data are missing from some
departments or the quality should be better in order to use the

DRG information. Therefore the DRG system was only used for fifty-eight acute-care hospitals in the 1990 Samdata report, all of which had their discharges grouped in DRGs.

The 1990 Samdata report, published in February 1991, shows that productivity increased in Norwegian hospitals from 1988 to 1989. Using DRGs as a basis for calculation, it was found that the increase in costs per patient was clearly lower than the increase in the general prices (consumer price index). The average patient load (case mix index) increased by 4 percent between 1988 and 1989. Hospitals in Oslo and Finnmark were found to have the highest operating costs. The lowest hospital operating costs were found in Horaland and Rogaland (Jørgensen and Pedersen, 1991).

The 1990 Samdata report has thus far caused little debate on DRGs. NIS is presenting the results at regional conferences, and the ministry is planning to discuss the use of DRGs with the county administrators.

In 1989 the Association of Local Authorities supported an information project on DRGs for all counties and hospitals. Except for Finnmark and Vest-Agder, all counties have arranged meetings for NIS to present DRG-based statistical reports for each hospital. They have also provided information about how DRGs work and how to use them. Despite this widespread effort, only ten hospitals are running DRGs on their own information systems. The patient information systems in Norwegian hospitals vary, so much that we currently have twelve different systems.

For some hospitals, there are technical problems with using the DRG software on their computers. To solve this problem, patient data needed for DRG grouping are extracted from the hospital data base and then grouped into DRGs on a personal computer. For hospitals unable to group DRGs on their own, NIS does the grouping and provides corresponding statistical reports.

Future of DRGs in Norway

There has been relatively little political debate about DRGs in Norway. So far DRGs have been perceived as a tool for making the hospitals more efficient. Since 1980 the political situation in Norway has been rather unstable; governments have come and gone. When the DRG project started in 1986, a Conservative government was in power. That was followed by a Labor government, which was overtaken by a Conservative government, which was in turn replaced by the current Labor government. Rather than causing disunity and uncertainty, the revolving governments have produced a consensus among parties to test new systems as a means of using tax dollars in the health care sector more efficiently.

The Association of Physicians has also reacted favorably to the DRG project in Norway. The group believes the system might result in more money for hospitals and inspire more efficiency and a fairer distribution of monetary resources to hospitals. Current hospital budgets are decided on the basis of historical data and arguments from powerful physicians.

In general, however, use of the DRG grouping in hospitals in Norway should still be looked on as experimental. Only in the payment experiment has the use of DRGs been mandatory. DRG use also remains mostly a financial issue. In the payment experiment, for example, DRGs have been used for patient classification and reimbursement. Some counties are also using statistical DRG information from NIS to adjust their hospital budgets. So far DRGs have not been used for external control or regulation or for internal management. In the payment experiment, efforts have been made to use DRGs as a measure for strategic planning, departmental budget setting, and management control.

Before the advent of DRGs, statistical information from hospitals was divided into resource information and medical information. Data have been collected mostly in response to county regulations and claims and to requirements from the Directorate of Health, the Ministry of Health and Social Affairs, and other national institutions. Any statistical results from the various reports previously described have been of little value in hospital planning, budgeting, and management.

It has been a goal for many years to improve the information system for the health care sector. Prior to DRGs, medical information was collected and entered in the hospital patient information system either by a clerical assistant at the clinical departmental level or by information people in the information department. At the national level, data from hospitals has been collected by different institutions.

As a result of the growing political interest in DRGs, physicians, nurses, and assistant nurses have become more interested in the system. The DRG-Based Payment Experiment revealed that knowledge about DRGs in general among health care practitioners is rather low. The use of DRGs as a payment method has sparked interest in their grouping logic, cost weights, and prices.

Interest in using DRGs as a managerial tool is also beginning to build. Physicians, however, find DRGs difficult to use because they are not accustomed to the notion of planning an activity and connecting that activity to costs. They need to be educated about how to use DRG information, and they need information about their own DRG costs. The cost accounting system must be improved to produce information about the different cost components in each DRG. In a few years this might be possible in some hospitals.

To understand and learn the DRG system, physicians claim they need to operate the system at the clinical departmental level. Only one hospital in the payment experiment currently is able to operate the DRG system on a clinical level. The hospital information system has to be improved on a national basis to a much greater extent for it to be effectively operated at the departmental level.

Norway has a decentralized health care system, and the counties and hospitals are allowed to use different computer systems for information purposes. Because, however, the Ministry of Health and Social Affairs still plays an important role in developing new methods, and because the hospitals are obliged to send a prescribed amount of medical data and resource information to the central level, the future use of DRGs will depend on what the Ministry of Health recommends. The DRG system needs to be medically updated, and the cost weights should be corrected and updated annually. This work must be centralized or it will not be possible to make comparisons across hospitals.

The country has invested more than NKr 6 million ($923,000) in research on DRGs since 1985. No case mix system other than DRGs has been considered, and the Ministry of Health and Social Affairs has no intention of developing its own method. The future use of DRGs in Norway will depend on the results of the DRG payment experiment. The political party in power and economic developments will continue to play a role as well.

Epilogue

Norway remains committed to ensuring that increases in public sector costs do not exceed increases in the gross domestic product. The gross domestic product was expected to increase through 1992–1993 at an annual rate of approximately 2.5 percent. The major part of this growth should come from the private sector, an increase in personal consumption, and gross capital expenditure. The Norwegian economy remains very dependent on its oil industry, which accounts for approximately 30 percent of the country's export product. Unemployment, which now stands at 7.7 percent, is an overriding public policy concern of the Labor government. One of the priorities will be to increase infrastructural programs.

To ensure that public sector costs do not exceed the gross domestic product, the government is committed to continuing efforts to promote rationalization in the public sector. Health care, as a dominant part of the public sector, is a concern in the context of controlling costs and monitoring efficiency and quality. Because the use of DRGs is an important part of this effort, the Ministry of Health and Social Affairs will continue to recommend the system. To use DRGs as a financing system, however, the payment experiment has to be evaluated, and Parliament was scheduled to make the decision in 1993. During the payment experiment, the ministry will take the responsibility for updating the DRG system and cost weights and standardiz-

ing hospital discharge data. This work will be done in cooperation with NIS.

It is likely that the method of financing hospitals will
change in Norway because the current system with its global
budget provides no incentives for efficiency in hospitals. For the
same reason, hospitals in Sweden, Finland, and other European
countries are changing their financing system. In Norway, the
way in which production and financing of health care are sepa-
rated and the fact that municipalities are responsible for buying
hospital care will also increase the demand for a case mix system
like DRGs.

The DRG system has yet to be used for quality improvement as recommended by the physician in the steering group in
1986. Whether differences in costs among hospitals will stimulate efforts to standardize medical performance remains to be
seen. The problem then will be to decide who should determine
guidelines for treatment. Should it be the regional hospitals, the
Directorate of Health, or consensus conferences? Guidelines
that must be followed might be considered restrictions in medical performance and physicians' clinical liberty, which was guaranteed by the 1984 Act of Physicians.

Critics of DRGs in Norway claim that the system focuses
too much on inpatient acute care in hospitals. To effectively
measure the productivity of hospitals and other health institutions, we need grouping systems for outpatient care, day surgery,
psychiatric care, and rehabilitation care, in addition to inpatient care. The Ministry of Health has decided to develop a
grouping system for outpatients. The research is being done by
NIS. A grouping system for psychiatric and rehabilitation care is
not currently planned. For these patients the ministry intends to
watch results from other countries.

Norway will continue to use DRGs in the coming years. It
will be a political decision whether DRGs should be used as a
payment system, but DRG use will always be connected to hospital financing in one way or another. The use of DRGs as a
managerial tool in hospitals will depend on the recommendation from the Ministry of Health and Social Affairs and incentives given to physicians for better management.

References

Aas, H. M. *Diagnose relaterte grupper* (Diagnosis related groups). NIS 3-85. Trondheim: Norwegian Institute for Hospital Research, 1985.

Aas, H. M., Freeman, J., Palmer, G., and Fetter, R. *The Making of Norwegian DRGs.* NIS 3-1989. Trondheim: Norwegian Institute for Hospital Research, 1989.

"Cost of Norwegian Patients." *Aftenposten,* June 23, 1990.

"Effektiviseringsvirksomhet i sykehussektoren" (Increasing efficiency in hospitals). Public commission report 59-1974, 1974.

Hogsnes, T. "The DRG-Based Payment Experiment." Oslo: Ministry of Health and Social Affairs, 1990.

Jørgensen, S., and Pedersen, P. B. *Samdata—Hospital 1991.* NIS 1-1991. Trondheim: Norwegian Institute for Hospital Research, 1991.

Magnussen, J. *DRG—Anvendelser og konsekvenser* (DRGs: Possibilities and consequences). NIS 6-1986. Trondheim: Norwegian Institute for Hospital Research, 1986.

"Medisinsk rasjonalisering" (Increasing medical efficiency). Public commission report 25-1981, 1981.

Ministry of Health and Social Affairs. *The DRG-Based Payment Experiment. Price List for Patient Treatment.* Unpublished document, 1990a.

Ministry of Health and Social Affairs. *Management in Hospitals.* Unpublished document, Sept. 1990b.

Ministry of Health and Social Affairs. *Government Bill No. 1.* (St. prp. No. 1) 1990–1991.

Regional Hospital in Tromsø. *Organization Chart of the Hospital.* Unpublished document, Dec. 1988.

Slåttebrekk, O. *What Does the Patient Cost?* NIS 1-1990. Trondheim: Norwegian Institute for Hospital Research, 1990.

"Sykehustjenester i Norge" (Hospital services in Norway). Public commission report 25-1987, 1987.

Nine

Denmark: Continuing Development and Potential Alternative Directions

Anita Alban

Health care in Denmark is a public-tax-based system. Because the system is decentralized, the state (Parliament) sets the laws but has little impact on the provision of services. This is left to the regions (which oversee hospitals and social security) and to a much smaller extent to the municipalities, which oversee care of the elderly, dental care in schools for children aged three to eighteen years, and visiting nursing care. (See Table 9.1 for an overview of the Danish health care system.)

Both the counties and the municipalities collect local taxes. Approximately 99 percent of county-based health care is tax financed, whereas in the municipalities, 50 percent of health services are tax financed and 50 percent are state grant financed. Every year the total budget for all public spending is negotiated between the state and the associations of counties and municipalities.

In the 1980s the budget cooperation between the state and the local governments was increased to secure an overall policy on public health care expenditures. Until 1983 the growth in spending at the local level was determined by recom-

Note: The author wishes to thank Kjeld Moller Pedersen, Paul Bak, and Jens Porup for reviewing this chapter.

Denmark 283

Table 9.1. Key Health Care Figures for Denmark.

Country area	42,930 sq. km.
Population, 1990	5.14 million
% of population over 67	14%
% of population over 80	4%
Life expectancy, 1987–1988:	
male	72 years
female	78 years
% of GDP spent on health care, 1987[a]	6%
Number of acute-care hospitals, 1988	97
Number of acute-care beds, 1988	29,900
Number of discharges, 1988	1.01 million
Number of bed days, 1988	7.94 million
Number of outpatient visits, 1988	3.69 million
Number of physicians (hospitals), 1988	8,696
Number of general practitioners, 1989	3,057
Number of full-time nurses (hospitals), 1988	51,806
Number of nurses (primary health care), 1989[b]	3,526

Type of service	1980	1985	1990
	(in billion Kroner)		
Hospitals	20	23	28
Social security[a]	5	6	7
Other health services[c]	2	2	3
Nursing homes[d]	8	12	13

[a] Includes fee to general practitioners (40%), specialists (14%), medicine (29%), dentists (13%), and physiotherapy (3%).

[b] Excludes nurses in nursing homes (social services).

[c] Includes expenses for children's dental care, visiting nurses, and home nurses. Does not include home assistants (care of the elderly). In 1985, there were 24,000 home assistants and 30,000 full-time employees in nursing homes.

[d] Includes staff of alternatives to nursing homes, such as protected housing.

mendations from the governmental level. Decisions were based on a formula that weighed growth in total expenditures for all counties against initiatives to lower growth in special areas. In 1983 the government reduced its grants to counties responsible for hospital services. (At the time about one-third of county finances came from the state grant and the remaining two-thirds from local taxes.) In the years following 1983 the counties were faced with further cuts in their general grant funds at the same time that the state recommended no increase in taxes. To add weight to its recommendations, the state introduced a surcharge under which local authorities that did not comply with recommendations were assessed a financial penalty, which was returned after several years without interest.

Since 1984 the general grant to counties has been progressively reduced, until in 1986 only 8 percent of basic financing came from the state grant, and today it is nearly zero. Some general grants still exist that are meant to redistribute or reallocate funds among counties on the basis of need (objective criteria) and revenue.

Financing Hospitals

Danish hospital services are decentralized. Sixteen hospital regions (counties) collect the taxes that finance hospital services. The hospitals are 99.9 percent publicly owned. Of the country's 27,235 acute-care beds, 1,200 are state owned (by Rigshospitalet in Copenhagen) and 35 are privately owned (by a private hospital). The remaining 26,000 beds are owned by sixteen counties, which finance hospital services through taxation.

In Denmark, hospitals operate within the politics or framework of the county in which they reside. The county loosely defines the role of each hospital according to the catchment area it serves. To some extent, the county also determines the area the hospital will serve and its degree of specialization. A fundamental objective for all counties is that their hospitals achieve efficiency and equity (defined as equal access). It is within this supply framework and a given global budget that the hospitals operate as individual firms.

Within hospitals, the strong administrator, as depicted in the U.S. literature (Lee, 1971; Feldstein, 1968) and the DRG literature, does not exist. Danish hospital administrators until recently had no say in determining what was produced.

In the wake of the economic decentralization of the 1980s, the counties created hospital management teams in which the administrator was supplemented by a senior clinician and senior nurse. The purpose of this change was to promote allocative efficiency between the functions such as radiography, laboratories, and kitchen services. Its philosophy is predicated on the belief that hospital behavior is determined more by internal bargaining powers than by allocative efficiency, as Clarkson (1972) points out and Muurinen (1986) shows with respect to residual revenues.

Today, a hospital's bargaining power lies at the departmental level. It is between the departments that competition for resources takes place within hospitals. If the cardiology department can convince the administrator that it can do better than (or at least as well as) the geriatric department, it will receive the available extra resources. However, no mechanism exists today that makes it possible to ensure that giving an extra DKr 2 million to the cardiology department will result in the money being used more efficiently than if it were given to the geriatric department.

There is no incentive mechanism in the Danish health care system that ensures that efficiency is an integral part of how a department is managed (by a clinician or by a clinician and a nurse). Beyond the framework of the catchment area and degree of specialization indicated above, departments are given no objectives for either the level of production or the case mix. They have no set budget. The resource constraints lie more or less explicitly in the number of beds, the size of the ambulatory care facilities, the size and mix of the staff, and the access to support services and other providers within the hospital.

Since 1979 Denmark has required complete nationwide registration of hospital inpatient data. All patients are classified according to diagnosis, date of admission, and date of discharge. All persons born alive are given a unique, lifetime identity number that is used for all contacts with public services. In this way such information as discharges per diagnosis and discharges per person per diagnosis is easily obtained at the national level, the county level, and the hospital level.

The 1990 World Health Organization classification scheme, ICD8, is used with a range of mainly Nordic modifications. In 1992 data on outpatient activity also became compulsory.

The National Board of Health publishes annual statistics on inpatient activity by hospital and by diagnosis. Most counties today have on-line data facilities and have daily access to information within their own region. Until recently most county health administrations distributed information monthly on activity to local hospitals and frequently to individual clinical departments as well. On-line facilities are now also available in many hospitals so that distribution of data is left to hospital managers.

Information on resources is more limited. The total budget is known for each hospital (for staffing, medical expenditures, laboratory and other test costs, and so on), but no data exist on patient costs. Only three hospitals had cost information (and budgets) at the clinical level in 1990, but the number is expected to increase markedly as calls for better patient data intensify.

No hospitals can yet link resources to activity at the patient level or to groups of patients. Since the early 1980s, a number of local studies have been undertaken to measure the impact of efforts to control the level of hospital expenditures, with mixed results.

As a result of efforts to regulate hospital budgets through state and local budget coordination, hospital expenditures registered zero growth between 1982 and 1989.

County budgets are allocated to local government services (high schools, environmental affairs, public health insurance, and hospitals). Budget negotiations begin with a budget framework that is given to each political committee in charge of a service (such as hospital services). The committee then allocates funds according to certain principles: the previous year's budget, equity based on an equal share per institution, priority setting based on political judgments, and a quota based on certain criteria.

Basing the budget on the previous year's budget was the dominating allocation principle until 1982–1983, when budget coordination was tightened. Since then priority setting has been the dominating principle. Political discussion leading up to the budget is based on available data. Resources are the dominant factor; activity plays a smaller but increasingly important role.

This shift in the principles that govern budget allocation has led to a growing awareness among county-level decision makers that relevant information is lacking. A number of initiatives have also taken place at the state level.

In the yearly statement of the Ministry of Finance in 1983 (Finansministeriet, 1983), the state government appealed to local governments that budgeting and expenditure control become decentralized within the public sector. The background for this appeal was the government's "program of renovation."

In 1983, the Ministry of the Interior (at that time responsible for health services) appointed a committee on productivity whose objective was to investigate and evaluate the possibilities of increasing hospital efficiency. As a second objective, the committee was given the task of proposing improvements in hospital management. The committee's recommendations, published in 1984 (Indenrigsministeriet, 1984), were, among other things, to establish global budgets as the allocation principle at the county level and to establish a hospital information system that would link resources to output as a way of decentralizing financial responsibility to the clinical level. Before this could take place it was felt that hospital management needed to be strengthened. A number of models were introduced, among which were strategies to include doctors and nurses on a management board.

At the same time that the productivity committee was developing its recommendations, the Association of Counties formed a working group of administrators to establish criteria for a hospital information system at the departmental and clinical level (Amtsraadsforeningen, 1984). The working group suggested that future work should concentrate on allocating resources to clinical departments in three areas: staff, nonstaff, and ancillary services. Like the productivity committee, the Association of Counties working group believed that departments were in the best position to manage their own budgets and could most directly ensure the efficient use of resources under output plans developed for each department.

Hospitals made considerable efforts to strengthen their senior management between 1984 and 1989. In 1990 only two counties had *not* established a tripartite management team (administrator, chief nurse, and chief doctor); half the counties had also established a dual management team (nurse and doctor) at the departmental level (Alban, Lehmann Knudsen, and Smidt Thomsen, 1990).

Diffusion of DRGs

In early 1985 the Ministry of Interior hosted a researcher who, as a senior civil servant, specialized in planning. The idea was to develop a health economics unit within the ministry to carry out the recommendations from the productivity committee. Two junior economists were also attached to the unit.

In November 1985 the Danish Hospital Institute housed a second seminar on the measurement of productivity and efficiency in the hospital sector. Discussion focused on the usefulness of the diagnosis-related groups (DRGs) developed in the United States. Interest stemmed from ongoing cooperative projects on DRGs at the Danish Hospital Institute and other hospital institutes in Norway and Sweden.

The senior civil servant and a junior economist from Denmark's Ministry of the Interior were invited to the seminar. They expressed interest in the DRG system but realized that it had to be adapted to the Danish environment. Although the Ministry of the Interior felt it was important to standardize the cost of the same procedure across different hospitals, it knew that the financial data on which to base such decisions was nonexistent. The ministry suggested that the initiative to introduce DRGs into the Danish hospital sector should come from the counties and that the ministry's role should be a coordinating one.

As a result of discussions at the November seminar, the Ministry of the Interior hired a consultant from the Health Board to convert the Danish Version of the ICD8 classification into ICD9-CM so that existing data on clinical activity could be grouped into DRGs. In early 1986 the ministry purchased the Yale University grouper. The DRG project continued for two more years, from 1986 to 1988.

The grouping of the Danish data was based on 1985

activity gathered from the National Hospital Information Register (*Land-spatientregisteret*). In the process of producing the reports, the Ministry of the Interior established an advisory committee that represented the Health Board, the Danish Hospital Institute, and the Association of Counties. The Ministry chaired the sessions, and the committee was strictly advisory.

In another initiative, the ministry developed new measures for standard costing and productivity for ninety-six acute-care hospitals in 1986 (Indenrigsministeriet, 1986). The purpose was to introduce a better basis for comparative analysis — one that took into account diagnosis profiles. The measures represented only five diagnostic groups that related to the activity of minor and major operations and hospital size. Feedback was limited and focused on the measures being too broad, but the idea was not rejected.

At the end of 1986, the Ministry of the Interior's senior civil servant in charge of the health economics unit left, and his position was never refilled. In 1987 the unit was closed down.

In 1987, a committee was established to investigate ways of controlling the counties' rising costs of hospital care. The initiative came from the Ministry of the Interior, but committee members came from both the ministry and the Association of Counties. All members were high-ranking civil servants. The committee published its report in November 1987 (Indenrigsministeriet, 1987). The report contained twenty-seven suggestions on how to improve hospital cost containment. Key among its suggestions was that a Ministry of Health be established. Others of its suggestions concerned hospital information systems:

- The Ministry of Health should take the initiative to ensure the collection of data on outpatient services (ambulatory care).
- The Ministry of Health, in cooperation with hospital owners, should introduce clinical budgeting. At a minimum, it should define the global budget and a measure of what constitutes activity in the clinical department no later than 1990.

- To improve information at the clinical level, the Ministry of Health should take the initiative to standardize registration of activity in the ancillary service departments.
- Ongoing efforts to convert clinical activity data into an on-line service are encouraged to continue. If the National Hospital Information Register data are authorized to be converted into DRGs in the future, users should have direct access to this facility. DRG tables should be made available to counties and hospitals for their own planning and analysis.
- To support counties and hospital administrators in their ability to compare costs across hospitals, it is suggested that the Ministry of Health take steps to improve productivity analyses based on the Data Envelopment Analysis approach. DRGs might form the basis for such data collection.

In September 1987 the Ministry of Health was established, and the financial secretariat had a new senior civil servant who was given the task of finalizing the DRG project. The secretariat's main responsibility was to promote and carry out the suggestions of the committee report of 1987 (Indenrigs-ministeriet, 1987).

In May 1988 the Ministry of Health held a meeting to announce the results of the DRG project, which were being simultaneously published in a report (Sundhedsministeriet og Indenrigsministeriet, 1988). At the meeting two people were invited in addition to the institutions represented on the advisory committee: a professor of health economics who had recently published a book on the subject (Moeller Pedersen, 1987) and a doctor interested in setting up a local study on DRGs.

In the report and at the meeting, the Ministry of Health expressed the view that the introduction of the DRG concept into the Danish hospital system should be seen as a means to achieve better planning. As a prospective payment system it had little relevance in Denmark, but the case mix idea was appealing.

Later in 1988 a personal-computer version of the grouper was made available by the Ministry of the Interior for interested

parties such as the National Board of Health, the Danish Hospital Institute, and the counties. A copy was distributed to the
National Health Board, the Danish Hospital Institute, and two
counties for local experiments. In 1989–1990 no initiatives were
taken by the Ministry of Health to continue work on DRGs.
During 1989 the senior civil servant in charge left the Ministry
of Health; his position was not refilled until April 1991, when it
was taken by the former chairman of the 1987 committee that
had suggested the introduction of DRGs as a means of controlling expenditures. With this change, DRGs were again on the
agenda of hospital management.

According to a two-year action plan published by the
Ministry of the Interior in May 1991, the strategy concerning
DRGs or a similar case mix system is (1) to establish a system of
cost weights based on diagnoses, (2) to encourage correct registration of diagnoses, procedures, and resource utilization in
hospitals, and (3) to further develop clinical budgets by introducing internal incentives.

At a Ministry of Health meeting in May 1988 two interested parties were present who later carried through local DRG
experiments. One represented a local health research unit in
Ringkoebing County, and the other (at the time a professor of
health economics) later became county director of health services in Vejle County.

Ringkoebing County Experiment

In 1987 Ringkoebing County founded a local health services
research unit. One of the doctors employed was very keen to
continue previous work on measurement of productivity. The
development of the personal-computer version of the Yale
grouper made such a local experiment possible, and it was
carried out at a small hospital with eighty-seven beds. The general results of the project, which also carried elements of quality
assurance, were published in the *Danish Medical Bulletin* during
1990 and 1991 (Bak 1990b, 1990c, 1990d, 1991). Another article
that addressed the DRG experience was published in a Danish
Hospital Institute report in 1990 (Ankjaer-Jensen, 1990).

Figure 9.1. Distribution of Length of Stay, Uncomplicated Appendectomy (DRG 167).

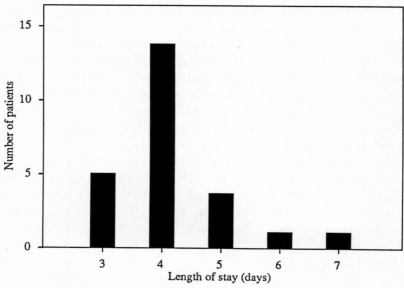

Source: Bak, 1990d.

Briefly, the local experiment was based on 2,000 discharges in 1988. The discharges used 255 DRGs, most of which contained very few patients. Only 16 groups had more than twenty patients in each. In many of these groups, the variation in average length of stay is large. The two examples shown in Figures 9.1 and 9.2 reflect a reasonable average length of stay (DRG 167) and an unreasonable one (DRG 127).

Bak concluded that DRGs as a patient classification system are not appropriate at the hospital level for internal planning purposes. However, the experience gained in the DRG project has been used to develop a management information system in hospitals in Ringkoebing County based on on-line tools. The work on grouping hospital activity continues. So far forty standard groups have been developed, and highly specialized departments are given one of their own. The groups have not yet been examined for resource homogeneity. Group-

Figure 9.2. Distribution of Length of Stay, Heart Insufficiency (DRG 127).

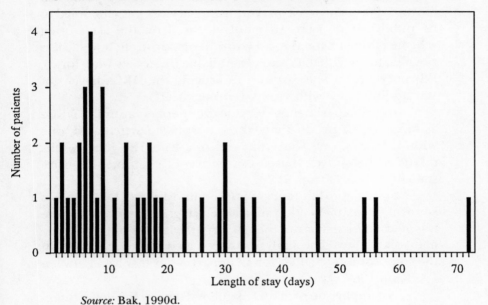

Source: Bak, 1990d.

ing is seen much more as an instrument for dialogue between the county hospital administration and the hospitals, as well as between hospital management boards and clinical departments (interview with Bak, February 1991).

Vejle County Experiment

In late 1988 the professor of health economics who participated in the May meeting at the Ministry of Health became director of health services in Vejle County. One of his earliest efforts was to start a local project on DRGs. The project's objectives were to test the Ministry of Health grouper and the usefulness of DRGs as a measurement of productivity to cost the services and to improve the U.S. groups.

A project leader (an economist) was attached to the project from January 1989 to January 1991. The preliminary results on the first objective were presented at a Danish Hospital Institute conference in October 1989 and were later published (Torup, 1990). The work on costing the services was scheduled to be published in 1991. It mainly focused on the accounting scheme of one hospital in an effort to demonstrate how far it is possible to go with data already available (interview with Torup, February 1991). The work on improving the DRGs never got started (interview with Torup, February 1991).

In the experiment to test the grouper and appraise DRGs as measures of productivity, three hospitals participated, one with 474 beds, one with 182, and one with 125. The results discussed below were based on the use of computer-intensive statistical tools (Torup, 1990).

Systematic differences in the composition of DRGs in two surgical departments that specialized in gastroenterology were revealed. At issue was not the few large variations but rather the many small ones. The analysis also revealed a systematic shift in the composition of DRGs for all departments involved between 1986 and 1987.

A comparison of actual use of bed days at the departmental level with expected use of bed days based on the DRG case mix revealed systematic differences. It is argued that DRGs are not very suitable for predicting average length of stay and that DRGs would be improved by being based on specialties in addition to diagnosis. This argument also seems to be valid for resource homogeneity across specialties.

The overall lesson of this study is that a grouping of diagnoses must be flexible if it is to serve different objectives (interview with Torup, February 1991).

Debate on DRGs

In 1984–1985 the Danish Hospital Institute worked on a study in cooperation with Copenhagen County and the National Health Board to link hospital episodes. The project was completed in the spring of 1985, and in June the institute invited a select group of interested parties (representatives, all senior economists, from the National Health Board, the state hospital, the Association of Counties, and four different local government administrations) to discuss the results and the future strategy chosen, which was to develop an information system that linked resources to activities at hospitals. The meeting produced a mutual agreement among participants that this strategy was the most important area to focus on.

On this basis a project began that looked at performance indicators as measures of productivity and efficiency at hospitals. To clarify whether DRGs had a part in this, it was decided to hold another seminar in November 1985. The seminar's objectives were to discuss the usefulness of DRGs at different decision-making levels in the hospital sector; to discuss the strategy of an interdisciplinary appraisal of DRGs (economists, doctors, and nurses); to discuss how to disseminate information on DRGs in Denmark (conferences, articles, folders, and so on); and to inform participants about the objectives of and preliminary experiences with DRG projects in Norway and Sweden.

Seminar participants occupied top positions in government and health care, representing doctors and nurses as well as hospital and county administrators. A number of representatives expressed concern with specific issues. The chairman of the hospital administrators' association announced, for example, that the association, after following the development of DRGs in several European countries, saw a need for further studies. The chief nurse and representative from the Association of Nurses emphasized that length of stay was closely related to nursing care and expressed her concern over the way the DRGs dealt with this problem. The National Health Board found that the basic idea was sound but preferred a grouping built on episodes and a classification involving both outpatients and long-term care.

The doctors wanted to await further work before they made up their mind. Their concern was mainly related to the clinical meaningfulness of the groups. The Association of Counties expressed concern that the DRGs solved the wrong problems. What was needed was an information system able to evaluate ongoing reallocations in the hospital sector. The meeting resulted in a Danish Hospital Institute strategy paper (Alban and Christensen, 1986) on DRGs, which concluded that the institute would undertake and initiate local experiments, participate in the work of translating the U.S. DRGs based on ICD9-CM into Danish DRGs based on ICD8, and continue to follow the development of DRGs in other Nordic countries and inform the Danish hospital sector of this work.

To clarify the usefulness of DRGs in Denmark, the Danish Health Institute asked a professor of health economics to prepare a report on the methodological considerations involved. The report (Moeller Pedersen, 1987) addressed the following concerns:

1.   DRGs have so far been used only as a tool for prospective payment. The use of DRGs as a means of measuring productivity and planning has been limited.
2.   Documentation of the ability of DRGs to contain costs is limited.
3.   Other effects of DRGs (such as increased cost awareness) still remain to be studied, in particular the introduction of DRGs for reasons other than prospective payment.
4.   As a classification system, DRGs are not superior. The individual DRGs are highly sensitive to small variations in statistical methodology.
5.   Basing DRGs in other countries on U.S. clinical practice may not be sound.
6.   The cost side of U.S. DRGs leaves much to be desired, and the cost weights cannot be used in the Danish environment.
7.   National cost studies should be undertaken. The costing of DRGs in the United States yields few lessons on methodology.
8.   The objectives in using DRGs must be clarified before undertaking any field experiments.
9.   The attractions of the DRG system are that it focuses on many "products" that are clinically meaningful and that it links resources to those products.

Local DRG Experiments

The Danish Hospital Institute's first local DRG experiment occurred in 1987–1988 in cooperation with a medium-sized (271-

bed) Danish hospital. It only tested the usefulness of DRGs as performance indicators at the clinical level, and the project was closed down before it got around to costing services at the DRG level (Hatting, 1988). When DRGs were used as an instrument for planning in a department of orthopedic surgery with fifty-one beds, nine groups described 51 percent of production and fifteen groups characterized 70 percent of production. Results were disappointing in the context of planning because it was common knowledge that many more groups had to be activated to describe a medical specialty.

In 1988 the institute was charged with evaluating the productivity of a highly specialized 1,000-bed hospital with twenty-one clinical specialties. To do so, like departments in four homogeneous (highly specialized) hospitals were compared for their performance on a range of measures that were supplemented by visualized diagnostic profiles. The grouping of diagnoses at the departmental level was left to the hospital's departmental management teams (chief physician and chief nurse), but the number of groups was restricted to a maximum of twelve, with the last group always being "other." The goal was for the management teams to identify their departments by diagnosis. As an aid in this task, they were told what their eleven most frequently used ICD8 groups had been in the previous year (1987).

The results for one department are reported in Alban, Lehmann Knudsen, and Smidt Thomsen, 1990. DRGs were not used because a survey revealed that too many DRGs would be necessary to provide a simple overview of a single department. The same conclusion reached by the two local experiments seemed to be confirmed for a highly specialized hospital in Denmark.

In 1990, the Danish Hospital Institute began another study of selected departments in the same hospital. The study's main purpose is to create a hospital information system that links resources to groups of output for outpatients and inpatients. It is not conditional that inpatient classifications be based on DRGs, but it is conditional that they be clinically meaningful, limited in number, and homogeneous in resource use. The approach of the Hospital Comparisons in Europe (HOSCOM) project is used as the resource allocation model (Roger France and others, 1991). As a part of this project, costing of a range of ancillary services is included. As of this writing, the study was expected to be completed in 1993.

In 1990 the institute also began a study in a 1,200-bed, highly specialized hospital with twenty-three clinical departments. The same methodology is being used as in the similar 1988 study, but the production groupings were selected by the hospital itself rather than the researchers.

In 1991 the institute began to carry out the same procedure in ten selected clinical departments (surgery and medicine) at the state hospital. However, the comparison is being made across time (1980, 1985, and 1990) rather than across hospitals for the departments chosen.

Once these studies are completed, efforts will concentrate on researching resource homogeneity.

DRG Networks

In 1984 Ernst and Whinney began marketing computer-based DRG programs in Denmark (Lundell and Aagaard, 1984; Aagaard and Lundell, 1985). One effort resulted in a seminar organized by the Danish Association of Hospital Administrators in February 1986. Speakers included a representative from Ernst and Whinney, the administrators, the Danish Hospital Institute, the Ministry of the Interior, and the University of Odense. The association invited Jacob Hofdijk from the University Hospital of Leiden, the Netherlands, as its special guest.

Ernst and Whinney's DRG enterprise never really caught hold in Denmark, however. A few small projects were carried out—for example, a nursing work load study at a hospital—but that was about all. One explanation for this might be the lack of interest shown by hospital administrators.

In 1986, under the impetus of their respective hospital institutes, the Nordic countries launched a formalized network on DRGs (initially comprising Sweden, Norway, Finland, and

Denmark, and in 1989 joined by Iceland). The group meets two or three times a year to exchange experiences informally.

In 1989 the Danish Hospital Institute joined the HOSCOM project in the European Community's program for Advanced Informatics in Medicine. The project was undertaken in cooperation with six other European countries. The institute led the efforts to develop resource models and a severity-of-illness index. The preliminary results have been published in *Health Policy* (Roger France and others, 1991).

In early 1990 the Ministry of Health asked the institute to develop the concept of a newsletter on financing in the health care sector. The newsletter was funded by the ministry, but editorial responsibility was given to the institute. In June 1990 the first issue was published under the theme of hospital re-source management. The newsletter was distributed to 1,500 interested parties at hospitals and to administrative and state and regional policy makers. It gave examples of case mix systems and described the DRG experiment in Norway and the testing of the DRG system in Vejle County, along with two other ongoing initiatives in Western countries (Danish Hospital Institute, 1990). As a follow-up to the great interest shown in the news-letter, a seminar was held in April 1991 in Copenhagen on the experiments on resource management in the United Kingdom.

Building on an Information System

This chapter seeks to appraise why DRGs became only one of many possible strategies for measuring efficiency in the Danish hospital sector. DRGs have undergone a fairly extensive evalua-tion process since 1985. Initially the concept met with consider-able enthusiasm because of its potential as an effective efficiency measurement strategy. Yet it is a star that over the last few years has lost a great deal of its luster. An analysis of what caused this decline is the focus of this section.

Denmark's publicly financed hospital system seeks to achieve efficiency (both allocative and x-efficiency), equity, and a security net (or "final resort") for the health sector; to educate (and sometimes ensure employment as well); and to conduct research. This discussion concentrates only on how to achieve efficiency in hospitals. The trade-offs between efficiency and equity or other hospital objectives are not discussed. The reason for this is that in recent years Denmark's focus has been on cost containment; the implications of such a stance for efficiency have been largely ignored (a problem not unique to Denmark). The discussion embodies the debate that occurred between 1985 and 1991.

The Hospital Information System

The purpose of Denmark's hospital financial information system is ostensibly to provide information that allows resources and activity to be considered together across all hospitals, that takes into account production in both inpatient and outpatient departments, that makes it possible for the decentralized decision-making entity to act efficiently, that makes it possible for the hospital directorship to act efficiently across clinics and departments, and that ensures that the benefits to the managers outweigh the costs. The arguments for setting up a hospital financial information system to work from the bottom up are strong. It is the clinicians and ward staff who generate costs, and it is at the clinical level that data are most disaggregated. In general, decision makers seem to recognize that the department is the data collector and cost center. It is unclear, however, whether the need for information acknowledged at the bottom is also acknowledged at the top. In Denmark there are four levels of decision making present in the managing of hospital services: the state, the county, the hospital, and the hospital departments.

Any financial information system must take as its starting point the decision makers it is to serve. Can one system, however, serve the objectives of different levels of decision making? Does the minister of health need the same information as the manager of a hospital department? Is it enough to aggregate information as we move from the bottom up? It can be argued that data should originate close to those who trigger resource use. At the departmental level, these should be the people who stand to gain the most by making sense of their own efficiency. If they

Table 9.2. Hospital Financial Information System Objectives and Outcomes.

Objectives	Outcomes
1. To provide a management framework by linking resources to outputs (or even better measures of efficiency)	Establish a total program budget of hospital expenditure by inpatient and outpatient activity
2. To measure quality of care	Produce definitions of goals of treatment that can be measured
3. To make it possible to plan within given areas, such as care of the elderly	Link resources and activities from which groupings are possible according to specific purposes
4. To promote an increased awareness of costs and greater economic responsibility among those who trigger resource use	Delegate economic responsibility to the departmental level
5. To promote a dialogue about priorities and objectives across levels of decision making	Establish case mix comparisons of homogeneous departments and hospitals
6. To be able to price services sold to other counties	Establish a global reimbursement system

lack that interest, incentives should be created to ensure that this happens. Any financial information system should be attractive to the management team at the departmental level in order to achieve the greatest possible efficiency within a given budget.

The added value of generating information at the departmental level is the expected validity of the data. If the department is responsible for its own planning and management, it is bound to affect the quality of the data, which is inevitably the key to the data's usefulness. Data that are seldom used and for which no one is responsible rarely have a high degree of validity.

To set up and successfully operate a single financial information system, there must be consensus at all decision-making levels about the underlying objectives and the mechanism involved. The main objective is clearly efficiency. The secondary objectives and their desired outcomes are listed in Table 9.2.

In the context of a single information system, it is important to consider whether any of the six secondary objectives in Table 9.2 are contradictory. The first two objectives are supplementary and a proxy for measuring efficiency. Planning of specific programs such as care of the elderly requires that resources be linked to throughputs (diagnoses), so there do not seem to be any contradictions among the first three objectives. It could be hoped that linking resources to throughputs would increase awareness of costs, at least if the right incentives were built in. Thus it seems that the objectives are more complementary than competing.

A dialogue between the decision-making levels at hospitals is bound to be based not only on resource use but also on the case mix of throughputs and on quality of care. The success of comparing hospital performances without taking case mix into account has been very limited and has made clinicians uncooperative. It is argued, therefore, that the definitions of case mix must be decided on the basis of a dialogue with those at the departmental level. However, those definitions must agree across hospitals if the same departments in different hospitals are to be compared. The first objective must therefore link resources to commonly agreed measures of output, agreed across similar departments in different hospitals.

The sixth objective will be met if the definition of throughputs is related to individual patients or patient groups that can be identified as out-of-county patients.

On the basis of this brief discussion, it would seem that the six objectives are not contradictory to such an extent that one or more must be abandoned to fulfill any of the others. However, not all decision-making levels can be expected to pursue all the objectives set for a financial information system.Therefore it is of some interest to get an idea of what it is that each decision-making level might aim for.

In 1985 the Danish Hospital Institute produced an assessment of the value of a single information system for the different levels of decision makers throughout the country's health care system (Table 9.3). Building an information system from the bottom up means that all data, at least to a certain extent, are used at the operational level in the department itself for plan-

Table 9.3. Need for Information at Different Decision-Making Levels.

Decision-Making Level	Need for Information
State	Performance measures, resource use, and throughputs
Ministry of Health and National Board of Health	• Comparisons across counties • Ad hoc surveys of selected groups of diagnoses to follow the trends of specialization
County Committee for Hospitals	Performance measures (high budget level) • Comparisons of productivity over time and across comparable hospital functions within and outside the region • Costs of services provided for other counties • Data for ad hoc analyses (planning for specific subjects: care of the elderly, chronically sick, and so on)
Hospital management	Performance measures (medium budget level) • Data on productivity (routine monitoring) • Data on quality of treatment • Costs of services provided for other counties
Hospital department	Performance measures (low budget level) • Data on productivity • Data on quality of treatment • Data for ad hoc analyses (planning for specific groups of patients within departments)

ning and for cost and quality control. As Table 9.3 shows, the data collected at the departmental level are aggregated to the hospital management level, then to the level of the hospital committee, and on up to the Ministry of Health. In the search for ways of dealing with all these multilevel demands within a single information system, one field of research naturally attracted attention: DRGs developed in the United States.

The question then arose: Which Danish objectives do DRGs meet? In the Danish hospital system, patients cross regional boundaries to obtain specialized treatment. When this happens, the county in which the patient lives pays for the services. This practice, which covers 5–10 percent of the hospital system's total budget, caused great interest in prospective reimbursement systems such as DRGs, especially among hospital administrators. The question is whether DRGs can meet any of the objectives sought in a single financial information system for hospitals in Denmark.

DRGs are built on the idea that each diagnostic group is clinically meaningful and homogeneous according to utilization of resources (Fetter and others, 1980), an appealing idea because it links resources to throughput (diagnosis). But DRGs cover only inpatient services, which means that they can only fulfill the objective mentioned earlier: to provide a management framework by linking resources to throughputs. There are no measures of quality of care built into DRGs, a condition that a peer review system resolves only to a limited extent (Department of Health and Human Services . . . , 1984). If an objective is to measure quality of care, it is necessary either to apply professional guidelines (some form of peer review system) or to build efficiency goals into each DRG.

DRGs as a Planning Tool

For planning purposes—such as making it possible to plan within given areas like care of the elderly—the use of DRGs is of doubtful value, at least for the Danish health care system. Fetter and others (1980) address the question of using DRGs in regional planning for hospitals, which they define as "the activity of organizing health care resources in a defined geographic region to achieve a desired state of affairs in terms of the availability of health care of acceptable quality and cost" (p. 36). They argue that "a regional planning model based on hospital case-mix can be used to suggest the most cost-effective means of distributing, e.g., a closed hospital's case-mix to the other hospitals in the region while still maintaining adequate access and quality and not exceeding the capacities of any hospital" (p. 37). This remains to be demonstrated, however. It is doubtful whether it will be possible to distribute resources on the basis of the DRG case mix to ensure the highest level of efficiency within the region.

If such a planning exercise showed, for example, that one-half of appendectomies should be referred to hospital A and the other half to hospital B, what would we then have to know? According to the 1985 version of DRGs (U.S. Federal Register, 1984), appendectomies cover DRGs 164–167. The cost weights attached to the four DRGs are 1.8130, 1.5986, 1.4179, and 1.0706. The referral system would need to be centralized and very detailed to distribute appendectomy cases fairly between hospital A and hospital B. When, for example, does one know that a case is complicated (DRGs 164 and 165)? Fetter's comments reflect a very narrow definition of hospital planning within a region. In a number of European countries, the planning agenda also covers planning between inpatient and outpatient care and increasingly across hospital and primary health care services — especially, for example, planning for the care of the elderly and mentally ill.

Because DRGs cover only inpatient care, they do not provide an adequate planning base for resource allocation between inpatient and outpatient care. In the current use of DRGs under Medicare, ninety-five DRGs come in pairs depending on age (under seventy or over sixty-nine years of age). Care of the elderly is often a subject for planning, but according to Des Harnais, Chesney, and Fleming (1988), the DRG assignment should not be based on age if the patients have no co-morbidities or complications. However, some Danish findings (Alban, Boll Hansen, and Christensen, 1988) seem to suggest that for the age group of 65–74 years, the length of stay is relatively higher for men than for women and that in the age group of 75 years or older the average length of stay is higher for women than for men. This tendency seems to a large extent to be correlated with the marital status (single or not) of the patient. Unless, therefore, the American DRGs are turned into Danish-relevant groups (known as DARGs) that take into account the special background here, DRGs do not have much to offer as an aid to Danish hospital planning.

DRGs as a Means of Increasing Cost Awareness

The notion that DRGs increase cost awareness at the lowest decision-making level has yet to be studied. Some evidence from the United States (Davis and Rhodes, 1988) points to DRGs as being fairly successful in this regard: "Studies have found no deterioration in the quality of care rendered to Medicare beneficiaries. Neither the mortality rate nor the rate of readmission increased" (p. 124). Others are more critical: "DRG incentives in themselves do not force either the achievement of operational efficiency or a realignment of authority within hospitals" (Sandford and others, 1987, p. 466). McCarthy (1988, p. 1684) puts it this way: "Any buyer who can set the price saves substantially, whether payment is in beads or booty or DRGs." McCarthy argues further that to increase cost consciousness instead of DRG consciousness, "incentives for the efficient delivery of care must be coupled with fair reimbursement" (p. 1684). In the United States, DRGs are used mainly as a method of prospective payment. They are not likely to be used as such in Denmark, and the same is probably true for other countries with decentralized health care systems. This means that a system built on groupings of diagnoses as proxies for output must look for other incentives than those that arise from not being paid according to a national average cost by case mix.

    In searching for efficiency and establishing corresponding objectives, cost reduction per se (without achieving efficiency) has so far not been discussed. There is no question, however, that in the United States prospective payment has cut costs in the hospital sector. The incentive to change is strong: whereas previously additional days of stay and more services were sources of more revenue, now they mean more costs. Although McCarthy (1988) has some doubts about whether this means higher efficiency, Berki (1985) has fewer reservations, arguing that "now hospitals will want to reduce the cost of services by reducing their amounts and by producing them more efficiently" (p. 71). According to Berki, the great potential of prospective payment lies in its power to set relative prices and in this way decide case mix. In the U.S. environment, this will give hospital managers strong incentives to alter the practice patterns of physicians to more conservative, consensus-based, cost-conscious practice styles and less aggressive intervention.

But will it necessarily lead to efficiency? Berki argues that the U.S. prospective payment system has reduced staffing to achieve efficiency by substituting personnel with lower qualifications for those with higher ones. In Denmark we have achieved the same result by cutting the personnel with lower qualifications. The steep rise in Danish health services expenditures in 1982 was the result of a 1981 agreement between the medical registrars and the Society of Counties that resulted in more hospital doctors. A comparison of expenditures with activities showed an increase of 11 percent vis-à-vis discharges, a decrease of 11 percent relative to bed days, and an increase in visits to outpatient clinics of 9 percent in the same period of time (1980–1986). Between 1982 and 1984 the Danish government put pressure on the counties to reduce expenditures. The results for 1980–1988 are shown in Figure 9.3. Even if DRGs have increased cost awareness, we cannot judge whether efficiency has improved or whether it has improved more or less than without DRGs.

DRGs as the Basis of Case Mix

One of the greatest attractions of DRGs is that they group patients with similar clinical attributes and output utilization patterns (Fetter and others, 1980). DRGs are a good basis for establishing case mix. The Danish experience has so far re-

Figure 9.3. Beds and Net Expenses (1988 Prices) for Danish Acute-Care Hospitals, 1980–1988.

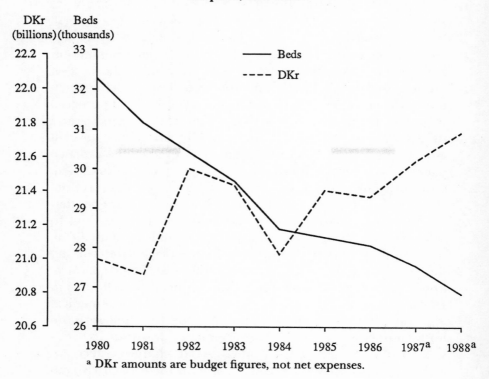

ᵃ DKr amounts are budget figures, not net expenses.

vealed, however, that it takes a substantial number of DRGs to describe case mix at the clinical level. In Alban, Lehmann Knudsen, and Smidt Thomsen (1990), ten Danish surgical departments that specialized in gastroenterology were surveyed and 325 DRGs were activated. The first 15 DRGs (in rank order) explain about 50 percent of bed day use, but it took 44 DRGs to explain 80 percent, and 71 to explain 90 percent.

The specific "garbage can" DRGs (DRGs 170–171, 182–184, and 188–189) took care of 12.6 percent of the bed days, and the general garbage can DRGs (DRG 467–470) another 5.7 percent. Further, we found that DRG 467 accounted for 12 percent of bed days in one of the hospitals investigated and 0 percent in another.

Costing Services

In the Danish health care environment the DRG method of organizing the costing of services does not make much sense. Medical salaries and outpatient care are fundamental features of the hospital service provided in Denmark (and, indeed, in a range of other European countries). It is also the case that the use of patient days to allocate routine nursing costs, as noted by Jenkins (1987), assumes that the level of nursing care required for all patients is the same on a daily basis, the amount of nursing time required per day is the same for each day of hospitalization, the age of the patient does not affect the amount of nursing time required, and the nature of nursing care is the same in all hospitals.

It is not the intention here to discuss how to cost services in European hospitals. Some of the problems that must be resolved, however, in the process of costing hospital services include the following:

- Definition of cost centers
- Keys for cost allocation (staff, beds, floor space, and so on)
- Which costs should be allocated
- Definition of overhead (all support services?)
- Which overhead costs vary with inpatient services and which vary with outpatient services
- Process for distributing provider services to cost centers

There are strong arguments for letting the final cost center be the hospital department. But the question of how best to allocate resource use (and at what rates) is still to be resolved.

Levels of Aggregation

DRGs are developed for the hospital's decision-making level: to assist the administrator generally and to assist in producing a given case mix at the lowest possible cost. The prospective payment system is set up in such a way that the net revenues for the hospital can only be maximized by reducing the length of stay or service intensity or both, thereby changing the practice patterns of physicians. There is also no doubt that a prospective payment system raises the cost consciousness (or perhaps DRG consciousness) of the hospital manager, who through product-line strategies can achieve reduced costs per case. The financial strategy of the hospital turns into a DRG strategy.

In Denmark as in many other European countries, a financial management information system ought to be designed to assist hospitals in the support of strategic and operational decision making. This in turn points to the lowest decision-making level as being crucial: the department. Today the bargaining power lies here. It is therefore essential that such an organization establish incentive mechanisms that ensure that the department is managed with efficiency as well as effectiveness. DRGs in a prospective payment system will not solve this problem.

DRGs are a powerful tool for reimbursement strategies that at their present stage need some second thoughts. In Denmark we would want to avoid the increasing inequalities of the U.S. Medicare system. DRGs might be appealing as a basis for calculating the global budget of hospitals within a region, but they would then have to take account of other objectives such as equal access, which might undermine their basic idea. What still is to be considered, however, is whether DRGs could be the basis of a specifically Danish departmental information system. For example, there seems to be some indication from Danish surveys that the age of 75 is crucial for length of stay.

The Danish experience also indicates that there may be too many DRGs to manage even at the departmental level and that the use of garbage can DRGs has got to be sorted out, perhaps by limiting the numbers or through some system of peer review. But even if the DRGs are turned into DARGs, we do not know if the costs linked to such groups will be homogeneous. This remains to be tested.

Current Attitudes to DRGs

The DRG diffusion process shows that a very limited number of key people influenced ongoing activities and that a lot of room was left to those who took the initiative. These included a local researcher, a professor of health economics who later became director of a regional health authority, two senior servants in the Ministry of the Interior, a consultant at the National Health Board who enthusiastically translated ICD8 into ICD9-CM codes, and the economists of the department of health economics in the Danish Hospital Institute who kept the kettle warm without letting any steam out.

The attitudes of the interested parties have changed over the years. It is now commonly recognized that DRGs are not the solution to achieving efficiency in the Danish hospital sector. Nonetheless, the experiments with DRGs have fed the discussions and led to new insights on the usefulness (and folly) of DRGs. At a conference on measurement of productivity and efficiency organized by the Danish Hospital Institute, the chairman of the Association of Doctors stated that the linking of resources was necessary at the clinical as well as the hospital level in order to set priorities and that this "could possibly take the form of a modified DRG system" (Goetrik, 1990, p. 78). Nurses, however, have been more specific about DRGs: so long as severity of illness and complexity of illness are not part of a diagnosis-related information system, "it is not appropriate for assessing resource utilization in nursing care" (Andersen, 1990, p. 44).

Future work on the establishment of relevant expressions of throughput will be based on the experience gained so far. Emphasis will be on the planning objective and, as a means of increasing cost awareness at the decentralized decision-making level, the departments. Discussion of strategic product lines as a means for hospital managers to achieve allocative efficiency has also been in the agenda in recent years as a result of the changed organization of hospitals.

The main emphasis in the counties will continue to be the development of resources and cost models that have the clinical department as the final cost center—the bottom-up approach. This work will be built on the assumption that it must be possible to apply to any suitable measure of output—DRGs, modified DRGs, or whatever.

Whether the ongoing process in the counties will be disturbed or enriched by the work recently initiated by the

Ministry of Health remains to be seen. At the central level, DRGs are again on the agenda, along with the development of cost weights as a way to improve the pricing of hospital services.

It is my conclusion that the point of no return has not yet been reached in Denmark. DRGs have been and remain part of ongoing discussions on developing performance indicators for hospital output. DRGs have promoted the notion of case mix in Denmark. They have helped to clarify the country's objectives in establishing a hospital information system. Their weaknesses—for example, the lack of any severity-of-illness measure—have prompted health care providers to think out the ideas introduced by Robert Fetter (Fetter and others, 1980). This entire process might have happened anyway, but it would not have happened as quickly without the advent of DRGs.

The Danish poet Piet Hein has this comment on innovations:

Mind
these three:
T. T. T.!
Hear
their chime:
Things Take Time

Epilogue

In April 1992 the senior civil servant in the Ministry of Health in charge of the DRG project left for a position in the Ministry of Finance. However, the project is continuing, and a report on the findings was scheduled to be published in 1992. The report was to be based on the findings of 1989 data from the National Patient Register and individual hospital budgets for all somatic hospitals in Denmark in 1989. As an approximation of Danish cost weights per DRG, the Norwegian figures were to be used after having been adjusted to the Danish average length of stay. The vacated post in the Ministry of Health has been filled, and at present it is uncertain how aggressively the DRG report will be marketed.

No single county has continued working with DRGs. The

Danish Hospital Institute has concentrated its efforts on the development of relevant cost-and-resource models along the lines of the HOSCOM project. However, some efforts have been devoted to the establishment of resource-homogeneous case mixes of selected specialties. At present the institute has an ongoing project in the county of Fuen.

In the spring of 1992 the Danish Hospital Institute published the experiences from the HOSCOM project in a report that put emphasis on the testing of different case mix systems and the development of a cost-and-resource model as the basis for a hospital information system.

References

Aagaard, L., and Lundell, J. "Diagnoserelaterede grupper — en situationsrapport fra USA" (DRGs — the state of the art in the United States). *Tidsskrift for Danske Sygehuse*, 1985, *61*(1), 3–5.

Alban, A. "Case-mix definition and departmental cost models." In F. H. Roger France and others (eds.), *Diagnosis Related Groups in Europe*. (2nd. ed.) Ghent, Belgium: UZ-Dienst., 1990.

Alban, A., Boll Hansen, E., and Christensen, U. *Opgaveglidning mellem sygehuse og kommuner* (Shifts of tasks within health care). Copenhagen: Danish Hospital Institute, 1988.

Alban, A., and Christensen, I. "Strategian for produktivitets og effektivitetsmålinger i sygehusvaesenet er lokale for søg." *DSI-Information*, 1986, *6*(1), 3–5.

Alban, A., Lehmann Knudsen, J., and Smidt Thomsen, I. *Ledelse paa sygehuse* (Management in hospitals). Copenhagen: Danish Hospital Institute, 1990.

Amtsraadsforeningen. *Afdelingsinformationssystemer* (Clinical budgeting). Copenhagen: Amtsraadsforeningen, 1984.

Andersen, Y. "Hvorledes kan produktivitets- og effektivitetsmaal for sygeplejen anvendes i det daglige?" (How can we use productivity and efficiency measures in daily nursing care?). In A. Ankjaer-Jensen (ed.), *Strategi for produktivitets- og effektivitetsmaal. Konferencerapport* (A strategy for measuring productivity and efficiency. A conference report). Copenhagen: Danish Hospital Institute, 1990.

Ankjaer-Jensen, A. (ed.). *Strategi for produktivitets- og effektivitets-maal. Konferencerapport* (A strategy for measuring productivity and efficiency. A conference report). Copenhagen: Danish Hospital Institute, 1990.

Bak, P. "Erfaringer fra arbejdet med DRG paa Ringkjoebing Sygehus" (Experiences from work with DRGs at Rinkjoebing Hospital). In A. Ankjaer-Jensen (ed.), *Strategi for produktivitets- og effektivitetsmaal. Konferencerapport* (A strategy for measuring productivity and efficiency. A conference report). Copenhagen: Danish Hospital Institute, 1990a.

Bak, P. "Klinisk-oekonomisk analyse som hjaelpemiddel til omstilling i hospitalsafdelinger, 1: Metode" (Clinical-economic analysis as a means to change in hospital departments. Vol. 1: Methods). *Ugeskrift for Laeger*, 1990b, *152*(28), 2032–2037.

Bak. P. "Klinisk-oekonomisk analyse som hjaelpemiddel til omstilling i hospitalsafdelinger, 2: Analyseeksempler" (Clinical-economic analysis as a means to change in hospital departments. Vol. 2: Examples from analysis). *Ugeskrift for Laeger*, 1990c, *152*(28), 2037–2041.

Bak, P. "Klinisk-oekonomisk analyse som baggrund for omstilling i hospitalsafdelinger, 3: Sammenligning med DRG-systemet" (Clinical-economic analysis as a means to change in hospital departments. Vol. 3: Comparisons with DRGs). *Ugeskrift for Laeger*, 1990d, *152*(28), 2041–2044.

Bak, P. "Fordeling af inlaeggelsesomkostninger" (Distribution of the expenses of admission to hospitals). *Ugeskrift for Laeger*, 1991, *153*(12), 844–846.

Berki, S. E. "DRGs, Incentives, Hospitals and Physicians." *Health Affairs*, Winter 1985, 70–76.

Clarkson, A. D. "Some Implications of Property Rights in Hospital Management." *Journal of Law and Economics*, 1972, *5*, 363–384.

Danish Hospital Institute. "Resource-styring på sygehuse" (Resource management in hospitals). *NYFIGEN*, 1990, *1*, 1–12.

Davis, D. K., and Rhodes, D. J. "The Impact of DRGs on the Cost and Quality of Health Care in the United States." *Health Policy*, 1988, *9*(2), 117–131.

Department of Health and Human Services, Health Care Financing Administration. *Medicare Peer Review Organization Manual.* (Publication 19) Washington, D.C.: Department of Health and Human Resources, 1984.

Des Harnais, S. I., Chesney, J. D., and Fleming, S. T. "Should DRG Assignment Be Based on Age? *Medical Care,* 1988, *26*(12), 124–131.

Feldstein, P. "Applying Economic Concepts to Hospital Care." *Hospital and Health Services Administration,* 1968, *3,* 68–69.

Fetter, R. B., and others. "Case-Mix Definition by Diagnosis-Related Groups." *Medical Care,* 1980, *18*(2) (Supplement).

Finansministeriet, Budgetdepartementet. *Budgetredegoerelse 1983* (Budget Strategy 1983). Copenhagen: Finansministeriet, 1983.

Goetrik, J. K. "Hvilke informationer er noedvendige for prioriteringer inden for sygehusvaesenet?" (Which information is necessary for priority setting within hospital care?) In A. Ankjaer-Jensen (ed.), *Strategi for produktivitets- og effektivitetsmaal. Konferencerapport* (A strategy for measuring productivity and efficiency. A conference report). Copenhagen: Danish Hospital Institute, 1990.

Hatting, A. "Produktivitet og effektivitet — nok en gang. Svaert, men ikke umuligt" (Productivity and efficiency once more: Difficult but not impossible). *Tidsskrift for Danske Sygehuse,* 1988, *64*(5), 187–192.

Indenrigsministeriet. *Sygehusenes organisation og oekonomi* (The organization and financing of hospitals). Copenhagen: Indenrigsministeriet, 1984.

Indenrigsministeriet. *Standardomkostninger og produktivitet for 96 somatiske sygehuse* (Standard costs and productivity of 96 acute-care hospitals). Copenhagen: Indenrigsministeriet, 1986.

Indenrigsministeriet. *"Amtskommunalt udgiftspres og styringsmuligheder"* (Financial pressure and management strategies of county councils) Betaenkning 1123. Copenhagen: Indenrigsministeriet, 1987.

Jenkins, L. "Reimbursing Hospitals by DRG." In M. Bardsley, J. Coles, and L. Jenkins, *DRGs and Health Care: The Management of Case-Mix.* London: King Edward's Hospital Fund, 1987.

Lee, M. L. "A Conspicuous Production Theory of Hospital Behavior." *Southern Economic Journal*, 1971, *38*, 48–58.

Lundell, J., and Aagaard, L. *Diagnoserelaterede grupper, DRG. Introduktion* (DRGs: Introduction). Copenhagen: Ernst and Whinney Management, 1984.

McCarthy, C. M. "DRGs—Five Years Later." *New England Journal of Medicine*, 1988, *318*(25), 1683–1686.

Moeller Pedersen, K. *Diagnose-relaterede grupper. DRG* (Diagnosis related groups: DRG). Odense, Denmark: Institute of Health Economics and Prevention, University of Odense, 1987.

Muurinen, J. M. "Modelling Non-Profit Firms in Medicine." In A. J. Culyer and B. Junsson (eds.), *Public and Private Health Services: Complementarities and Substitutes*. London: Basil-Blackwell, 1986.

Roger France, F., and others. "Hospital Comparisons Using a EuroHealth Data Base for Resource Management and Strategic Planning." *Health Policy*, 1991, *17*(2), 165–178.

Sandford, L., and others. "Economic Incentives and Organizational Realities: Managing Hospitals Under DRGs." *Milbank Memorial Fund Quarterly*, 1987, *65*, 463–485.

Sundhedsministeriet og Indenrigsministeriet. *DRG-systemet. En af-testning af systemet paa danske udskrivninger fra 1985* (Testing DRGs on Danish discharges from 1985). Copenhagen: Sundhedsministeriet og Indenrigsministeriet, 1988.

Torup, J. "Diagnoserelaterede grupper som praestationsmaal paa afdelingsniveau—en analyse med udgangspunkt i sygehusene i Vejle amtskommune" (DRGs as performance indicators at the departmental level: An analysis conducted at the hospitals of Vejle county). In A. Ankjaer-Jensen (ed.), *Strategi for produktivitets- og effektivitetsmaal. Konferencerapport* (A strategy for measuring productivity and efficiency. A conference report). Copenhagen: Danish Hospital Institute, 1990.

U.S. Federal Register, Aug. 31, 1984, *49*, 34780–34790.

Ten

Germany: An Outsider in DRG Development

Günter Neubauer

It is commonly agreed in Germany (although not necessarily among academics) that the health care system works well and its principles are worth preserving. Reforms are seen as necessary only insofar as they do not alter these principles. We will begin our discussion of the German health care system with a short description of its principles and then go on to an examination of the hospital sector. Following that, we will analyze the objectives of the current health policy.

Overview of German Health Care

Germany's mandatory health care system (for further information see Ferber and others, 1985) can be characterized by four principles that take into account both the financing and the delivery of health care. These principles are mandatory insurance; solidarity within the mandatory sickness funds; pluralistic, decentralized sickness funds and health-care providers; and self-managing bodies for the sickness funds and the health care providers (*Selbstverwaltungen*).

Note: The author wishes to thank Gertrud Demmler and Peter Rehermann of the Universität der Bundeswehr for reading this chapter.

Table 10.1. Key Health Care Figures for Germany, 1988.[a]

	West Germany	East Germany	Total
Country area (sq. km.)	248,700	108,300	357,000
Population (millions)	62.3	16.4	78.7
% of population over 65	10.8	—	—
Life expectancy in years (female)	78.65	76	77
Life expectancy in years (male)	72.13	70	71
Income per capita, 1990	$22,759[b]	$8,818	$19,894
Expenditure on health per capita, 1987[c]	$1,093	—	—
% of GDP spent on health, 1989[c]	8.24%	—	—
Number of hospitals	3,069	441	3,510
Number of acute-care hospitals	1,754	—	—
Number of hospital beds	672,834	164,101	836,935
Number of acute-care hospital beds	456,041	—	—
Number of physicians	177,000	42,000	219,000
Number of physicians in hospitals	85,000	17,300	102,000
Number of physicians per 10,000 pop.	28.4	25.6	27.8
Number of hospital physicians per 10,000 pop.	7.5	9.5	7.8
Percentage of mandatory insured	90	—	—
Contribution for health care as percentage of income (average in 1991)	12.25	12.8	—
Upper income limit for insurance, 1991	DM4,875[b]	DM2,250	—

[a] All data are for 1988 except where otherwise indicated.
[b] $1 = DM1.7
[c] Data from Organization for Economic Cooperation and Development, 1990.

In the following section we will discuss both the meaning of these principles and how they are embodied in actual practice. (For basic demographic and financial data on German health care, sees Table 10.1.)

Mandatory Insurance

All employees whose incomes are below an upper limit have to be insured by one of the different mandatory sickness funds. In 1991 the limit was a monthly income of DM 4,875 ($2,868).

Below this level, family members are insured automatically without having to make their own contributions. Employees who pass the ceiling have the right to stay in their sickness fund or to opt out in favor of private insurance. Above the ceiling, about half of all employees leave; in doing so, they forfeit any right to return to a sickness fund later on.

Out of the total population of Germany, 90 percent are insured by mandatory sickness funds. Of the other 10 percent, only 3–4 percent are insured privately. The rest are those who receive direct support from their employers: for example, soldiers, police, and civil servants. (The latter have only 50 percent coverage and normally buy additional private coverage of 50 percent.) A lot of Germans with mandatory insurance also buy complementary private insurance, mainly to ensure more comfort in case of hospitalization.

The private health insurance sector plays an important ideological role in Germany, but the reality shows that the health industry is dominated by the sickness funds.

The Principle of Solidarity

Solidarity is the key word for different kinds of income redistribution within a single sickness fund. First, high-income members pay more than low-income members under the same circumstances; contributions to the funds are related only to wages. Second, at comparable income levels, people who represent a large health risk pay the same as people who represent a small health risk. This practice naturally favors the elderly. Third, members with many dependents pay the same as single members at a comparable income level. This practice is intended to support large families.

One result of this manifold redistribution is that contributions are not linked to health risks, which means that in a free market the system would not be stable. At the moment there is a heated debate on how far competition and solidarity can be combined and what level of regulation is necessary to support both.

Decentralized Sickness Funds

The sickness funds have some important rights that make them independent of the government. Probably the most important is the right to raise contributions according to expenditures. This allows them complete financial independence of any state funding. The sickness funds have a corresponding duty of contracting with the providers, which are also organized in self-regulating bodies. (This process will be described below.)

Whenever the provider does not agree to a contract, a neutral referee committee makes the decision. Thus, contracting is not really free because each side is obliged to sign a contract if certain conditions are fulfilled.

The lowest level of autonomy is given in the range of covered services. Here the government sets the same level of all the sickness funds; only in a very few and relatively unimportant fields do the covered services differ among the sickness funds.

The pluralistic structure of the sickness funds means that different kinds of sickness funds are operating inside the scheme for compulsory social insurance. There are local sickness funds covering all areas of Germany, sickness funds for clerks, company-run sickness funds, and some others for farmers, miners, craft workers, and sailors. All of these nearly 1,200 funds are autonomous in raising contributions.

In spite of its decentralized structure, the system is highly regulated by law. There are some tendencies to more centralization, but there is strong resistance to such tendencies, particularly on the regional level. At the moment, no planning at the federal level is allowed. Twice a year there are so-called concerted actions in which the Ministry of Health (established in January 1991), the federal associations of the sickness funds, and all health care providers discuss their objectives for the near future. They then recommend a figure for the annual increase in health-care expenditures. However, they have no power to enforce this recommendation or any other guidelines. Only the states are entitled to plan hospital services.

The Hospital Sector

The hospitals are also pluralistically organized according to their ownership. About half of the hospitals (60 percent of the beds) are owned by the communities (cities or counties) and the states (university hospitals). Voluntary organizations like churches, welfare associations, and foundations run about 40 percent of the hospitals. Less than 10 percent are run by private proprietors for profit.

The supply of hospital services is planned by the individual German states. The states draw up hospital plans that define which hospitals are needed and lay out a specific role for each hospital depending on its location, size, and equipment. All hospitals so included in the plan are privileged that the state is obliged by law to finance them. These hospitals are also entitled to get a contract with the sickness funds.

Hospitals outside the hospital plan have to finance their investment by their own revenues—mostly payments by the sickness funds and private insurance. There are a couple of specialized clinics outside of the hospital plans. As they get the same per diem rates as the subsidized hospitals, they have to be more efficient than their competitors.

Hospitals are, as already mentioned, financed in a dualistic way. Investment costs (which include buildings and new long-term equipment) are financed by the states. Replacement of short-term technical equipment is paid by lump sums per bed.

Operating costs are financed by the sickness funds and private insurance. Operating costs are about 85 percent of total costs and depend in part on investments. Often the sickness funds complain about financing the consequences of politically determined investment decisions.

This dualistic financing is strongly debated because of its inefficient incentives and because in these days some states are not providing enough money for hospital investment. This is particularly true for the new (eastern) states. Possible solutions include monistic financing by the sickness funds or—for the

new states—financing by the federal government. This latter
possibility is opposed by the western states, which see in it a
threat of federalism. Perhaps for a limited time there will be
consent for federal support for the eastern states.

Hospitals are reimbursed through a flexible budget calculated using per diem rates and prospective patient days. The
budget is flexible in that an adjustment is done after the budget
period. For additional patient days, the hospitals get only 25
percent of the total per diem rate. Similarly, they have to accept
reductions in the budget of 25 percent for each patient day less
than the expected number. The argument for this procedure is
that 75 percent of all operating costs are fixed costs. (Under the
most extreme form of this argument, a hospital without any
patients would receive 75 percent of its budget).

Most critics, however, focus on the per diem rates, which
are equal for all patients in a given hospital. Thus, a hospital with
less severe cases can do its work more easily than a hospital with
more severe cases but the same level of supply. The case mix does
not play any role in reimbursement.

At the moment, the sickness funds try to classify hospitals
by their level of supply and to group patients by the ICD9 code.
The sickness funds try to include both factors in their negotiations with individual hospitals. The hospitals oppose these attempts with arguments contesting their validity, particularly the
validity of the ICD9 code.

The ICD9 code must be used by all hospitals in the three-
digit version. The codings have to be done by the physicians,
who are quite unwilling, and thus the statistics are quite unrelia-
ble. So there is an accepted need for alternative methods that
take the case mix into account. This was the first step in the
discussion of diagnosis-related groups, or DRGs (Sauerzapf,
1980; Stiftung, 1987).

Cost Containment

One of the main objectives of German health policy is cost
containment. As both costs and contributions to sickness funds
began to increase very quickly, the government tried to contain

the costs to ensure the competitiveness of industry (employers pay 50 percént of contributions) and to reduce negative incentives for employees. In 1991 the average contribution to sickness funds was 12.25 percent of gross income. (The maximum contribution is DM 604, which is paid half and half by employer and employee.)

Cost containment is also an objective because of the need to improve efficiency in the system and because health care providers have not always had an adequate level of income. In January 1989 a new reform law was enacted that called for expenditures to be linked with income development. Other important changes have hit the pharmaceutical industry, the hearing-aid industry, and other less important health care provider groups. Still under debate are a reform of the organizational structure of the sickness funds (Deutscher Bundestag— Referat Öffentlichkeitsarbeit, 1990), the introduction of obligatory insurance for people in need of nursing care, and a reform of the hospital services.

The most important task for any future reform of the hospital services will be the reimbursement system. The intention is to cut down the supply of hospital beds by shortening the length of stay and concentrating the expensive equipment in a few hospitals. As explained above, the reimbursement of hospitals is based on flexible budgets calculated on a per diem basis. The government believes that this payment should be more differentiated in the direction of the actual costs per treatment. Two approaches to improving the payment system are under consideration.

The first is the development of a catalogue of expensive medical procedures like organ transplantations and dialysis for which the hospital can claim special reimbursements (*Sonderentgelte*) (Wissenschaftliches. . . , 1990). As of 1991, this catalogue had been enlarged to include minor medical procedures. Use of these special reimbursements has met with resistance because calculating the reimbursements is not very easy. As indirect costs contained in the budget are rather high and differ considerably from hospital to hospital, only the direct costs can be compared. This means that the impact of special reimbursements on the budget is difficult to calculate.

A second approach is the development of a case-based payment system (this will be discussed below). It is still an unanswered question whether the special reimbursements and the case-based payments will be merged in the near future.

Besides reimbursement, quality assurance has been a target for reform. Since January 1990 all hospitals have been required to establish quality assurance tools, though there has been no consistency in this effort. The government can be expected to make a new push in this direction.

A more organizational aspect of the reform effort is the push for more efficient management of hospitals. In particular, the communal hospitals are often administered rather than managed. As part of the communal administration, they are often burdened with a lot of regulations that hinder them from reacting in a flexible way to changing circumstances. Reform in this area is recognized as urgent, but neither the federal government nor the states have the legal competence to intervene in the communities. Only the increasing financial problems can force single communities to free their hospitals from narrow communal ties.

DRGs and Their Alternatives

In the 1970s health expenditures began to increase faster and faster. This was particularly true in the hospital sector, which accounts for 30 percent of total spending and is thus the most important subsector of the health care system. Consequently, cost containment policies focused on hospitals. However, the federal structure in Germany requires the consent of the second chamber of the Parliament (representing the states) for any cost containment law. The states refused their consent to a cost containment law including the hospitals, so the first law (enacted in July 1977) excluded hospitals. A new attempt to include the hospitals in July 1980 also failed.

Finally, in 1982, a cost containment law for the hospitals was enacted, but its instruments were blunt. The law mandated the inclusion of the hospital sector in the annual concerted action and tries to influence the hospital sector by efficiency control and recommendations by the financing and provider bodies regarding special problems like staffing (see Vollmer and Graeve, 1990).

In 1983 the Minister of Labor and Social Affairs appointed an advisory board to develop proposals for a more efficient hospital financing system. The main proposal of the advisory committee was to split the reimbursement into two components: a fixed per diem rate for the "hotel costs" and a fee for the medical services. This proposal was strongly opposed by the sickness funds, which feared an expansion of services.

In the years 1985 and 1986 a couple of modifications were made to the hospital financing law and the hospital reimbursement system. Among the main changes: The states got the exclusive investment financing authority; the contracts between hospitals and the sickness funds did not need final consent by the state any longer; and the contractors became free to negotiate different reimbursement modes, including case-based payments like DRGs.

In the early 1980s the discussion of DRGs as a basis for reimbursement began in Germany. It was initiated by academics who visited the United States and learned about DRGs there. The incentives of case-based payment had been generally discussed even before that time, but there had never been a reasonable grouping system.

It is striking that from the very beginning attention focused on the introduction of a new reimbursement mode. The effects on transparency of services and on internal management were considered welcome side effects but were not seen as important objectives, as seems to have been the case in other European countries.

The discussion first came to official attention in 1984 when the federal government commissioned the company Ernst and Whinney and a partner hospital to examine DRGs (Ernst and Whinney, 1986). Since that time more and more managers of sickness funds and hospitals have paid attention to DRGs.

DRGs were put in the programs of conferences, and speakers on the subject were invited mostly from academia. I know, however, only one person, Professor Hansen (now at the University of Hamburg), who visited Yale University and worked with Bob Fetter for some time. The interest and activities of Hansen were more oriented to data processing, so he did not influence the content of discussion in Germany very much.

From 1982 until 1986 the Robert Bosch Foundation sponsored a commission on hospital financing (Stiftung, 1987). Its objective was to propose different organizational and financial frameworks. Many members of this commission were well known academics and practical experts. The discussion centered on defining the position of the states, the need for hospital planning, and the advantages of free, selective price contracting. The results of the Bosch commission found a wide audience and crowded out the more specialized debate on DRGs for a while.

After the end of the Bosch commission in 1986, the Bosch Foundation financed a study of alternative modes of reimbursement of hospitals. In this study, for which I had responsibility, we compared a lot of different grouping systems and analyzed their advantages and shortcomings. The study ran from 1986 to 1988 (Neubauer and others, 1989).

In the summer of 1987 the federal government organized an expert meeting to develop guidelines for its hospital policy. The main topics of discussion were the results of the Ernst and Whinney study and further developments in hospital reimbursement. The Ernst and Whinney study enumerated a long list of obstacles to be overcome before DRGs could be applicable to German hospitals. The system itself was criticized for not taking into account severity of illness and the reason for hospital admission. The partner hospital in the study stressed the dangers that economic constraints and fixed costs posed to sound medical practice. Both Ernst and Whinney and the hospital asserted that DRGs could not be used in Germany anytime soon. The hospital was adamant on the subject, whereas Ernst and Whinney held that an introduction might be possible in five years or so. The results of the study were not altogether encouraging to the administration, so it proposed two parallel developments: special reimbursements for expensive procedures and a test of an alternative to DRGs known as patient management categories (PMCs).

Later in 1987 the Bosch Foundation organized a colloquium on alternative reimbursement systems. After heated debate between DRG and PMC proponents, it was agreed that PMCs promise an easier application in Germany because the system is more clinically specific. This was the decisive argument for participating clinicians, who would be obliged to code the patients directly. After this colloquium it was decided to start a clinical test of PMCs.

The Kiel Experiment

In the meantime, beginning in 1985, a small ophthalmological clinic in Kiel (Rüschmann and others, 1988) started to contract case-related payments for the first time in Germany. The grouping system used was very pragmatic and primarily cost-oriented. Starting with the ICD9 four-digit code, the clinic divided the patients into ten groups, each containing ICD9 codes with similar costs. At the time this project represented all that many politicians and health industry managers knew about DRGs. As a result, politicians often used the term DRGs inaccurately to mean *any* case-related payment system.

The case-related payments in Kiel encouraged a lot of people to favor such a development because the results were very striking. The clinic shortened the average length of stay by 30 percent and made profits with relatively low payments. By contrast, the nearby ophthalmological hospital of the University of Kiel had a longer length of stay and higher costs.

The sickness funds used the results of the small clinic against the university hospital in arguing for a single price for the same procedure. This argument was only partly valid, but it helped the funds to demand more such experiments. At the moment the Kiel experiment is still running, but its limitations are becoming more and more evident.

Development of PMCs

As mentioned above, in 1988 the federal government commissioned me to test the plausibility, validity, and reliability of PMCs. The test of validity and reliability was done in three surgical departments; the test of plausibility was done for nearly all PMCs by experienced clinicians working in a number of different hospitals. Most of these clinicians accepted the underlying philosophy that PMCs are based on the reasons for admission (symptoms), the diagnosis, and the main therapeutical decisions (see Figure 10.1). One characteristic of the PMC classification system is its hierarchical structure; only one PMC should be used for a given diagnosis — the one with the highest use of resources. Multimorbidity, however, involves classification of PMCs from more than one model. In these instances, there was conflict between economic and clinical criteria, or conflict that has not yet been satisfactorily resolved.

The reliability of the coding done by the physicians was a central question. Involving the physicians directly in coding is not done in the United States or most European countries. The results were mixed and depended on the educational level and the engagement of the physicians. The method of organizing the coding also seemed to be important: whether it was done by only one physician or by all physicians, with or without control, with or without additional payment.

The validity test included the construction of a case-related accounting system and an extension of the data processing system. The results were encouraging; the explanatory power of the system was high and the coefficients of variance low — as U.S. experiments had similarly shown (Thomas and Ashcraft, 1991). More important, the system can be managed by the hospitals.

The case mix of two of the surgical departments was nearly the same, while the third department was more specialized (see Figure 10.2). We found that twelve to fourteen PMCs accounted for 50 percent of the treated patients.

Figure 10.1. Logic Structure of PMCs.

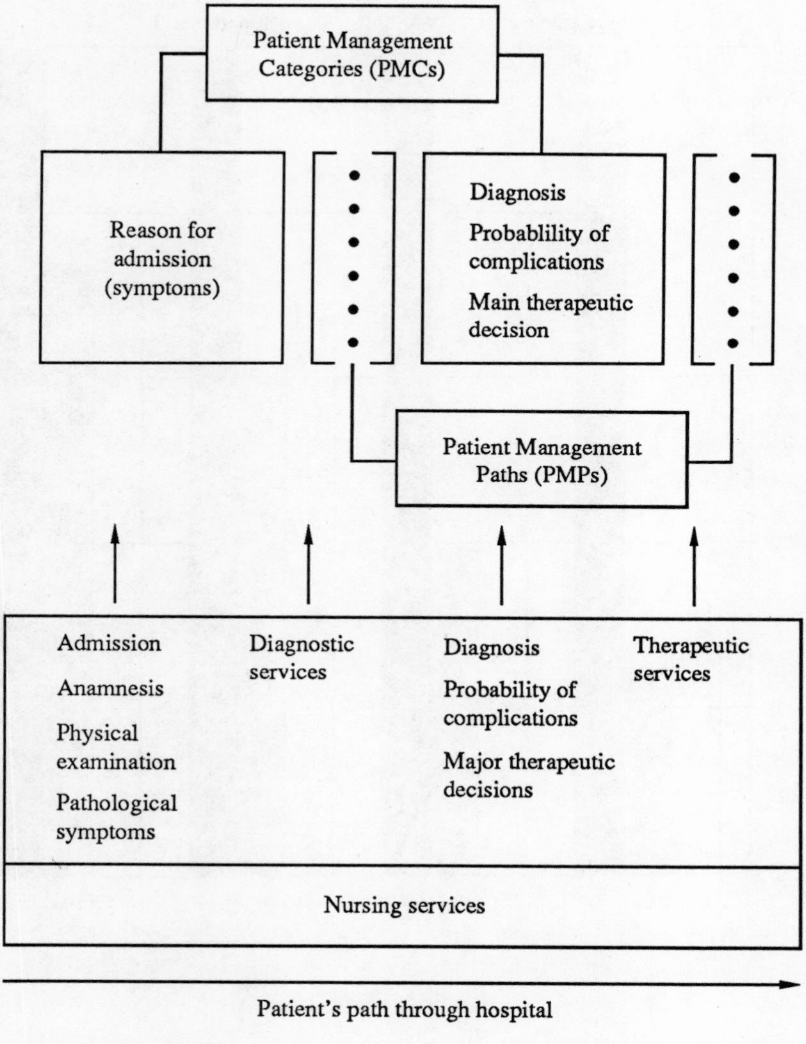

The results for one pilot hospital in the test of the valid of PMCs (measured by R-square and the coefficient of variance) are shown in Tables 10.2 and 10.3. The homogeneity of PMCs is shown in Table 10.3 by the coefficient of variance.

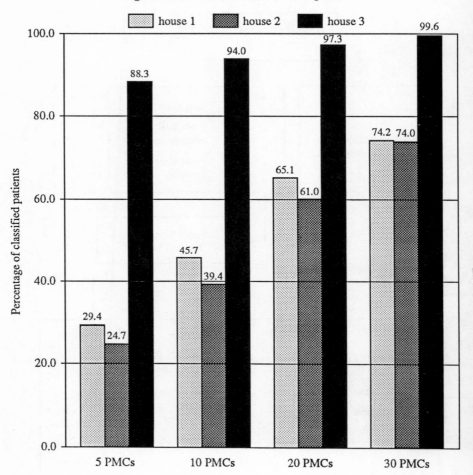

Figure 10.2. Case Mix of Three Hospitals.

We have also calculated costs per PMC on the basis of our differentiated documentation per patient. In Figure 10.3 we show different PMCs and their costs.

All in all, the test results of the PMC system seem to be a good basis for further development in the next few years.

Table 10.2. R-square for Different Variables of One Pilot Hospital.

	PMC level	
	with outliers[a] (n = 823)	without outliers (n = 731)
	R^2	R^2
Average costs per case[b]	0.444	0.649
Direct costs[c]	0.471	0.639
Nursing[d]	0.377	0.632
Medicaments	0.424	0.479
Ancillary services[e]	0.421	0.464
Length of stay	0.363	0.629

[a] Trimming method is described in Neubauer and others, 1990, p. 79.
[b] Costs per case include physician salaries.
[c] Direct costs are nursing, ancillary services, operations, medicaments, direct physician services.
[d] Intensity of nursing is defined by four intensity categories, which are weighted by different costs.
[e] Includes labor, x-rays, and so on.
Source: Neubauer and others, 1990, Supplement 2, p. 108.

Diffusion of PMCs

The diffusion of PMCs in Germany will depend on financial support from the federal government, on acceptance of PMCs by hospitals, physicians, and sickness funds, and on further convincing test results. There are already a couple of hospitals that are willing to introduce PMCs. Some of these are hospitals that would like to offer more specialized medicine than the hospital plan provides for; others are hospitals that would like to achieve more autonomy.

Hospital physicians are still generally reluctant, however. To understand their reasons it is necessary to know that the head of a department normally has the right to treat private patients in the hospital. Revenues from private patients are often three to five times higher than the physician's salary—a good reason for head physicians to resist any move that might jeopardize their right to treat private patients. Many physicians are simply not sure what the consequences of PMCs will be.

Table 10.3. Coefficient of Variance (CV) for One Pilot Hospital and
Selected PMCs.

PMC	with outlier		without outlier	
	n	$CV \times 100$	n	$CV \times 100$
0607[a]	43	36	38	28
1104[b]	47	31	47	31
1203[c]	99	38	81	31
1901[d]	43	56	39	33
3501[e]	65	64	58	52
4101[f]	48	53	41	47
4136[g]	83	43	83	43

[a] 0607: Gallbladder: elective cholecystectomy.
[b] 1104: Appendicitis: elective appendectomy.
[c] 1203: Hernia—abdominal: elective herniorrhaphy, recurrent.
[d] 1901: Femur FRX—proximal: operative repair.
[e] 3501: Head injury: linear skull fracture/scalp laceration.
[f] 4101: Vascular disorder: peripheral with operation.
[g] 4136: Vascular disorder: varicose veins.
Source: Neubauer and others, 1990, Supplement 2, p. 121.

By contrast, the sickness funds are showing great willingness to agree upon per-case payments. They see the advantages of a higher visibility in hospital performance and—most importantly—of an easier comparison of the levels of reimbursement. They hope to find ultimately a fair performance-related payment.

The decentralized structure of the German health care system allows a lot of independent experiments if there are hospitals and sickness funds willing to contract for such experiments. The sickness funds are also able to finance a preparatory phase, which allows adaptations to be made in, for example, the internal accounting system. At the beginning of 1991 a couple of such experiments were under way.

What is the role of the states and the federal government in all this? The federal government was only recently elected, and its program is still being worked out. Several possible scenarios will be discussed below; what is certain, however, is that the federal government will not obstruct a development it initiated itself.

Figure 10.3. Cost Structure of Selected PMCs.

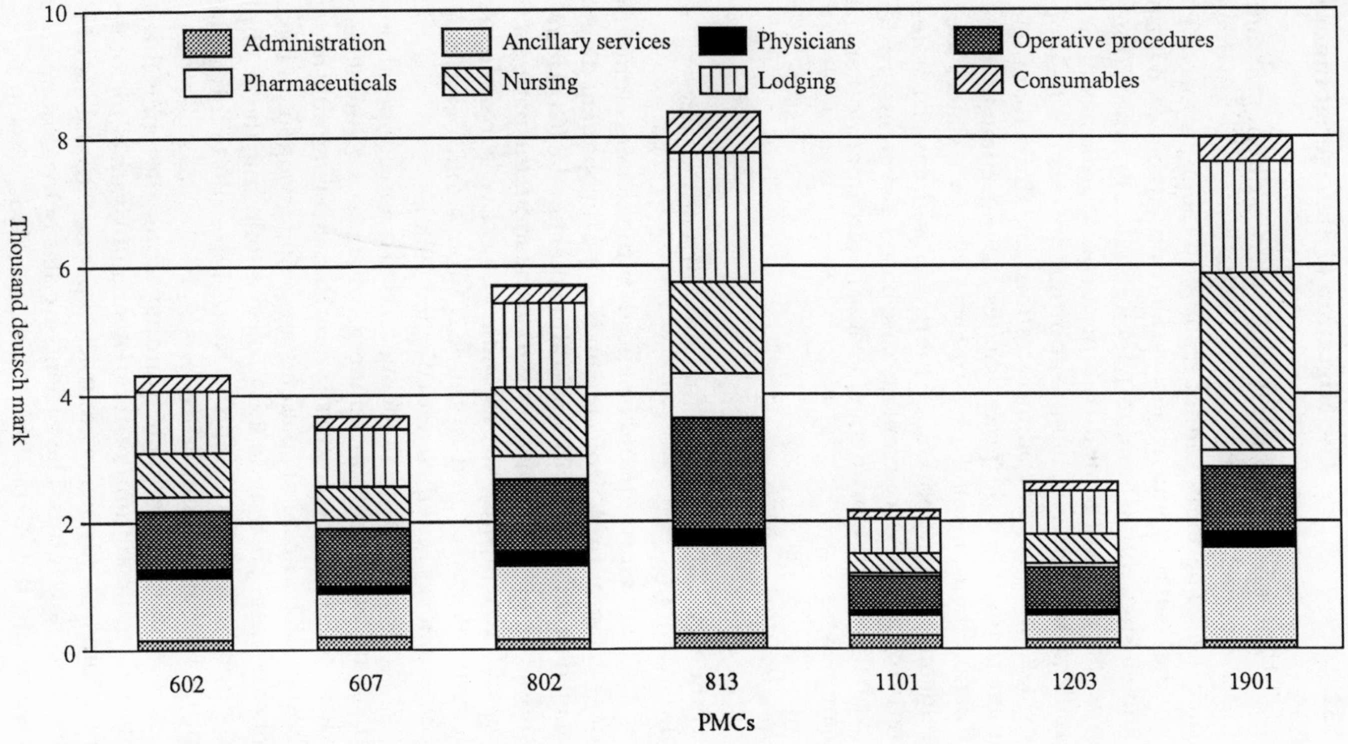

Legend:
- Administration
- Pharmaceuticals
- Ancillary services
- Nursing
- Physicians
- Lodging
- Operative procedures
- Consumables

Y-axis: Thousand deutsch mark (0, 2, 4, 6, 8, 10)

X-axis: PMCs (602, 607, 802, 813, 1101, 1203, 1901)

The position of the federal states is different. Some are fostering development; some are indifferent; some are dragging their feet. The states cannot really stop the diffusion of PMCs, but they can postpone it because all contracts between hospitals and sickness funds have to pass the state administration. It is true that the state administration can only forbid a contract that is illegal in some way, but the approval process can be long and exhausting. The state administrations are afraid that their hospital plans will lose power. States having enough money to finance their hospital investments (southern states) are thus reluctant, while poor states (northern and eastern states) are favoring the development of case-based payments (including capital costs) independent of PMCs, DRGs, or any other classification system.

Non-PMC Projects

Three non-PMC projects that are currently under way merit discussion here.

The first is run and financed by the sickness funds in the city of Hamburg. A project team is collecting patient diagnoses at all hospitals in the city and coding them in the ICD9 four-digit code. The primary objective is to learn about the patient mix of the different hospitals. A secondary objective is to compare the lengths of stay related to the ICD groups and determine the consequences for efficiency (Werner, 1990).

A second project is being carried out in cooperation with the state of Baden-Württemberg, where a patient-related services and cost accounting system has been established in a hospital. The hospital's patients are being grouped on the basis of cost classes; in a sense this project is following the example of the ophthalmological clinic in Kiel. The results of this grouping project are still unpublished.

A third experiment running along the same lines was started in the autumn of 1990. A small private clinic of twenty beds run by a physician contracted per-case payments with the local sickness funds. The patients are also being grouped by cost classes and the ICD9 three-digit code. This classification was chosen because of its simplicity. The ICD9 codes are already mandatory for all hospitals and known to all partners, and the cost classes follow the usual philosophy of cost reimbursement. If there is a surplus or a deficit, the consequences are limited by a compensation system. The decisive shortcoming of this approach is that each hospital has different groups, and thus reliable comparison is not possible. As all of the projects described here know about the PMC test, they could change to that classification system.

The Future of PMCs

In other European countries, DRG experiments are clearly dominant. Besides Germany only Spain has some experience with PMCs. Up to now Germany seems to have been in an outsider role.

This impression is confirmed by the Advanced Informatics in Medicine research program. Only a few subprojects are taking PMCs into account, but even this has not really reduced the predominance of DRGs.

In Germany the federal government is feeling besieged because of its isolated position, even though it may have the stronger arguments. The administration would thus like an extended discussion of PMCs, as otherwise diffusion of PMCs could become stalled.

The basic lines of development in Germany can be forecast for the next five years. There is no realistic chance for an introduction of DRGs; even experiments or projects with DRGs are unlikely. Only if the European Community as a whole starts to emphasize the general use of DRGs could the situation change. At the moment the European Community is not authorized to make such recommendations.

What *will* happen is that hospital financing will be supplemented by more special reimbursements. There is a possibility that the federal government will force the contractors (hospitals and sickness funds) to agree upon special reimbursements; they could even become mandatory, but this would require a change in the financing law as part of a general hospital reform.

What is also certain is that PMCs will be tested and used in a broader way than now. There will be a German version of PMCs after a couple of modifications are made. It is unclear whether the coding will be done by physicians, by recorders, or by an advanced software. Some indicators point to the last possibility. It depends on the cooperation of the physicians; for further pilot projects, it will be possible to find enough cooperative physicians, but in the long run it should be done by a grouper software. This will also reduce the danger of data manipulation. PMCs will not become mandatory in the next five years, but in the long run they may. In the near future PMCs will be the basis for a couple of selected case payment projects and some hospital and departmental budgets.

An important factor in the future will be the development of quality assurance. If researchers succeed in combining methods of quality assurance with PMCs, then the introduction of PMCs will accelerate. The chances of such a combination are even at the moment.

Last but not least, the development of PMCs will depend on the financial resources the federal government devotes to further pilot projects. At the moment many contractors are afraid of the risks involved in changing their reimbursement mode. Financial support can encourage them. At the moment, however, the federal government and the richer western states are fully engaged in helping the poorer eastern states. Hospitals in the eastern states need an enormous financial input for modernizing and reconstruction. All available resources will probably be transferred there for the next five years. This will slow down the development of any new hospital financing system.

In addition, the ongoing integration of the eastern and western states will probably reduce the federal government's ability to reform the hospital sector. If there is any reform, it will be a moderate one. On the other hand, a slower development will give time to examine and test different variations in PMCs — and other alternatives as well.

Epilogue

Since the summer of 1991, discussion in Germany has focused on the topic of hospital reform. All those involved have stressed the need for a more performance-related remuneration. There are three different (but not independent) approaches to the issue.

First, reform of hospital department budgets is proposed as one route to more transparency and efficiency of outputs.

Second, special reimbursement of well-defined surgical procedures (about 220 items) is suggested as a quick first step to increased efficiency. All hospitals should be obliged to record the kind and number of these procedures for remuneration by the sickness funds. Prices for the procedures should be negotiated by the regional associations.

Third, an increasing number of experts and politicians see a case-based payment system as the best overall solution. The discussion has focused on only a few kinds of patient classification systems, with the result that the difficulties of introducing a mandatory patient classification system are being underestimated. The Federal Hospital Association is continuing to argue against case-based remuneration, pointing to the negative results in the United States.

A few hospitals in addition to those described earlier are now experimenting with patient classification systems. In one project I am involved with, PMCs are being used for reimbursement in three surgical departments at different hospitals. Case-based reimbursements are still part of the prospective department budgets at these hospitals. The number of cases is prospectively calculated and will be retrospectively balanced. Another small orthopedic clinic is using PMCs for case-based payments without retrospective balancing.

Some other hospitals are preparing for future PMC-related reimbursement experiments. A few hospitals are using patient groups calculated by cost for reimbursement. Here the case mix is built by grouping defined International Classification of Diseases codes.

Hopefully, case-based remuneration will be generally allowed in the Hospital Reform Act, which is expected to pass in 1993. Hopefully, also, the patient classification systems will be restricted to only a few—including, I predict, PMCs.

References

Bundesminister für Gesundheit (ed.). *Erprobung der Fallklassifikation "Patient Management Categories" für Krankenhauspatienten* (Development of classification system for hospital patients). Baden-Baden, Germany: Nomos, 1992.

Deutscher Bundestag—Referat Öffentlichkeitsarbeit (ed.). *Strukturreform der gesetzlichen Krankenversicherung: Endbericht der Enquête-Kommission des 11. Deutschen Bundestags* (Structural reform of the mandatory sickness funds: Final report of the enquête commission of the 11th German Bundestag). Bonn, Germany: Bonner Universitätsbuchdrukerei, 1990.

Ernst and Whinney. *Modellversuch zu alternativen Pflegesatzformen in Krankenhüsern, Vorstudie zu diagnoseabhängigen Fallpauschalen* (Pattern experiment for alternative modes of reimbursement in hospitals: Pilot-study for diagnosis-related case lump sums). Bonn, Germany: Bundesministerium für Arbeit und Sozialordnung, 1986.

Ferber, C., and others. *Kosten und Effizienz im Gesundheitswesen* (Costs and efficiency in health care). Munich: Oldenbourg, 1985.

Neubauer, G., Demmler, G., and Rehermann, P. "Erprobung der Fallklassifikation 'Patient Management Categories' für Krankenhauspatienten" (Test of the 'Patient Management Categories' classification for inpatients in Germany), final report, including two supplements. Munich: Universität der Bundeswehr, 1990.

Neubauer, G., and others. *Von der Leistung zum Entgelt—neue Ansätze zur Vergütung von Krankehäusern* (From performance to reimbursement—new valuations for reimbursement of hospitals). Gerlingen, Germany: Bleicher, 1989.

Organization for Economic Cooperation and Development. *Social Policy Studies No. 7: Health Care Systems in Transition.* Paris: DECD, 1990.

Rüschmann, H. H., and others. *Diagnosebezogene Festpreise in der Krankenhausfinanzierung, Analyse und Ergebnisse des "Kieler Modells"* (Diagnosis-related payments in financing hospitals: Analysis and results of the Kiel experiment). Kiel, Germany: Schmidt & Klaunig, 1988.

Sauerzapf, M. *Das Krankenhauswesen in der Bundesrepublik Deutschland* (Hospital care in West Germany). Baden-Baden, Germany: Nomos, 1980.

Stiftung, R. B. (ed.). *Krankenhausfinanzierung in Selbstverwaltung, Teil I: Kommissionsbericht* (Financing hospitals by self-management). Gerlingen, Germany: Bleicher, 1987.

Thomas, J. W., and Ashcraft, M.L.F. "Measuring Severity of Illness: Six Severity Systems and Their Ability to Explain Cost Variations." *Inquiry*, 1991, *28*, 39–55.

Vollmer, R. J., and Graeve, K. H. *Krankenhausfinanzierungsgesetz — KHG* (Hospital financing act). Bonn: AOK-Verlag, 1990.

Werner, B. "Möglichkeiten der Beratung der Krankenkassen durch den Medizinischen Dienst auf dem Krankenhaussektor: Erste Ergenbuisse aus dem 'Project Krankenhäuser'" (Possibilities of consulting health insurers in hospitals: First results from Project Hospitals) *Die Ersatzkasse*, 1992, *70*, 97–105.

Wissenschaftliches Institut der Ortskrankenkassen (ed.). "Sonderengtgelte" (Special reimbursements). *Krankenhausinfo 2/90* "Sonderentgelte" (newsletter). Bonn: Wissenschaftliches Institut der Ortskrankenkassen, 1990.

Eleven

DRGs in Western Europe: Lessons and Comparisons in Managerial Innovation

John R. Kimberly

We have now considered the fate of diagnosis related groups, or DRGs, in each of nine countries in Western Europe. The story in each country is interesting in itself, although in no case is the story over. We are simply freezing the action at a particular point in time, knowing full well that the action continues to unfold but wishing to take stock of what has transpired thus far.

Beyond these nine individual histories, however, we can make some observations about the migration of DRGs in particular and perhaps of innovation more generally. Indeed, one of the objectives of this book is to determine what may be learned about the migration of DRGs when we compare the experiences of our nine countries. This requires us to go beyond the country-by-country accounts and focus on the questions and patterns that emerge from such a comparison.

Diffusion: How Fast and How Far?

Perhaps the first question we might ask is how the nine countries now stand with respect to the extensiveness and rapidity of diffusion. We have tried to capture the dynamics of the diffusion of DRGs within and between our nine countries, and each of the country chapters has concluded with a description of the status of DRGs in mid to late 1991. Looking across the nine countries, we find that in two countries, Portugal and Norway, commitments have been made to DRGs at the national level. Although the specifics are different, decisions have been taken in both of these countries to tie DRGs directly to the financing of health care. In Germany, on the other hand, there has been very little enthusiasm for their use, and in Denmark, after considerable experimentation, it appears likely that future developments will go in other directions. In the remaining five countries — Belgium, England, France, Sweden, and Switzerland — the level and extensiveness of experimentation varies considerably. Relatively steady and incrementally increasing amounts of activity have characterized developments in Sweden, Belgium, and England, while in France there has been greater turbulence, with periods of relatively intense activity followed by periods of greatly diminished political support and hence less activity. Switzerland has seen less activity, in general, than any of these four. In fact, one might argue that although Denmark appears to be moving in other directions, it has actually experimented more extensively with DRGs than Switzerland has.

If one were to conceptualize countries as potential adopters of DRGs, and if one were to use Rogers's (1983) categories, one would say that two countries have "adopted" DRGs, two have rejected them, and the other five are in a "trial" period, having neither fully adopted nor rejected them. Despite the intuitive appeal of these categories, however, for the purpose of understanding the fate of DRGs in Western Europe they are deficient in at least two respects. First the nature of the innovation itself is ambiguous; second, the diffusion of DRGs to a given country may occur independent of whether they are used at the national level.

The Ambiguity of Innovation

We began our research with a certain model of innovation and processes of adoption and diffusion as our guide. This model presupposed the existence of an innovation whose attributes could be fully described and whose diffusion could be carefully and fully documented and subsequently described and analyzed.

In the case of DRGs and, we now suspect, most new developments, certain assumptions in this model are seriously flawed. First, the model implicitly assumes stability or stasis in the conception of innovation itself. If innovations are viewed as new products, processes, or programs — that is, as concrete representations of underlying ideas or theories — then the focus of attention is necessarily on the representation rather than on the underlying idea. If we focus, for example, on 2, 4-D weed spray, or hybrid corn, or CAT scanning, we tend to overlook the fact that each of these innovations is embedded in a *process* of development, that each may be modified substantially in the course of its life, and that each will undoubtedly be supplanted at some point by something newer.

For the reader interested in theories of innovation (and able to read French), the strikingly original work of Michel Callon, Bruno Latour, and their colleagues on the evolution and metamorphosis of innovations is strongly recommended (Latour, Maguin, and Teil, 1990). In their view, innovation is a process in the course of which relatively significant but often invisible changes in technical structure occur. They argue, for example, that the technology underlying the idea of the camera has undergone significant transformations since the first camera was invented and that what we call a camera today has virtually nothing to do technologically with the original (Latour, Mauguin, and Teil, 1990). This point is reinforced by the different technical strategies that Kodak and Sony have adopted for the next generation of cameras (although perhaps "image-producing devices" would be a more accurate descriptor). The larger point of relevance here is that the innovation process virtually guarantees that change, not stability, is the norm and thus suggests that one should expect change in products as they mature.

In the case of DRGs, a common concern among various parties in the nine countries was the extent to which this innovation might be modified or improved. One factor that explains the variability in the speed of DRG diffusion is the differing judgments about the probability that newer (and presumably better) versions might be forthcoming. A considerable amount of the research that was undertaken in each country was oriented toward determining the extent to which a given country's data fit the U.S. model. Generally it was found that the fit was acceptable; however, there was much discussion of the fact that the fit was never perfect.

What constitutes an acceptable fit in any particular instance could, of course, itself be the subject of an interesting analysis, as acceptability has both technical and political dimensions. Our view is that one factor contributing to the relatively slow pace of decision making with respect to DRGs in some countries was the anticipation that improved DRGs or viable alternatives to DRGs might become available—and hence prudence dictated minimal action. In some cases, minimal action was based on a genuine belief in potential improvement; in other cases, the possibility of improvement was used politically as a justification for doing nothing.

In a related vein, the possibility existed for any given country to create its own system (that is, its own grouper) and thus to improve the fit. This possibility was not widely pursued as the availability of off-the-shelf technology overwhelmed concerns about possible inappropriateness. Where alternative groupers did become commercially available, as in France, more uncertainty entered the decision process because the results from the alternatives were not identical with the results of the Yale grouper. Although these differences should have been expected, they added ambiguity to the decision process and have contributed to the measured pace of the diffusion process in England, France, and Sweden.

The first flaw in the underlying logic of Rogers' model, then, is an implicit assumption about stasis, whereas change seems to be the norm. The model, in our view, unintentionally creates the impression of certainty, whereas from the perspective of potential users, adopters, or investors, ambiguity and uncertainty with respect to the innovation are no doubt more common.

The second flaw in the model is that it fails to connect the innovation of interest to what I have called "the ebb and flow of invention" and as such leaves open the question of how any particular concrete representation of ideas relates to the larger context of the circulation of ideas in general (Kimberly, 1981). In the case of DRGs this thinking might prompt us to question whether the DRGs themselves are the fundamental innovation of interest for the contexts of diffusion—in this case the nine countries we included in our study—or whether it may not be the more generic penetration of an operations management logic into the health care systems of these countries. By introducing DRGs at the national level, the Ministries of Health in these countries would effectively be accepting the appropriateness of what can only be defined as a new logic; not adopting DRGs, however, would not necessarily imply a rejection of this logic, as there are other specific, concrete representations of the logic that could be used instead.

For this reason, we believe that there is some ambiguity regarding the nature of the innovation we are considering when we examine the diffusion of DRGs. Is the innovation really DRGs, or is it something more fundamental and potentially more profound in its implications for the health care system? We should argue that one of the factors slowing the diffusion of DRGs in some cases—notably France and Belgium but others as well—is the recognition by physicians that adoption of DRGs has implications that go far beyond case mix comparisons. Although it may not be in the interest of the advocates of DRGs to make this explicit—to do so could increase the risk of controversy substantially—the fact remains that the potential is there, and the way in which the advantages of the innovation are represented and communicated becomes an important part of the story.

The question of what the innovation in this case really is is hardly academic. In observing the diffusion of DRGs, the central importance of ambiguity and perhaps of understatement is apparent. The more general point is that how a new initiative is represented by its advocates to those with a significant interest in the outcome will most certainly affect what ultimately happens.

Who Is the Adopter?

One of the most interesting aspects of the DRG story, as noted in the opening chapter, is the fact that its developers saw its primary potential benefit as a tool for improving the internal management of hospitals, whereas it was adopted by the federal government in the United States as a payment mechanism. As researchers, policy makers, and hospital managers outside the United States observed the development and implementation of DRGs, they saw different uses for them, and most naturally focused on the use that was closest to their own needs.

One result of the fact that there are at least two distinctly different uses for DRGs is the development of two different markets for them, a management market and a policy market. In Europe, of course, these two markets are not perfectly distinct. Public policy and hospital activities are more closely tied together in Europe than in the United States, and as a result hospitals in general have less autonomy in the former than in the latter. Nevertheless, it is still possible for individual hospitals in the countries we have included in this book to use DRGs for internal management purposes independent of what occurs at the national policy level. The converse, of course, is not possible: once DRGs are used for payment at the national level, individual hospitals have no choice but to use them as well.

How the two markets and the players involved have interacted with respect to DRGs differs from country to country. In Portugal, for example, the two appear to have been closely allied and aligned. In Belgium, it appears that the government acted in ways that had the effect of protecting the hospitals from the payers. In other cases, such as France, the interactions appear to have been more contentious.

The development of two different markets for DRGs complicates the job of determining patterns of adoption and raises the question of just who the adopter is. Are we only concerned with the policy market and therefore only concerned with the use of DRGs as a policy tool by a unit of government? Or are we interested in their diffusion to hospitals independent of direct government intervention?

Our answer to this question is linked closely to our earlier discussion of ambiguity. In our view, the logic underlying DRGs is what is new to the health sector. Introduction of this logic, whether it be at the level of the state or at the level of an individual institution delivering health care, portends significant changes in the relationships among parties to the production process. For this reason we are interested in *both* markets for DRGs and believe that the fact of two markets influences the diffusion process.

To summarize, DRGs were first introduced into Western Europe between the late 1970s, when one of the developers of the approach, Robert Fetter, spent a sabbatical at the Catholic University of Louvain in Belgium working with Jean Blanpain, and 1984. This latter date is approximate since it is virtually impossible to document precisely when the approach was first introduced in each and every instance. Despite, or perhaps because of, ambiguity surrounding the innovation itself and questions about who the customer for DRGs really was, by late 1991 two countries were committed to using DRGs on the national level and five others were quite actively involved in various trials and tests intended, among other things, to help shape decisions about their utility. In two countries it appeared unlikely that DRGs would be widely used, in one instance after considerable testing and experimentation had been done. Perhaps most significantly, although the scope of these trials varied considerably, they involved hospitals and hospital information systems in every instance, a fact to which we will return later.

The Importance of Context

In discussing the migration of certain ideas about government and social welfare policies from the United States to Great Britain, Marmor and Plowden (1991, p. 812) noted that ideas "do not travel well because they are good or bad, clever or dumb.

Ideas are elements in policy warfare whose take-up is determined not by their intrinsic validity but by the local setting—its
culture, present moods and circumstances, and structures." We
would make a similar argument for the influence of context on
the migration of innovation. Context conditions the levels of
receptivity to innovation. A favorable context can hasten the
spread of innovation, while a less favorable context can act as a
real brake on the process.

The importance of what they call "receptive and non-
receptive contexts for change" has been highlighted by Andrew
Pettigrew and his colleagues in their study of the fate of changes
introduced at the district health authority level in National
Health Service in Britain (Pettigrew, Ferlie, and McKee, 1992).
Although their work focuses principally on the organizational
level, the message coming from their work is highly relevant for
our analysis of the diffusion of DRGs: one cannot hope to
understand their fate in the absence of an understanding of the
context into which they were introduced.

In preparing the histories of DRGs in each of our nine
countries, the authors were asked to describe the health care
context of their country. They were asked not only to describe
the basic contours of their system but also to highlight areas of
current concern and policy debate. Despite the considerable
ideological and operational differences from one country to the
next with regard to how health care is financed and how health
planning is organized, we were struck by two dimensions of
context that were similar from one country to the next: pressures
to modernize the national administrative apparatus and the
search for ways to stem the rising costs of health care. Together,
these pressures strongly enhanced receptivity to administrative
changes that promised greater efficiency in general and to
DRGs in particular.

Although the origins of the pressure to modernize administration may vary somewhat from one country to another, an
active search for ways to improve the effectiveness of the administrative apparatus—not only in health care, but across the
board—is under way in each. New administrative approaches,

tools, or practices that offer promise of enhanced effectiveness will thus find particularly fertile soil.

DRGs are one such tool. They require a considerable investment in information infrastructure, in computing capability, and in technical expertise. In this sense, they are viewed as modern; their requirements are consistent with widely shared views of how future health care administration should be structured. They have become available at a particularly propitious point in time, and one should not underestimate the importance of this factor in creating a favorable context for their diffusion.

The acuity of the problem of rising health care costs varies somewhat among the nine countries, with Switzerland apparently being less sensitive to this issue at present than any of the other eight. In no case, however, was there an absence of concern, and in some cases, such as France, Norway, Portugal, and Sweden, concern was widespread and politically highly visible.

DRGs were implemented in the United States as part of an overall effort to introduce incentives for efficiency and cost savings into the health care system. This fact became widely known in Western Europe, and the U.S. experiment was closely watched by health policy experts in those countries. Despite the mixed results on cost control coming out of the United States, the experiment was frequently used by reformers to justify experimentation with DRGs in other countries. In the United States, it could be argued that the decision of the federal government to use DRGs as part of the prospective payment system was a function both of the pressure to do something to control costs on the one hand and of the coincidental availability of DRGs as a tool being tested in the state of New Jersey (Smith, 1992). To the extent that this argument has merit, it appears to be applicable in at least some (and probably most) countries in Western Europe as well.

The Ready Availability of DRGs

We argued above that the twin pressures to modernize the administrative apparatus and to control the costs of health care

created a favorable context in the nine countries for the diffusion of new administrative techniques that promised to increase
efficiency and reduce costs. Case mix management approaches,
in general, would have meshed well with these contextual constraints. Why, at least initially and through late 1991, have DRGs
been the principal approach considered and used? We have
identified seven factors that together help to answer this
question.

DRGs were being used on a national basis in the United States.
The single most important influence on thinking about options
in Western Europe was the fact that the prospective payment
system implemented in the United States was based on DRGs,
was designed to create incentives for increased efficiency, and
was intended, therefore, to help slow cost increases. The fact of
its adoption generated both credibility and interest and encouraged those interested in reform to consider how the approach
might be used in their own cases.

*DRGs were the first case mix management system to make the
transition from research to policy.* The fact that DRGs were the first
approach to case mix management to be available to users gave
them a sort of "first mover advantage" with respect to alternatives. First mover advantage is multidimensional, but in the
case of DRGs, they became the approach that was discussed,
and, although alternative approaches have been developed that
compensate in some ways for the shortcomings attributed to
DRGs, they became the standard of reference. Being first does
not guarantee becoming the standard, of course, but it does
create the opportunity. In this instance, at least through 1991,
that opportunity was not lost.

*The relevance of DRGs for particular countries could be assessed
empirically.* Often, the diffusion of innovation is slowed by what
has become known as the "not invented here" syndrome. There
is a tendency for people to reject new programs or products that
do not appear to take the special characteristics of their own
situations into account. To reject something as "not invented
here" is to say that it (whatever it might be) simply does not fit
because it came from outside. Here we return to the migratory
paradox referred to in Chapter One. Why might the French or

the Germans or the Swedish be enthusiastic about an innovation developed in the United States? Might that fact in itself not produce skepticism and perhaps rejection?

One of the interesting features of DRGs is that hospital discharge data from any given country could be analyzed (often after having been recoded) and a judgment made about how well those data fit the DRG model. If there were large discrepancies, then (at least in theory) it could be argued that DRGs were not appropriate. To the extent that the data fit the model, it could be argued that despite having been developed elsewhere, the tool was appropriate.

Although the data from some countries were more discrepant with the model than those from others, in no case were the discrepancies of sufficient magnitude to lead to a negative conclusion regarding DRGs. Since there were no absolute and incontrovertible criteria for making the assessment, this result is not surprising. The availability of a sophisticated analytical process was, in our judgment, significant in reinforcing the enthusiasm of proponents and in disarming potential opponents. It also provided a data-based means for determining whether an innovation developed abroad fit the circumstances of any particular country. Thus, the potential constraining effects of the migratory paradox were minimized by the capacity to make comparisons.

The technology for producing DRGs was readily available at a reasonable price. The developers of DRGs in the Health Systems Management Group at Yale made the Yale grouper available at a very reasonable price. Although some might argue that the higher the price the greater the value one imputes to the product (and thus that too low a price is ill-advised), in the case of DRGs researchers in other countries were frequently the first customers. Had the Yale grouper been priced commercially, it is highly likely that at least some research groups might not have been willing to make the investment. In any case, price was certainly no barrier to access, and the DRGs actually entered the majority of our nine countries through the research door.

Consultation and technical assistance were available directly from the developers. Fetter and Thompson created a group of researchers and technical specialists at Yale—the Health Systems Management Group—and this group was able to provide a variety of services to clients in a number of different countries under contract. The standard contract was divided into three phases: a first phase in which the technical feasibility of assigning DRG numbers to discharge abstracts was assessed; a second phase in which the adequacy of the utilization model defined by the DRGs for the country's hospitalization data was evaluated; and a third phase in which the DRG-based cost and budgeting model developed in the United States was adapted to the needs of the particular country.

Although the technical assistance added value per se, the political legitimacy that was created by working with the Yale team should not be ignored. Norway and Portugal, the countries that have gone the farthest with DRGs, both had contracts, as did Sweden, England, and France. Neither Germany nor Denmark, the two countries that have moved in other directions, had contracts, nor did Belgium or Switzerland.

We certainly do not mean to imply that having a contract with Yale guaranteed that DRGs would be implemented. On the other hand, by creating the possibility of a feasibility study, the Yale group facilitated both serious exploration of technical issues and eventual political support. Whether intentionally or not, the contracting mechanism the Yale group used was a very effective marketing device.

DRGs were flexible as a classification scheme. Even after the production of the original version of DRGs, the developers made it a point to keep abreast of various criticisms that were made of the product. They not only stayed very much in touch with these criticisms, they also began to work on a refined version of the product, using ideas that had served as the basis for potentially competing products such as disease staging and patient management categories. These ideas complemented the original work on DRGs, and the combination effectively kept DRGs ahead of the competition. The refined version became available in 1987, again at a very reasonable price, and allowed DRGs to remain at the center of policy discussions in the countries examined here.

The refined DRGs required minimal additional investment on the part of the user. It is at least conceivable that had the DRGs not been flexible, and had the refined DRGs not been based on the same underlying logic, technology, and infrastructure as the original version, their fate might have been much different. But in point of fact, no further investment on the part of users was required to use the refined version except for a modest financial outlay for the product itself. No new technology was needed, no additional training was required, and no new personnel had to be hired. This situation contrasts markedly with many generational improvements in innovations, which often face the user with substantial additional investment in order to take advantage of the improvements. It would be difficult to overestimate the importance of this factor in keeping DRGs on the health policy agendas of those countries still experimenting with them.

To summarize, we can explain the relatively rapid diffusion of DRGs to our nine countries as a function of two factors: the near-simultaneous emergence of pressures for administrative modernity and fiscal responsibility in health care and the fact that DRGs themselves were the first case mix management approach on the market. They had already been used on a national scale in the United States, their relevance for other countries could be assessed empirically, they were relatively inexpensive and thus attractive to researchers, there was prestigious and qualified technical assistance available, they were flexible, and minimal additional investment was required to acquire and use the refined version. This combination of factors together made it both relatively easy to invest in DRGs and relatively difficult to ignore them.

Facilitating Factors

In addition to the contextual and facilitating factors noted above, there are other factors that appear to explain the diffusion of DRGs, some of which are associated with the specifics of politics, administrative structures, and economics in particular countries, some of which have to do with the efficacy of champions, and some of which are related to the networks of people actually using DRGs.

Country Contexts

When we consider the details of the stories in each of the nine countries, we are tempted to say that each one is unique and that explanations of the spread of DRGs are necessarily lodged at the country level. In some respects, of course, this argument is valid. Each story is different and involves a unique combination of contexts, actors, agendas, and resources.

Particularly striking to us is the interplay between political agendas at the national level (which may change dramatically with changes in the party in power) and the legitimacy and support that may be provided to specific initiatives linked to these agendas.

There is certainly no news here for the political scientist; these linkages constitute a major focus for research in the discipline. For those whose theories rest on assumptions about rational expectations, however, there is cause to wonder. If nothing else, the earlier chapters of this book speak volumes about how politics influence innovation. When innovation is high on the political agenda, as it has been in Portugal and Norway, the process moves along smartly. When it is off the agenda or has an ambiguous status, the process is slowed considerably, often to a crawl and occasionally to a dead stop. In Europe, where the links between national policy and the management of individual health care institutions tend to be tighter than in the United States, the influence of politics on innovation is particularly evident.

Perhaps the most vivid illustration of the braking effect of politics on innovation is provided by France, where the PMSI project has survived three major government changes, but where the ever-shifting sands of political priority have, at least until very recently, resulted in redefinition of the role of DRGs in such a way that little progress has been made in advancing a consistent national policy for their use.

We had initially expected to find a positive relationship

between the existence of a reasonably sophisticated medical information infrastructure in a given country and the diffusion of DRGs. In fact, there appears to be very little relationship of this kind. Although it is the case that use of DRGs requires such an infrastructure, both Norway and Portugal had to build one from the ground up. Commitment to the importance of DRGs in Portugal led to investment in the necessary infrastructure, while in Norway the search for more efficient management structures for hospitals triggered the investment. The Danes, on the other hand, had such an infrastructure and ultimately moved in a different direction, as did the Germans without the infrastructure.

Our conclusion is that this aspect of country context did not per se influence the diffusion process to any significant degree. One might ask how the process might have unfolded had a sophisticated infrastructure already been in place in every country. Our speculations here are quite mixed. One might argue that diffusion would have moved faster because the DRGs depend on such an infrastructure, but one might also argue that the existence of the infrastructure is itself an indicator of administrative modernity and that diffusion might have been slower absent pressures to modernize. One might also argue that had the infrastructure already been in existence, it would also have been in use, and the fact of usage would make it extremely difficult to change, thus slowing the diffusion process.

In a similar vein, we had expected to find a relationship between the centralization of policy making and administration and the diffusion of DRGs. The more centralized the apparatus, we reasoned, the easier it would be to mandate use of DRGs. Furthermore, in more centralized countries, people *expect* central authorities to take positions, and this expectation often creates ambiguity and paralysis when it is not met. Our nine countries vary considerably in their degree of centralization. Denmark, Germany, and Switzerland are highly decentralized, while England, France, and Portugal are more highly centralized. Belgium, Sweden, and Norway are somewhere in between. Thus far, however, centralization per se does not appear either to have increased or decreased the proba-

bilities of diffusion. The explanation is at once more complicated and more interesting.

Importance of Champions

Studies of innovation in other contexts have frequently noted
the importance of true believers or champions. Champions are
individuals who, for whatever reasons, believe deeply in the
promise of innovation and are prepared to go to great lengths to
see the innovative process successfully managed. Champions
have been found to be particularly important in the new-prod-
uct development process, where uncertainty about both the
performance of the new product and its profitability is extremely high. These people, because of their unwavering belief
in the potential of the product being developed, protect the
process from critics and detractors and manage to obtain
enough resources to permit the development process to be
completed, often in the face of severe pressures to abandon the
effort.

In the case of the diffusion of DRGs to Western Europe,
we recognize the importance of such champions and find some
parallels with what others have found in studying the innovation
process in other settings. In each country, one can identify a
person or a small group of people who came to believe that the
use of medical information for management purposes was
important and needed to be developed. In many cases, such as
France, the use of medical information for management purposes and the use of DRGs were nearly synonymous. In some
cases, however, such as Denmark and Germany, they were not,
and decisions were taken that led to other approaches than
DRGS.

As important as the existence of champions, however,
appears to be their ability to coopt others and thus widen the
network of people knowledgeable about and committed to the
innovation. Whether DRGs entered a particular country initially through research channels, as in England or Sweden, or
through political and administrative channels, as in Portugal or
Norway, the challenge for the initiators has been to mobilize

political and technical support for both the underlying idea and its concrete representation. Furthermore, a relatively small number of particularly agile individuals have managed to become personally involved in the multiple and somewhat overlapping networks emerging around computerized medical records, patient classification systems, and DRGs in Europe and in so doing have been able to increase their influence considerably.

Interestingly, the way this has been done has differed widely among the nine countries examined, and different groups of champions have had different views of what the DRGs are good for. In some cases, such as Sweden and Switzerland, the mobilization process was dominated by researchers; in other cases, such as Norway and Portugal, it was dominated by political actors; and in still others, such as Belgium, England, and France, there was a great deal of interchange between the research community and the political infrastructure, with researchers often becoming very active in the politics of support and political figures relying heavily on the advice and counsel of researchers. In all cases, however, the role of champions has been significant. As we will see below, despite some striking differences in approach and orientation at the outset, over time there appears to have been some convergence among the various countries — convergence that has its roots not in the specifics of particular stories but rather in the strong institutional pressures that are developing in Europe.

Emergence of User Networks

The migration of DRGs across the Atlantic in the first place was greatly facilitated by connections between people who were players in the health care systems of their individual countries and who also had been infected with the idea of using medical information for management purposes or with the idea of DRGs. An example of such a connection comes from the French chapter, where one can observe the contact made between Robert Fetter and the future director of French hospitals in the course of a seminar in the French Alps in 1979, a contact that led directly to the French PMSI project.

Such contacts have a somewhat random quality, however, and one key mechanism for encouraging a more systematic spread of DRGs was the annual week-long Health Care Executive Education Program held at the School of Organization and Management at Yale University. Organized by Fetter and initially offered in 1978, this program attracted between fifty and sixty health care managers, physicians, and policy makers each year through 1988, when Fetter retired from Yale. Its principal focus was on the application of operations management logic to health care organizations through DRGs, and it was in these sessions that the initial network of true believers was created. Not everyone who attended, of course, became a convert, but the seeds were planted, and a series of sessions for program alumni helped to reinforce the ties that were created.

In the early and mid 1980s the composition of these groups expanded to include people from outside the United States. As best we can tell, people from England, France, Sweden, and Switzerland attended the Yale Executive Summer Program, and their attendance marks the beginning of the development of personal networks of DRG enthusiasts abroad. The other important information channel, of course, was publication in scientific and professional journals, and the single most significant article in this regard was the piece by Fetter and his colleagues that appeared in the supplement to *Medical Care* in 1980. The influence of this article is specifically referred to in the chapters on England and Sweden, but its influence was no doubt considerably broader as more people used it as a point of reference in discussions either of the use of medical information for management purposes or of patient classification systems.

Information about innovation is a necessary but hardly sufficient condition for its diffusion. The emergence of networks of users in particular countries and across national borders served to build the sufficient conditions. These networks were both formal (as in the case of England, where a users' newsletter was developed) and informal, in that information of all sorts, nontechnical as well as technical, was shared on a reasonably regular basis among research groups. The importance of these networks for sustaining interest in and attention to DRGs cannot be overestimated. Not only did they provide a sense of legitimacy for those involved, they also provided an ever-increasing access to potential recruits.

On top of these networks forming within countries, others began to form across national borders. The Scandinavian network noted in the chapters on Denmark, Norway, and Sweden is one good example, but there are others as well. Meetings among researchers from different countries wishing to share experiences and findings began to be organized, the first taking place at the University of Louvain in Belgium in April 1983 under the leadership of Francis Roger France, author of the chapter on Belgium. The first international conference on DRGs, organized by Robert Fetter, was held in London in December 1986 and brought together researchers from throughout Europe to discuss ongoing efforts in various countries to use DRGs. In addition, as the result of a 1985 study commissioned by the Council of Europe on the use of computerized medical records in hospitals, individuals from eighteen countries formed an entity called Patient Classification Systems–Europe to discuss various different patient classification systems (among which were DRGs).

Finally, in 1989, the European Community launched a large-scale research program called Advanced Informatics in Medicine (AIM). At least two of the major international projects that were funded through AIM dealt with case mix management. There were many issues under study: the harmonization of hospital discharge data, the development of classification systems for ambulatory care and nonacute hospital care, patient-oriented cost accounting systems, and case mix–based budgeting methods. Not surprisingly, many of the champions were active participants in these two projects, thus getting the new logic firmly positioned on the agenda of the European Community.

These emerging networks have had a significant impact on the diffusion of DRGs in our nine countries by facilitating the sharing of technical and nontechnical information, by encouraging discussion of successes and failures, and by creating subtle and not-so-subtle pressures to climb on the DRG bandwagon. As the chapter on Germany so clearly illustrates, when many countries are going in a particular direction, it is extremely difficult for any particular country to move in another, no matter how valid the reasoning. The multiple networks emerging around DRGs represent a strong institutional force — DiMaggio and Powell (1983) would call it a mimetic force— favoring diffusion. As they grow and develop, they create structures that become increasingly durable and resilient and thus add to the staying power of the innovation itself.

Development of a DRG-Based Research Industry

One way of thinking about why innovations take is to consider what aspects of any particular innovation become part of the fabric of everyday organizational life. The more this occurs, the greater the investment the system has in the innovation, and the more difficult it becomes to "exnovate," that is, to remove or discontinue using the innovation. The more this occurs, in other words, the more the innovation has become legitimized and hence institutionalized.

In the case of DRGs, two things in particular have resulted in greater institutionalization. First, a vital, though modest, research industry has grown up around their evaluation and implementation. Research teams have been formed for the specific purpose of working on DRGs, generally within existing research organizations such as CASPE in England, the Swedish Planning and Rationalization Institute, or the Danish Hospital Institute, but occasionally in newly created entities such as the Medical Information and Hospital Management Commission in France or in cross-institutional collaborative ventures as in Switzerland. As these research teams have grown and as their work has become more visible, it has become increasingly difficult to ignore what they do. The longer they continue, the more difficult it will become to shut them down without their consent. Their creation and continued existence, then, are momentum-generating.

Second, as these research teams have grown and as intra- and inter-country networks have emerged, an increasing number of individuals have acquired DRG-related skills and competencies. This increasing stock of asset-specific resources on a national level represents both a sunk cost and a barrier to switching. Increasing levels of investment in experimentation with DRGs, in other words, have increased the supply of people with particular competencies, and this supply itself has become a force for continuing the investment.

Momentum and Migration

As noted in the beginning of this chapter, our analysis of the diffusion of DRGs to Belgium, Denmark, England, France, Germany, Norway, Portugal, Sweden, and Switzerland is necessarily incomplete. We arbitrarily brought our efforts to construct the histories of the diffusion process in each country to a close as of the fall of 1992, but in each case, the process continues to unfold. Thus, our concluding observations are not in any sense final.

With this caveat clearly stated, we would like to offer three observations. First, an important factor in the diffusion of DRGs and, we suspect, in the diffusion of innovations more generally, is the development of momentum. Momentum is born of the multiplication of interest in the innovation itself. The indicators of momentum are manifold: the development of research efforts, attention in the scientific literature, recognition in the popular press, the appearance of focused conferences, and the emergence of networks, to name just a few.

Momentum does not guarantee diffusion. Increased viability increases vulnerability, and increasing momentum may have the effect of catalyzing opposition, as in the case of Denmark. But for the practicing manager or policy maker, our work strongly suggests the usefulness of taking action explicitly designed to produce momentum.

A second observation concerns the connectedness of actors and contexts in the diffusion process. We have seen the importance of relationships both within and between countries, relationships that both create and reinforce momentum and that in some cases are deliberately managed and in others appear to emerge more organically. No matter what their origins, these relationships — within and between groups of physicians, researchers, policy makers, and others — are central ingredients in the process by which an innovation becomes visible and begins to take hold in a given context. For the practicing manager or policy maker, the implication is clear: creating and effectively managing connectedness among groups of people whose support for innovation is essential can have significant benefits. No opportunity to build connectedness should be overlooked.

Finally, there may come a point in the diffusion process of any innovation when irreversibility is achieved. By irreversibility we mean that the process evolves to such an extent that what has been done cannot be undone. We believe that the point of irreversibility has been reached in each of the countries considered here, but that the irreversibility is lodged not in the DRGs per se but rather in the underlying logic. We believe that a significant shift has taken place in the way all parties to the health care process think about the products of the hospital, patterns of resource consumption within the hospital, and the way in which the production process should be monitored. The DRGs provide one very useful technology for assessing and measuring each of these dimensions, but alternatives are available. No matter what specific technology is used, however, it is difficult to imagine a return to the earlier ways of viewing the production process in hospitals. In this sense, the process of innovation of which the DRGs are a part is irreversible, and its effects will be felt not only in Western Europe but around the globe, for decades to come.

References

DiMaggio, P. J., and Powell, W. W. "The Iron Cage Revisited: Institutional Isomorphism and Collective Rationality in Organizational Fields." *American Sociological Review*, 1983, *48*(2), 147–160.

Fetter, R. B., and others. "Case Mix Definition by Diagnostic Related Groups."*Medical Care*, 1980 (Supplement), *18*(2), 1–53.

Kimberly, J. R. "Managerial Innovation." In P. C. Nystrom and W. H. Starbuck (eds.), *Handbook of Organizational Design.* New York: Oxford University Press, 1981.

Latour, B., Mauguin, P., and Teil, G. "Comment suivre les innovations: Le Graphe Sociotechnique" (How to follow innovations: The socio-technical graph). *Gérer et Comprendre,* Sept. 1990, pp. 62–79.

Marmor, T., and Plowden, W. "Rhetoric and Reality in the Intellectual Jet Stream: The Export to Britain from America of Questionable Ideas." *Journal of Health Politics, Policy and Law,* 1991, *16*(4), 807–812.

Pettigrew, A., Ferlie, E., and McKee, L. *Shaping Strategic Change.* London: Basil Blackwell/Oxford, 1992.

Rogers, E. *The Diffusion of Innovation.* New York: Free Press, 1983.

Smith, D. *Paying for Medicare: The Politics of Reform.* New York: Aldine-DeGruyter, 1992.

Index

363

Index

371

Mason, A., 29, 58
Maud, R., 116, 120
Mauguin, P., 342, 362
Mauroy, P., 90
Mayo Clinic (United States), 65, 67
Medical Information and Hospital Management Commission (IMAGE) (France), 112, 113–115, 120, 122, 129, 359
Medical Information Department (France), 114, 119, 124–125, 126
Medicare (United States): cost weights from, 150, 170; and DRG uses, 305, 306, 310; grouping for, 140–141, 144; and prospective payment, 64, 137, 138; and resource allocation, 234, 235, 236, 237
Medisgroups, 47
Medisys (Sweden), 143, 150
Medizinal-Tarif-Kommission (Switzerland), 181
Meurisse, M., 73, 81
Millet, A., 102, 129
Mills, I., 39
Mills, R. E., 103, 128
Minder, C., 184, 211
Mines, L'Ecole des. *See* Scientific Management Center
Ministère des Affaires Sociales et de la Solidarité (France), 65, 85n, 129
Ministry of Finance (Denmark), 287, 312, 315
Ministry of Finance (Sweden), 139, 157, 158, 171
Ministry of Health (Denmark), 293, 299, 303, 304, 312
Ministry of Health (Germany), 320
Ministry of Health (Portugal): Department of Finance in, 236, 239, 241; and evolution of DRGs, 225–226, 228, 229–230, 232–233; and health care policies, 218, 221
Ministry of Health and Social Affairs (Norway): and diffusion, 263–265, 268, 269, 275; and future, 277, 278–279, 280; and

health care system, 257n, 259, 260–263, 281; and incentives, 274–275; and Payment Experiment, 271–272, 281
Ministry of Health and Social Affairs (Sweden): Delegation for Social Research at, 152; and future, 168, 171–172; and health care context, 132, 139, 151, 153
Ministry of Labor and Social Affairs (Germany), 325
Ministry of Local Government (Norway), 262
Ministry of Public Health (Belgium): and health care context, 60, 62, 71–72; Institute of Hygiene and Epidemiology at, 77; issues in, 74, 76–77, 78, 79–80
Ministry of Science Policy (Belgium), 66, 67, 71
Ministry of Social Affairs (Belgium), 60, 71
Ministry of the Interior (Denmark), 287, 288–291, 298, 311, 315–316
Minvielle, E., 109, 129
Mitterand, F., 91, 115
Moeller Pedersen, K., 290, 296, 316
Moisdon, J. C., 87, 104, 128, 129
Molet, H., 128
Montpellier hospital (France), 122
Morges hospital (Switzerland), 204
Morraz, A., 195, 211
Mullin, R., 143, 226, 227, 228, 253
Municipality Health Services Act of 1984 (Norway), 258
Mutual-benefit societies, in Belgium, 61–62, 77–78
Mutualité Agricole (France), 117
Muurinen, J. M., 285, 316
Myhre, H. O., 265

Nancy hospital (France), 122
Napoleon III, 61
National Board of Health (Denmark): and attitudes, 311; and diffusion of DRGs, 288–289, 291, 294–295; and financing,

376

Index